THE FLORIDA GULF COAST
TRAVEL+SMART™ TRIP PLANNER

THE FLORIDA GULF COAST

TRAVEL◆SMART™ TRIP PLANNER

Jan Kirby

John Muir Publications
Santa Fe, New Mexico

Acknowledgments

The author wishes to thank Mike Kirby for his contributions to the chapters on Pensacola, Panama City, Apalachicola, Tallahassee, Clearwater, and Naples; and Ruth Bross, manager of the Chamber of Commerce Tourist Bureau in downtown St. Petersburg, for sharing her vast knowledge of St. Petersburg and its beautiful beaches. Many thanks also to the well-informed, friendly staff members and volunteers in tourist bureaus from Pensacola to Naples, and to the residents of the Florida Gulf Coast for their helpful information.

John Muir Publications, P.O. Box 613, Santa Fe, New Mexico 87504

Printed in the United States of America.
First edition. First printing February 1997.

ISSN 1092-597X
ISBN 1-56261-318-9

Editors: Carol Perry, Elizabeth Wolf
Design: Janine Lehmann and Linda Braun
Graphics Coordination: Jane Susan MacCarter
Cover Photo: Jeff Greenberg/Leo de Wys, Inc.
Back cover photos: *top*—Charles Hornbrook
                      bottom—Sarasota Convention and Visitors Bureau
Map Style Development: American Custom Maps—Albuquerque, NM USA
Map Illustration: Julie Felton
Production: Marie J. T. Vigil, Nikki Rooker
Typesetting: Elsa Kendall
Printing: Publishers Press

Distributed to the book trade by
Publishers Group West
Emeryville, California

HOW TO USE THIS BOOK

This *Florida Gulf Coast Travel✦Smart Trip Planner* is organized in 14 destination chapters, each covering the best sights and activities, restaurants, and lodging available in that specific destination. Thanks to thorough research and experience, the author is able to bring you only the best options, saving you time and money in your travels. The chapters are presented in geographic sequence so you can follow an easy route from one to the next. If you were to visit each destination in chapter order, you'd enjoy a complete tour of the best of Florida's Gulf Coast.

Each chapter contains:

• User-friendly maps of the area, showing all recommended sights, restaurants, and accommodations.
• "A Perfect Day" description—how the author would spend her time if she had just one day in that destination.
• Sightseeing highlights, each rated by degree of importance: ✮✮✮ Don't miss; ✮✮ Try hard to see; ✮ See if you have time; and No stars—Worth knowing about.
• Selected restaurant, lodging, and camping recommendations to suit a variety of budgets.
• Helpful hints, fitness and recreation ideas, insights, and random tidbits of information to enhance your trip.

The Importance of Planning. Developing an itinerary is the best way to get the most satisfaction from your travels, and this guidebook makes it easy. First, read through the book and choose the places you'd most like to visit. Then, study the color map on the inside cover flap and the mileage chart (page 12) to determine which you can realistically see in the time you have available and at the travel pace you prefer. Using the Planning Map (pages 10–11), map out your route. Finally, use the lodging recommendations to determine your accommodations.

Some Suggested Itineries. To get you started, six itineraries of varying lengths and based on specific interests follow. Mix and match according to your interests and time constraints, or follow a given itinerary from start to finish. The possibilities are endless. *Happy travels!*

SUGGESTED ITINERARIES

With the *Florida Gulf Coast Travel+Smart Trip Planner* you can plan a trip of any length—a one-day excursion, a getaway weekend, or a three-week vacation—around any special interest. To get you started, the following pages contain six suggested itineraries geared toward a variety of interests. For more information, refer to the chapters listed—chapter names are in boldface, and chapter numbers appear inside black bullets. You can follow a suggested itinerary in its entirety, or shorten, lengthen, or combine parts of each, depending on your starting and ending points.

Discuss alternative routes and schedules with your travel companions—it's a great way to have fun, even before you leave home. And remember: don't hesitate to change your itinerary once you're on the road. Careful study and planning ahead of time will help you make informed decisions as you go, but spontaneity is the extra ingredient that will make your trip memorable.

Wakulla Springs State Park

Best of Florida's Gulf Coast Tour

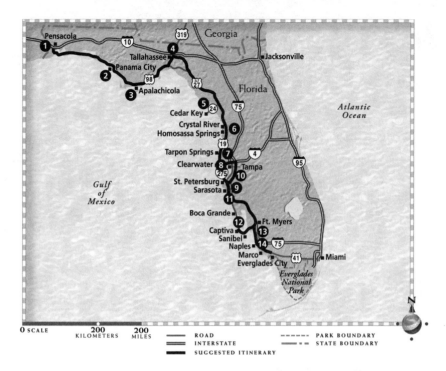

To see the very best of Florida's beautiful Gulf Coast region, start in Pensacola and continue south to Naples as shown on this "Best of the Gulf Coast" tour.

① Pensacola

② Panama City

③ Apalachicola

④ Tallahassee

⑤ Cedar Key

⑥ Crystal River/Homosassa Springs

⑦ Tarpon Springs

⑨ Clearwater

⑧ St. Petersburg

⑩ Tampa

⑪ Sarasota

⑫ The Gulf Islands

⑬ Fort Myers

⑭ Naples

Time needed: 3 weeks

Nature Lover's Tour

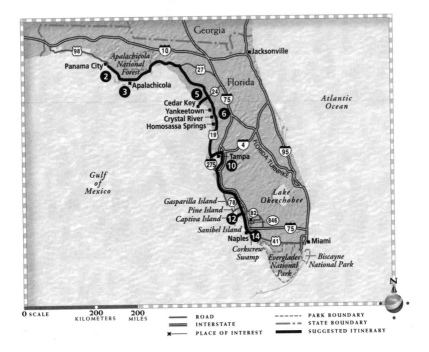

The beauty of Florida's west coast—sandy beaches, low-lying river country, and barrier islands—make this tour a nature lover's delight.

② **Panama City Beach** (Shell Island, fishing, swimming, The Museum of Man in the Sea)

③ **Apalachicola** (oyster beds, Apalachicola National Forest, Florida National Scenic Trail and Trout Pond)

⑤ **Cedar Key** (state museum, historic coastal village, wildlife, islands)

⑥ **Crystal River/Homosassa** (river tours, swim with the manatees)

⑩ **Tampa** (Florida Aquarium, Busch Gardens, zoo)

⑫ **The Gulf Islands** (famous shelling, boating, beaches, fishing)

⑭ **Naples** (Corkscrew Swamp)

Time needed: 2 weeks

Arts and Culture Tour

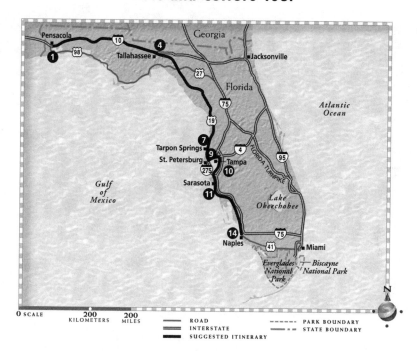

Florida's art and culture reflect the influences of both the early Spanish explorers and settlers and the area's earliest inhabitants, American Indians.

❶ **Pensacola** (Pensacola Historical Museum: Indian culture, The Museum of Industry, Spanish maps, fabrics and costumes)

❹ **Tallahassee** (Alfred B. Maclay State Gardens, Black Archives Research Center and Museum, San Luis Archaeological and Historic Site)

❼ **Tarpon Springs** (Greek Orthodox Church of St. Nicholas, Arts and Crafts Festival in April, Spongorama Exhibit Center, St. Nicholas Boat Line Tour)

❾ **St. Petersburg** (The Museum of Fine Arts, Salvador Dali Museum, Sunken Gardens, The Pier)

❿ **Tampa** (The Florida Aquarium, Museum of African-American Art, Henry B. Plant Museum, Ybor City State Museum)

⓫ **Sarasota** (Asolo Center for The Performing Arts, The John and Mable Ringling Museum of Art, The Circus Museum, Selby Gallery)

⓮ **Naples** (Collier County Museum, Trolley Tours, Philharmonic Center)

Time needed: 2½ weeks

Family Fun Tour

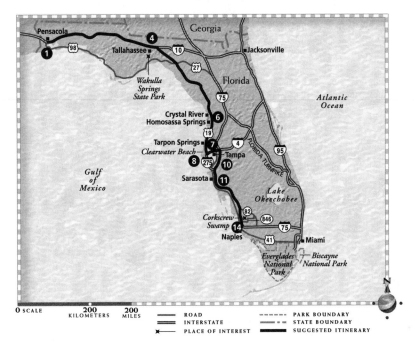

From sandy beaches to kid-friendly museums and attractions, Family fun abounds on Florida's Gulf Coast.

❶ Pensacola (National Museum of Naval Aviation, Flight Adventure Deck, Pensacola Naval Air Station tours, Wildlife Rescue and Sanctuary)

❹ Tallahassee (Tallahassee Museum of History and Natural Science, Florida State Capitol tours, Native American Heritage Festival in September, Edward Bell Springs State Park, swimming)

❻ Crystal River/Homosassa (swim with the manatees, river tour)

❼ Tarpon Springs (Coral Sea Aquarium, St. Nicholas Boat Line sponge diving, gift shops, Pappas Restaurant)

❽ Clearwater Beach (marine aquarium, Captain Memo's Pirate Cruise)

❿ Tampa (Adventure Island, Busch Gardens, Lowry Park Zoological Garden, Children's Museum of Tampa, Florida Aquarium)

⓫ Sarasota (The Gulf Coast World of Science, The Circus Museum, Mote Marine Aquarium, Sarasota Jungle Gardens)

⓮ Naples (Corkscrew Swamp Sanctuary, Frannies Teddy Bear Museum)

Time needed: 2 weeks

History Lover's Tour

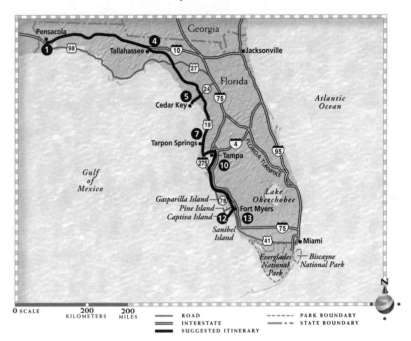

Those interested in history will find much to see and do in Florida's West Coast region.

❶ Pensacola (National Museum of Naval Aviation, Historic Pensacola village, Museum of Commerce, Civil War Soldiers Museum)

❹ Tallahassee (walking tours, Florida State Capitol, The Knott House Museum, the Old Capitol)

❺ Cedar Key (Cedar Key Historical Society Museum, Historic Island Hotel, Cedar Key State Museum)

❼ Tarpon Springs (George Inness Jr. Pictures, Tarpon Avenue Antiques, sponge docks)

❿ Tampa (Tampa Museum of Art, Henry B. Plant Museum, Ybor City State Museum, Preservation Park)

⓬ The Gulf Islands (Miller's Marina, Pink Elephant Restaurant, shelling)

⓭ Fort Myers (Fort Myers Historical Museum, Thomas A. Edison Home, Henry Ford Winter Home, J.C. Sightseeing Boat Cruises, Seminole Gulf Railway)

Time needed: 2 weeks

Beachcomber's Tour

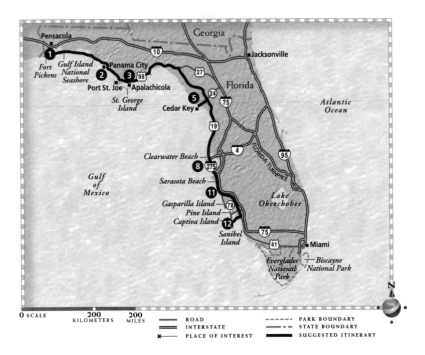

The Gulf beaches are heaven for beachcombers. Live shelling exists in many sheltered bays for those seeking a perfect specimen—please, take only one or two of these rare finds.

❶ Pensacola (Fort Pickens, Gulf Islands National Seashore)

❷ Panama City (scuba diving, Shell Island boat shuffle, fishing)

❸ Apalachicola (oyster beds, Port St. Joe, oyster shucking in November, St. George Island, St. George State Park)

❺ Cedar Key (crabbing and oystering, picnicking, restaurants)

❽ Clearwater (shelling, Sand Key Pinellas County Park, Clearwater Marine Aquarium, Caledesi State Park Ferry, Ferry Tour to Tarpon Springs)

⓫ Sarasota (Longboat Key, Lido Key, St. Armond Key, Siesta Key)

⓬ The Gulf Islands (shelling, The Plantation Inn, Captiva Cruises to neighboring islands, J.N. "Ding" Darling National Wildlife Refuge, Island Historical Museum, Sanibel/Captiva Conservation Foundation)

Time needed: 1 to 2 weeks or more (for 1 week, see last three destinations)

USING THE PLANNING MAP

A major aspect of itinerary planning is determining your mode of transportation and the route you will follow as you travel from destination to destination. The Planning Map on the following pages will allow you to do just that.

First, read through the destination chapters carefully and note the sights that intrigue you. Then, photocopy the Planning Map so you can try out several different routes that will take you to these destinations. (The mileage chart that follows will allow you to calculate your travel distances.) Decide where you will be starting your tour of the Gulf Coast. Will you fly into Tampa or Tallahassee, or will you start from somewhere in between? Will you be driving from place to place or flying into major transportation hubs and renting a car for day trips? The answers to these questions will form the basis for your travel route design.

Once you have a firm idea of where your travels will take you, copy your route onto the additional Planning Map in the Appendix. You won't have to worry about where your map is, and the information you need on each destination will always be close at hand.

Planning Map: Florida's Gulf Coas

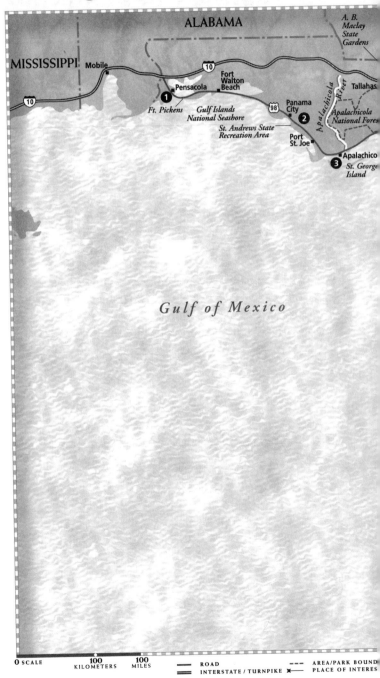

ALABAMA

MISSISSIPPI

Mobile

A. B.
Maclay
State
Gardens

Fort
Walton
Beach

Pensacola

Tallahas

1

Ft. Pickens

Gulf Islands
National Seashore

Panama
City

Apalachicola
National Fores

St. Andrews State
Recreation Area

Port
St. Joe

2

Apalachico

3

St. George
Island

Gulf of Mexico

GEORGIA

Jacksonville

Wakulla Springs State Park

Suwannee

Cedar Key **5**
Yankee Town
Homosassa Springs Crystal River **6**
State Wildlife Homosassa
Preserve Springs

Weeki Wachee Spring

Tarpon Springs **7** Tampa
Caladesi Island State Park Clearwater **8**
10
St. Petersburg **9**

Ringling Museums
Sarasota
11

Gasparilla Island

Boca Grande
Captiva
Captiva Island **12 13**
Pine Island Sanibel
Sanibel Island

Naples **14**
Marco

Everglades City

FLORIDA

Orlando

Atlantic Ocean

FLORIDA TURNPIKE
FLORIDA TURNPIKE
FLORIDA TURNPIKE

Lake Okeechobee

Ft. Myers
Corkscrew Swamp

Ft. Lauderdale

Miami

Everglades National Park

Biscayne National Park

N

FLORIDA GULF COAST MILEAGE CHART

	Apalachicola	Cedar Key	Clearwater	Crystal River	Fort Myers	Homosassa	Naples	Panama City	Pensacola	St. Petersburg	Sanibel Island	Sarasota	Tallahassee	Tampa	Tarpon Springs
Apalachicola	–	211	311	267	436	274	471	63	139	331	446	376	84	331	297
Cedar Key	211	–	130	56	255	63	290	274	350	150	299	195	183	150	116
Clearwater	311	130	–	74	125	67	184	374	450	20	169	65	238	20	14
Crystal River	267	56	74	–	199	7	234	330	406	94	219	139	164	94	60
Fort Myers	436	255	125	199	–	206	35	499	575	105	20	72	398	129	139
Homosassa	274	63	67	7	206	–	227	337	413	87	212	132	171	87	53
Naples	471	290	184	234	35	227	–	552	628	140	55	107	433	164	297
Panama City	63	274	374	330	499	337	552	–	76	394	519	439	119	394	361
Pensacola	139	350	450	406	575	413	628	76	–	470	683	515	195	470	437
St. Petersburg	331	150	20	94	105	87	140	394	470	–	169	45	253	24	34
Sanibel Island	446	299	169	219	20	212	55	519	683	169	–	92	412	149	182
Sarasota	376	195	65	139	72	132	107	439	515	45	92	–	326	57	78
Tallahassee	84	183	238	164	398	171	433	119	195	253	412	326	–	275	224
Tampa	331	150	20	94	129	87	164	394	470	24	149	57	275	–	34
Tarpon Springs	297	116	14	60	139	53	297	361	437	34	182	78	224	34	–

WHY VISIT
THE FLORIDA GULF COAST?

Many people consider the Florida Gulf Coast the "real Florida." Here more than 500 miles of gently curving coastline offer visitors three distinct natural regions. Floridians call these special places the Panhandle, the Nature Coast, and the Gulf Island Coast. Extending from Pensacola to Naples, these strikingly different areas provide some of the most interesting drives in America—when you know where to look—and that's what this book is all about.

The Panhandle: The sugar-white sandy beaches and warm waters of the Panhandle area, all the way from Pensacola to the "Big Bend" near the famous Suwannee River, attract swimmers and boaters, while bountiful gifts from the sea delight fishermen and diners.

The Nature Coast: The Nature Coast begins south of Tallahassee in Florida's lush, green "spring country." Here millions of gallons of crystal-clear water rush from more than 300 natural springs. Wide rivers created by the springs wind through wetlands and sawgrass and cypress hammocks to the Gulf of Mexico. An astonishing variety of wildlife greets visitors all along the way. Glass-bottomed boats are a favorite way to see the springs. Snorkeling, scuba diving, and canoeing provide do-it-yourself adventures.

Unlike in the Panhandle in the north and on the barrier islands south of the Tampa Bay area, there is no coastal road following Florida's central west coast section. But plenty of well-paved access roads lead from the main highways into this special part of the Sunshine State— short side trips well worth taking.

The Gulf Islands: South of Tarpon Springs the wide, white beaches of the barrier islands begin. These narrow, sandy island communities, connected to the mainland by causeways, offer visitors yet another exciting aspect of west coast Florida's diversity. Condominiums, big hotels, and a variety of entertainment venues make this area an exciting change from the shoreline to the north.

Clearwater Beach begins the string of well-settled barrier islands protecting the coastline south to Naples. Attractions, universities, businesses, and entertainment are plentiful along the adjacent mainland and on the islands themselves. Beach fun includes swimming, shell collecting, volleyball, windsurfing, and just relaxing in the warm Florida sunshine.

HISTORY

Spanish explorers found Florida back in the 1500s, and the shallow "Straits of Florida" off the Florida Keys became the graveyard of many Spanish galleons transporting gold and silver shipments from Central America across the Atlantic to Spain. Treacherous unmarked shoals and violent tropical storms—typical of the narrow passage between the island of Cuba and the Florida peninsula—wreaked havoc on the treasure ships.

Some of the historic riches have been uncovered by modern treasure hunters at great expense and loss of life. Historic records tell us of even more ancient ships lost at sea, listing rich cargoes of gold, silver, jewels, and priceless artifacts. Many are still out there, buried on the ocean floor off Florida—somewhere.

At first the exploring Spaniards thought that Florida was an island, perhaps related to the Bahama Islands just 50 miles to the east. It was Juan Ponce de Leon of "Fountain of Youth" fame who gave Florida its name. He'd happened upon it when he arrived at what is now St. Augustine, naming his discovery *Pascua Florida*, "Feast of Flowers."

For two long centuries Spain struggled to control Florida, fighting and trading land back and forth with England. In 1819 Spain finally sold the troublesome territory to the United States. The boundary to "West Florida," established by the English, remained disputed until 1821. Finally, Spain traded it to the United States in return for Texas.

Florida was declared a territory of the United States in 1822, and settlers flocked to the inviting new land. But they weren't in for a peaceful welcome. The Seminole Indians had been here first, and they didn't take kindly to the newcomers. *Seminole* means "runaways," and these Indians from various tribes were originally refugees from the Carolinas. They were united by their hostility toward the United States government. Seven years of raids and skirmishes known as the Seminole Indian War concluded with most of the Seminoles resettled on lands west of the Mississippi. But several tribes fled to South Florida, to add their rich Native American heritage to the state's multicultural mix.

At the end of the Seminole Indian War, more settlers were lured to Florida by the Armed Occupation Act of 1842. Some 160 acres of land were offered to anyone who would settle the land and defend it against the Indians.

In 1845 Florida became a state, then seceded from the Union to join the Confederacy in 1861. Florida was readmitted to the Union in 1868. It was after the close of the Civil War that major growth began in earnest for the Sunshine State. Wealthy developers including Henry M. Flagler and Henry B. Plant cast shrewd, speculative eyes on the potentially rich markets of Central and South America. The development of ports and railroads in Florida made economic sense. Flagler built his railroad down the east coast all the way to Key West. Plant built his down the west coast to Tampa. Competition between the two men continued with Flagler's elegant Ponce de Leon Hotel opening in St. Augustine in 1888. Not to be outdone, Plant opened his gold-turreted Tampa Bay Hotel in 1891. The historic structure now houses the University of Tampa and the Plant Museum.

Despite killer hurricanes and the stock market crash of 1929, citrus groves and tourism continued to flourish in Florida. Florida sunshine was widely touted as a cure for lung disease and other ailments, and people from Northern states flocked to its beaches, springs, hotels, and sanitoriums.

During World War II, German submarines lurked off West Florida's sandy beaches. In the mangrove swamps around Clearwater Bay, Donald Roebling designed the famous *Alligator Amphibian*, which accompanied U.S. troops fighting in the South Pacific.

Little more than a decade later, in 1958, the first U.S. satellite, *Explorer I*, was launched into space from Cape Canaveral. That successful flight encouraged the organization of the National Aeronautics and Space Administration (NASA) later in the same year. Throughout the 1960s space flights continued from Florida. In 1969 *Apollo 11* carried Neil Armstrong and his crew into space. When Armstrong took his "giant step for mankind" on to the surface of the moon, millions of awed television viewers watched and cheered.

In 1971 Florida focused on the long-awaited opening of Walt Disney World. Tourism boomed as children and adults alike were dazzled by the Magic Kingdom. They twirled on the Teacup Ride and climbed the three-story Swiss Family Robinson Tree House. Docile Clydesdales pulled open-air trolleys down Main Street U.S.A. while Mickey Mouse, Donald Duck, and their friends strolled Disney World streets. Prosperity had arrived in Central Florida.

Florida continues to expand in every direction—from outer space to Walt Disney World, from populous beaches to the lonely mystery of the Everglades. There's a growing awareness here, too, of the need to protect and preserve this unique and precious natural environment for future generations of wildlife and people.

CULTURES

Florida's many cultures make it an outstanding example of the United States' "melting pot." Over the years explorers from Spain, England, and France have all staked claims to various parts of the state. Up in the Panhandle, five different flags have flown over the city of Pensacola. Governments of Spain, France, England, the Confederate States, and the United States have all had a hand in shaping the culture here; museums and carefully preserved historic buildings depict this fascinating diversity. During the Fiesta of Five Flags each June there are art shows, parades, and a dramatic re-enactment of the landing of founding father Don Tristan de Luna on Florida shores in 1559. There's a U.S. Naval Air Station in Pensacola, too, and the National Museum of Naval Aviation offers a glimpse of another important aspect of the state's cultural heritage.

Colorful Native American cultures dot Florida's west coast. A Native American Heritage Festival is held each September in Tallahassee, honoring the Miccosukee, Creek, and other Indian tribes. Native American arts and crafts highlight the annual event.

The Crystal River State Archeological Site is one of Florida's most spectacular pre-Columbian Indian sites. Beginning more than 2,100 years ago, the riverside area served as a ceremonial center for about 1,600 years. Today visitors can view an authentic ancient temple as well as ancient burial and refuse mounds.

The Greek culture of Tarpon Springs has to be one of the Gulf Coast's most delightful ethnic influences. Music and dancing, colorful costumes, and wonderful Greek foods attract visitors year after year. The cultural heritage here is lovingly preserved by caring citizens, an active religious community, and a savvy chamber of commerce.

Tampa's Ybor City (EE-bore) became a cigar manufacturing center in 1885, when Don Vincente Martinez Ybor, a Cuban exile, opened Tampa's first cigar factory. The idea caught on, and soon the area was home to more than 200 factories—making Ybor City the "Cigar Capital of the World." Spanish, Italian, and German workers came to join the Cuban cigar makers, and the vigorous community took on a multicultural flavor. Despite an embargo on Cuban tobacco since the Castro regime took over Cuba in 1959, Ybor City remains the center of Cuban culture in Tampa. It has also become a major entertainment center for Tampa's younger set, with restaurants and nightclubs open late. Antiques and collectibles shops provide daytime diversions aplenty, and the Ybor State Museum offers a glimpse into Tampa's colorful cigar industry history. A legendary Spanish pirate named Jose Gaspar is the focus of an annual February festival. The "Gasparilla" celebration begins with a mock "invasion" of Tampa Bay by a handsome Spanish galleon, crewed by extravagantly costumed prominent citizens. The vessel is escorted from Tampa Bay up the wide Hillsborough River by hundreds of private boats, large and small. Finally the symbolic ship ties up to the wharf, signaling the beginning of the big, float-filled Gasparilla Day Parade. The partying lasts for several days and has become a favorite tradition among visitors and residents. This is just one of many festivals on Florida's Gulf Coast. The area lends itself to year-round celebrating. The mild climate is perfect for outdoor fun, and the region's colorful past offers plenty of reasons for festivity.

THE ARTS

The arts take many directions along the Gulf coast of Florida. Artists, photographers, writers, and performers are influenced by the unique surroundings. Visitors are often surprised by the diversity and quality of west coast Florida museums. Two of the state's finest are located in downtown St. Petersburg. The Museum of Fine Arts owns an impressive collection of works by master artists and regularly mounts special showings of paintings and artifacts. The Salvador Dali Museum houses the world's premier collection of Dali works.

Sarasota is well-known as an artistic center, and the John and Mabel Ringling Museum Complex is perhaps the focal point of this cosmopolitan city's art community. Within the sprawling complex visitors may enjoy both indoor and outdoor art shows, and can visit the famed Asolo Center for the Performing Arts with its authentic eighteenth-century opera house. Sarasota has long been associated with the Ringling Bros. Barnum & Bailey Circus, and kids of all ages still enjoy visiting the Circus Museum and watching live circus acts during the summer and winter seasons.

Check local papers for announcements of the arts and crafts shows and sales. Oil and watercolor paintings, pottery, and handmade jewelry make some of the very nicest souvenirs.

Watch, too, for park performances. This is a great area for "Concerts in the Park," "Shakespeare in the Park," and the like. Art festivals in Cedar Key and Dunedin are only two of hundreds of such events, usually held in the spring. Sea oats and sand dunes, colorful native birds, lush vegetation, and famous sunsets over the Gulf provide a never-ending source of inspiration for artists and photographers from all over the world.

CUISINE

Crab cakes, cabbage palm salad, seafood chowder, and hush puppies—that's the basis for a seafood dinner, Florida style. At the Captain's Table Restaurant in Cedar Key, the cakes are loaded with generous chunks of sweet, freshly harvested crabmeat. Try catfish and hush puppies in Homosassa. They're wonderful with beer, but any cold drink will do. Fresh oysters, shucked on a platter with a spicy hot sauce or a squeeze of lemon? Where else but Apalachicola? Grouper sandwiches are typical Florida fare, usually served in a basket with fries and coleslaw.

Seafood rules on Florida's west coast, and it's always available. Red snapper, black and red grouper, flounder, and kingfish are just a few of the many species served fresh daily. Shellfish abound too. All sizes of shrimp live in the Gulf waters, along with a fine variety of tasty crabs, petite bay scallops, and "Florida lobster" tails (actually a crawfish).

The Panhandle is *the* place for oysters. Apalachicola's famous oyster beds produce nearly 80 percent of Florida's oyster crop—from an astonishing 10,000 acres of productive oyster beds. Little wonder, then, that Apalachicola hosts a seafood festival! It's held the first weekend of November and features oyster-shucking and -eating competitions along with a fine parade. Oyster bisque is another not-to-be-missed Apalachicola specialty.

Bay scallops are often featured in Florida restaurants. Unlike their larger cousins up North, bay scallops grow in comparatively shallow water just 3 to 6 feet deep. Maybe you'll find your own scallops in July or August, while snorkeling or wading along the coastline.

Stone crabs are especially delightful. These crabs live in holes on the sandy bottom of bays and the Gulf of Mexico, and are protected by law during the summer months. When the crab is harvested, only the largest claw is taken and the animal is released. (Don't worry. It quickly grows a replacement.) The claws are immediately boiled or steamed and eaten hot or cold. Crack the big thick claws and eat the sweet crabmeat with melted butter and maybe a little lemon juice.

When it comes to Florida lobster, only the tail is worth eating. These crustaceans are also protected during the summer months, and catching them in season has become a favorite sport for divers in the Florida Keys. The meat is served hot or cold and makes a great salad as well as lovely main-course fare. Splitting the tail with heavy shears and broiling it is a favorite method of preparation.

Mullet aren't as plentiful as they once were. (They used to be so thick, the old-timers claim, that men used to chase them to shore while the women scooped them up in their aprons!) The popularity of mullet roe on the world market has diminished the supply, but you can still find fried or smoked mullet on the menu at some dockside restaurants.

If you want to catch your own seafood supper, do so only during official harvesting seasons. Since the rules change periodically, it's best to ask about new restrictions before fishing along the Gulf coast. Bans on gathering shellfish are strictly enforced. Bait stores typically offer the latest information, along with free fishing publications, tide tables, and fishing licences.

Seafood is by no means the only cuisine enjoyed on Florida's Gulf Coast. Visitors enjoy Greek, Spanish, Cuban, Mexican, German, and Asian specialties and more, as well as world-class steaks and ribs.

Recommended restaurants are listed in each destination chapter.

FLORA AND FAUNA

The semi-tropical and tropical Florida Gulf Coast is divided roughly into three different vegetation areas: the Panhandle, the Nature Coast, and the Gulf Islands.

Driving south from Pensacola in the Panhandle, visitors notice a surprising variety of trees. Pine trees and oaks are much in evidence here. The largest of Florida's three national forests, the Apalachicola National Forest, affords a good look at high, pine-shrouded bluffs and dense cypress and hardwood groves. The park is easily accessible from Highway 319 passing through Ochlockonee River State Park to the town of Sopchoppy, where a well-marked trail leads visitors past a good variety of native trees and vegetation. Sharp-eyed travelers may spot a wary Florida 'gator along the banks of the Ochlockonee, or see a bald eagle or a rare red-cockaded woodpecker atop a long-needle pine.

The national forest features a Trout Pond area designed especially for the physically limited. Here wide, hard-surfaced access to an interesting forest pond is provided, with easily accessible swimming and fishing facilities. Elevations in these Florida "highlands" range from 10 to 100 feet.

Next comes the Nature Coast, true "spring country" in the central section of Florida's west coast. Here vegetation is lush and colorful around the giant freshwater springs. The springs form wide rivers that flow to the Gulf. Miles of cypress swamps are lined with spikes of cypress "knees" protruding from river bottoms. These knees, pointing a few feet above the water, are part of the cypress tree's root system. Opinions vary as to the function of these odd-shaped structures, but woodworkers love them for their beautiful grain and mellow color.

This is pine hammock country, where winding passages of sharp-edged sawgrass lead to the Gulf, providing habitat for hundreds of birds and animals ranging from raccoons and otters to the occasional black bear and panther. Alligators are plentiful here in the wetlands. Once near endangered status, the Florida alligator now exists in sufficient numbers to be somewhat of a nuisance. 'Gator' accidents are relatively rare, but tourists need to remember that they are dangerous and—when hungry—will go after anything they can swallow. That includes small dogs. Alligators can be fascinating to watch from a safe distance. Never feed them.

If you're on the water on a warm summer night, you might hear the 'gator's distinctive "gronk-gronk" call. Shining a flashlight may reveal red eyes glowing in the dark—the creature swims with only its eyes above the surface. "Shining 'gators" from a dock can sometimes reveal a surprisingly large number of them gathered together!

There are at least 30 alligator farms in Florida, and many area restaurants feature tasty 'gator dishes for adventurous diners. Some specialty butcher shops carry the meat too. Only certain sections of the head and tail meat, which tastes remarkably like veal, are considered edible. A little Dijon mustard served on the side is a good accompaniment for alligator dishes.

The Gulf Islands begin just south of Tarpon Springs and include the islands of Sanibel and Captiva. The long, narrow string of barrier islands, most of them connected to the mainland by causeways, continue south to Naples, past Sarasota and Fort Myers Beach. The protected bays and harbors sheltered by these islands make this one of Florida's most beautiful areas. This is picture-book country, with sand dunes and sea oats, streets lined with tropical palms, and amazing sunsets streaking the sky with improbable colors almost every evening.

The National Audubon Society maintains the Corkscrew Swamp Sanctuary near Fort Myers and Naples. Convenient boardwalks enable sightseers to view South Florida's wildlife and vegetation at close range. (Visitors may also experience small biting flies here occasionally, so bug repellent is a good idea.)

Florida is a land full of color. People here grow beautiful gardens despite salt air and occasional high winds. Sea grapes and viburnum are salt-tolerant plants, and the brightly hued, hardy hibiscus thrives in several varieties. Petunias, snapdragons, pansies, and all annual flowers planted in October thrive until May. Vegetable gardens started in the fall mature in the spring. Hardy periwinkle are one of the few flowers able to survive during the hot summer months from July through September.

In the growing season from October to May, shade-loving impatiens brighten the bases of giant live oaks, and huge "elephant ears" line riverbanks. Spanish moss drapes gracefully from oak tree branches, though most gardeners try to "keep ahead" of the lacy grey plant. In springtime towering lavender Jacaranda trees and a blaze of bright azaleas welcome the season in this amazing land of sand, flowers, lush vegetation, and creatures on the edge of the Gulf of Mexico.

THE LAY OF THE LAND

Florida is almost entirely surrounded by ocean. A low-lying peninsula separating the Atlantic Ocean from the Gulf of Mexico, the state is 432 miles long from the top of the Panhandle to the tip of the Florida Keys. The peninsula is about 150 miles wide, and at the widest part of the northern Panhandle it measures 367 miles from east to west. The west coast includes all of the Panhandle, and the area south along the coast to Naples and beyond. The beaches of the Panhandle extending south toward Cedar Key are noted for their pure, quartz-crystal sand. Some experts recognize this sand as some of the whitest in the world. Writers have compared it to snow or sugar. It's this special sand that gives the Gulf water along the Panhandle its remarkable aquamarine color.

There are 27 artesian springs within the central area of the west coast that create many of the wide rivers and wetlands leading to the Gulf of Mexico. Seventeen of these are "first-magnitude" springs, those producing more than 65 million gallons of water per day. Florida has almost twice as many of these first-magnitude springs as does any other state. Notable ones include Blue, Alexander, Jupiter, Silver, and Waukulla Springs. The subtropical barrier islands south of Tarpon Springs begin with Dunedin Beach and Clearwater Beach in the Tampa Bay area. South of the entrance to Tampa Bay, across the Sunshine Skyway Bridge, the islands continue. They extend along the coastline of Sarasota and Fort Myers, hugging the bays and inlets. Among these are Captiva Islands, Sanibel where, according to legend, the dreaded pirate Jose Gaspar kept his helpless female captives. The marshy lands south of Naples splay out into the famed "Ten Thousand Islands."

The barrier islands, so called for the protection they give the mainland from storms and erosion, form tranquil bays perfect for boating and water sports. During the past 50 years, development of these islands and keys has been rapid, if not always wise. Condominiums, motels, restaurants, businesses, entertainment attractions, and many lovely homes are the result of this development. Both residents and visitors enjoy these unique coastal islands, swimming and shell-collecting on the peaceful, almost deserted remote beaches.

THE NATURE COAST

Florida's newly designated Nature Coast, and the huge, first-magnitude springs within it, combine to create one of the finest coastal wilderness areas found anywhere in the world. Thanks to the farsighted efforts of ecology-minded people, future generations will be able to enjoy the beauty and quiet of these pristine rivers and lowlands and will reap the harvests of the warm, shallow Gulf waters.

The "Big Bend" area of Florida's west coast was formally renamed "The Nature Coast" by Governor Lawton Chiles in October 1992. The designation includes seven coastal counties: Wakulla, Jefferson, Taylor, Dixie, Levey, Citrus, Hernando, and Pasco, plus the town of Dunnellon. The idea for the Nature Coast came when a concerned group of chamber of commerce leaders realized the need to develop an overall plan for the preservation and use of this fragile, naturally productive spring and wilderness environment. Governor Chiles agreed to the plan. Today more than 40 percent of the Nature Coast is preserved as state and national parks, with others planned for the future.

The Nature Coast thrives naturally, maintained by millions of gallons of fresh water produced by hundreds of spectacular springs. These amazing springs originate 200 to 300 feet below the limestone base underlying Florida. An even larger supply of fresh water is located even deeper within the earth; this is designated the artesian aquifer. This giant reservoir is trapped by a layer of clay and nonporous material above it. When cracks occasionally develop in this nonporous material, water escapes to the Florida aquifer, which is contained only by limestone. When the limestone dissolves, it leaves holes for the crystal-clear water to reach the surface, forming the famous springs. North Florida springs originate in the artesian aquifer, making many of them first-magnitude springs.

Wakulla Springs, south of Tallahassee in North Florida, is the largest spring in the world, producing more than 1 billion gallons per day at peak periods. Explorations into its depths have mapped more than 10,000 feet of underwater tunnels, some reaching 320 feet. Silver Springs record average flow is greater than that of Wakulla, however. Plans are underway to explore Wakulla's tunnels further. (See "Sightseeing Highlights" in Chapter 4, Tallahassee, for details.)

Florida is world-famous for its 27 first-magnitude springs, the most found in any one state in the country. The springs also provide relaxation and enjoyment to many people as they discover the incredible beauty, lush vegetation, and different species of wildlife in this natural attraction. The springs actually "create" the Nature Coast by forming its productive rivers and wetlands before mingling with the salt waters of the Gulf.

Anyone who has paddled a canoe over these clear springs, or watched through a glass-bottom boat on a narrated tour of the larger spring parks, will never forget looking into this magic world below: fish appear from an intriguing opening near the bottom—is it really the bottom?—and the water quietly pushes through the ash-like sandy floor to the surface of the spring. The rising water reflects the sunlight and brilliant hues of fish swimming unafraid in its transparent depths. Underwater landscapes of the springs come in many shapes, from small bubbling places in the shallows under a tree limb to an enormous quiet pool, gently flowing downstream through the trees and foliage along the shore. The water temperature usually remains 72 degrees Fahrenheit all year, sometimes a few degrees warmer in southern Florida, especially near Venice, south of Sarasota, where the hot mineral springs spa reaches 96 degrees.

The tropical foliage surrounding the large springs and rivers keeps riverbanks from eroding and forms habitat for wildlife, including the endangered and lovable manatee. Manatees seek warm water during the colder winter months, often swimming far upstream to find it.

One of the most famous examples of rivers and springs working together is the historic **Suwannee River**, subject of Stephen Foster's nostalgic song "Old Folks at Home." The Suwannee is one of Florida's largest rivers, winding more than 200 miles across Florida from the Okefenokee Swamp in Georgia to its final destination, the Gulf of Mexico. Along the way, it is fed by more than 22 major springs, including those at **Manatee Springs State Park**, (352) 493-6072, on the banks of the river. Manatee Springs produces 116.9 million gallons of water daily, making it one of the area's largest springs. Manatees often swim the 23 miles upstream from the Gulf of Mexico to visit the park during the winter months. The 2,075-acre park can be reached by turning west off U.S. 19 about 2 miles north of Chiefland onto State Road 320, which ends at the park. The facility offers visitors opportunities for picnicking, bicycling, hiking, nature study, fishing, swimming, and boating. The park campground has 86 camp sites equipped with picnic tables, grills, and water, plus some with electricity. A ranger station gives information and assistance when needed. One of the most popular activities is the 8.5-mile wilderness bicycle trail system. Handy route maps are available at the entrance to the park.

The biggest attraction here is the beautiful spring itself. A boardwalk adjacent to the spring run allows an unobstructed view into the river swamp, where cypress, gum, ash, and maple trees border the river. Seasonal canoe rentals at the concession stand make exploring and fishing possible; a launching ramp allows visitors to bring their own boats.

OUTDOOR ACTIVITIES

Water sports naturally top the list of favorite activities along Florida's west coast. The miles of white sand beaches and the mild water temperatures attract sailors and power boaters, snorkelers, scuba divers, swimmers, and just plain "soakers."

Florida has more than its share of swim teams, and age-group competitions offer year-round healthy fun for folks of all ages. Most large apartment and condominium complexes have one or more pools, usually heated, as do many private homes. Tennis courts are a common sight here too, and some city or community recreation departments maintain them for the pleasure of citizens.

Sport fishing is available from private and municipal marinas, and "head boat" or "party boat" fishing is offered from numerous Gulf-side locations. Half-day and full-day charters and regularly scheduled boat trips make deep-sea fishing available to the whole family.

Canoeing along Florida's spring-fed lakes and rivers lends a perspective one couldn't get any other way. Mapped-out "canoe trails," in varying degrees of difficulty, are available to canoeists. Bird life is plentiful on the rivers, and some of the more spectacular wading birds come close enough to boats and docks to permit exciting wildlife photography. Visitors are invited to swim in most spring waters. Many spring areas have "no alcohol" signs posted, and authorities are very serious about enforcing the anti-littering ordinances.

Golf courses, both public and private, are plentiful. Several baseball teams winter in Florida. Their practice games bring the real thing to fans—even the best hot dogs.

Parasailing over the Gulf is a fast-growing sport. A giant parachute towed by a boat far below offers an unparalleled view of an area. Broad beaches and shallow waters make the sport a safe, yet exciting, experience.

For detailed information about Florida's many activities, read the destination chapters of this book. Visit or call local chambers of commerce for up-to-date schedules of events.

PRACTICAL TIPS

HOW MUCH WILL IT COST?

The cost of your trip depends on what you plan to spend. Florida offers a wide range of housing, transportation, and entertainment options. Water sports like swimming, snorkeling, and even scuba diving can be free—if you bring your own equipment. Beaches are free in most places, and every beach is required to have one or more public access points. State and county parks have excellent picnicking spots, and restrooms are generally very clean. Many offer showers too. Services such as canoe rental and transportation vary in price; check with the many tourist information and welcome stations for current information.

Larger, more tourist-oriented places provide more to see and do—and they cost more. Excellent campgrounds are available throughout the state— some plain, some fancy. Remember, the closer you get to the beach, the more things cost, especially during the main tourist season, from January through mid-April.

Summer rates are lower than winter ones. Consider making reservations in efficiency motels instead of eating all meals in restaurants. Chambers of commerce and tourist welcome centers can provide lists of appropriate possibilities. Elegant homes and condominiums are often rented by their owners for longer stays, usually a month or more.

Make reservations well ahead to plan expenses, and remember: the sunshine, sand, and Gulf waters are free.

CLIMATE

Summer in Florida is hot and humid. The humidity brings moisturizing benefits for all—and discomfort for some. Retreat to air-conditioned comfort on those hot, muggy afternoons. Saltwater swimming may be helpful for stiff joints and muscles.

The climate during the high tourist season, November to May, is delightful. Occasionally the weather disappoints vacationers who have only a week to spend in the Sunshine State, but for the most part, travelers can expect to enjoy outdoor living and wear summer clothing. Fall and spring are happy blends of summer and winter. Moderate winds cool the atmosphere, and humidity ranges from 50 to 60 percent. Winter winds, however, carry the remains of those nasty Northern cold fronts. It can get quite chilly, so pack a sweater or light jacket.

During hurricane season, between June and November, tropical storms and hurricanes can bring strong winds and torrential rain. Once in a while there's a whopper like Hurricane Andrew, which, in August 1992, caused millions of dollars in damage to the Homestead area south of Miami. Florida media and guest accommodations are prepared to advise you in the event of a storm.

Afternoon rain showers can come up so quickly that it can be raining on one side of the street and sunny on the other! Floridians welcome these showers, enjoying the cooler air that usually follows. If thunder and lightning threaten, stay inside. The storm will be gone in a few minutes.

WHEN TO GO

The Florida west coast has something to offer visitors year-round. Summertime is vacation time for families, and the beaches are the place to be. Buy a big straw hat and enjoy soaking in the warm Gulf waters. ("Soaking" is an art form taught by Florida Crackers to

FLORIDA GULF COAST CLIMATE

Average daily high and low temperatures in degrees Fahrenheit.

	Apalachicola	Fort Myers	Pensacola	Tallahassee	Tampa
Jan.	61/46	75/52	61/43	64/41	71/50
Mar.	68/54	80/57	69/51	72/48	76/56
May	82/68	89/66	84/66	87/63	87/67
July	87/75	91/74	90/74	91/72	90/74
Sept.	85/72	90/73	86/70	87/69	89/73
Nov.	69/53	80/59	70/49	71/46	77/56

Yankees—just relax and float around. No swimming laps allowed.)
Remember, this is the subtropics. Take it slow and easy and slather on the
sunscreen.

Plan to be outdoors in the mornings until noon. Then go inside and
enjoy air conditioning until after 2 p.m. Florida's summer lasts from June
until October, with the hottest months July, August, and September.

Not many Floridians swim in the Gulf in January and February—
It's too cold. But it doesn't seem to bother Northern folks much.
However, lots of hotels and motels have heated pools, and the sun is
always warm if you find a sheltered spot out of the wind. Golf and other
active sports are available year-round, but better to plan for the moderate
temperatures of fall, winter, and spring.

My favorite months are April and May, when the winter cold fronts
fade and beach temperatures are ideal. Fall, with its possible tropical
storms, is risky but delightful.

Crowds generally peak the week after Christmas and for several
weeks around Easter, when students' Spring Break and vacation times
coincide. But college vacation time has not been a problem on the west
coast, where living is slower paced and the beaches are geared toward
relaxation.

WHAT TO BRING

Summertime in tropical Florida requires light, airy clothes. Loose cotton shirts and shorts are most comfortable. A lightweight long-
sleeved white shirt is handy for sun-sensitive skin. Straw or canvas hats
help to keep heads cool. Bring lots of sunscreen and plan to use it. Treat
Florida's summer sun with great respect. Remember, Florida is closer to
the Equator than are Northern states, and skin burns much faster here. A
lightweight raincoat or umbrella in the car is wise protection against
unexpected tropical showers. Sport coats and ties for gentlemen are
rarely needed, but bring them just in case. Some of the upscale restaurants and hotels still require them, but the trend toward casual dress
seems to be more and more pronounced each year.

Shoes and cover-ups over swimsuits are necessary in hotel lobbies
and elevators. Buy inexpensive sandals to kick off when you want to wig-
gle your toes in the sand. (Never leave your room key unattended on
your beach towel or "hidden" in a shoe while swimming.)

Bring a cooler in the car and to the beach. Snacks with cheese and
fruit can replace expensive restaurant meals. It's important to drink

enough liquids in the heat, and people perspire even while swimming. Children especially need to be encouraged to drink juice or a favorite soda while playing or paddling in the water. It's a good idea to keep cameras in the shade to protect the film.

If you have room, bring golf clubs, tennis racquets, scuba gear, and other sports equipment. You'll save hefty rental fees (and your equipment will probably be of better quality than that at rental facilities).

TRANSPORTATION

The ideal way to see Florida is by car, recreational vehicle, or motorcycle—in other words, on your own (or rented) wheels. Public transportation is good, when and where it is available.

An Amtrack Auto Train station is located in Sanford, near Orlando, providing one way to avoid the long drive north. Car rentals are available just about everywhere, including airport locations. A quick call to rental agencies is the best way to get current rates, which can change often in Florida, where competition is keen. Make sure to ask about "drop off" costs between jaunts. Sometimes it's cheaper to pay the weekly rate.

Another option is renting a boat, either a captained vessel or do-it-yourself "bare boating," for those who qualify. Quite a few west coast cities with large marinas offer rentals by the day, week, or month. It's a fun way to see a different side of the Sunshine State.

Motor homes and camping trailers may also be rented in this area. Excellent campgrounds abound, but remember to reserve space ahead of time. Some folks stay two or three months in well-equipped RV parks. They know the Gulf Coast is a good place to be when the snow flies!

CAMPING, LODGING, AND DINING

Camping on Florida's west coast during the peak tourist season is usually a less expensive option than staying in hotels or motels. But camping here is not cheap by most veteran campers' standards. Overnight charges may range up to $50 a night. Monthly rentals bring the rate down in most places. The closer the campground is to the Gulf, the higher the rates will be. Off-season rates drop by about half. Some facilities will store RVs. Shop around before making reservations.

Lodging can be especially interesting in out-of-the-way places. Consider renting a townhouse or a waterfront time-share facility. They can be surprisingly inexpensive, especially if shared with friends. Of course, a place on the beach is more expensive—but usually worth it.

Suite hotels are increasingly popular. They're usually new, too, and conveniently located. Some of the older motels and efficiencies, often located a block or so from the beach, are worth a look for next year— they're often filled with repeat visitors, booked a year in advance.

RECOMMENDED READING

Reading opens up the lives and history of this unique state. Marjorie Kinnan Rawlings wrote *The Yearling* from her home in north central Florida, where she lived for many years. Ernest Hemingway's *The Old Man and the Sea* could have been written about any fisherman living in tropical waters. Hemingway lived for many years in Key West, Florida. Have fun reading Jeff Klinkenberg's *The Real Florida: Key Lime Pies, Warm Fiddlers, A Man Called Frog and Other Endangered Species*. Klinkenberg is famous in Florida for his perceptive description of native Floridians and the wildlife of the area. *Tropical Son, Essays on the Nature of Florida*, by Jonathon Harrington, and *Up For Grabs, A Trip Through Time and Space in the Sunshine State*, by John Rothchild, also help readers understand Florida and its place in the world today.

RESOURCES

Chambers of Commerce/Visitors Centers:
Pensacola (904) 874-1234
Panama City (904) 785-5206
Tallahassee (904) 488-6167
Cedar Key (904) 543-5600
Tarpon Springs (813) 937-6109
Clearwater (813) 461-0011
St. Petersburg (813) 821-4069
Greater Tampa (813)228-7777
Sarasota (800) 522-9799
Fort Myers (800) 366-3622
Boca Grande (941) 964-0568
Naples (941) 262-6141

1
PENSACOLA

Pensacola is located in the center of Florida's Panhandle along the Gulf of Mexico. More than 400 years ago Don Tristan De Luna and his 1,400 troops came ashore on the beaches of Pensacola Bay. Since then five flags have flown over Pensacola, and the city has changed hands more than a dozen times in exchanges involving Spain, France, England, the United States, and the Confederacy. The first permanent settlement was Fort San Carlos, built in 1698. The city's historic sites and natural attractions, from the restored downtown to the pristine, protected beaches, lend a sense of time-lessness to Pensacola. Yesteryear is on display at several sites in and around Historic Pensacola Village, which features museums, historic homes, and a Colonial Archaeological Trail that leads visitors through different eras of the area's history and even to a real, ongoing archeological dig.

But there's more than history here. Vacationers will find all the holiday accoutrements with plenty of individual activities and enough family-oriented fun to keep the clan interested. Nightlife is definitely part of the action here, with New Orleans only four hours away and the Pensacola Naval Air Station right outside of town. In short, Pensacola can be laid-back, educational, or a real thrill. Take your pick. ◼

PENSACOLA

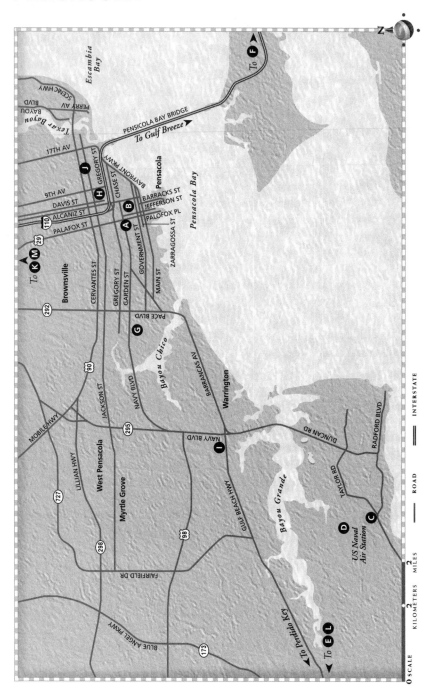

Sightseeing Highlights

Ⓐ Civil War Soldiers Museum

Ⓑ Historic Pensacola Village and
    Colonial Archaeological Trail

Ⓒ National Museum of Naval
    Aviation

Ⓓ Pensacola Historical Museum

Ⓔ Pensacola U. S. Naval Air
    Station

Ⓕ Perdido Key State Recreation
    Area

Ⓖ Seaside

Ⓑ T. T. Wentworth Jr. Florida
    State Museum

Ⓖ Wildlife Rescue and Sanctuary

Lodging

Ⓙ Bay Breeze Bed & Breakfast

Ⓚ Executive Inn

Camping

Ⓛ Perdido Bay KOA

Ⓜ Tall Oaks Campground

Food

Ⓗ Grouper Seafood and Steak
    Restaurant

Ⓘ Oyster Bar

Note: Items with the same letter are located in the same town or area.

A PERFECT DAY IN THE PENSACOLA AREA

Start this Perfect Day while it's still cool, with a morning of swimming, diving, hiking, and picnicking at Fort Pickens. Then check out the National Museum of Aviation, where more than 100 history-making aircraft are on display, from an FF6 Hellcat to the Skylab Command Module. Later head for The ZOO and botanical garden. For a more leisurely day, take a morning canoe trip down one of Pensacola's fresh-water steams, then spend the afternoon exploring some of the historical areas. Either way, don't forget to take a relaxing evening walk on the beach.

SIGHTSEEING HIGHLIGHTS

✩✩✩ **Civil War Soldiers Museum**—This 4,200-square-foot museum includes more than 80 well-interpreted exhibits from a private collection of memorabilia, letters, and artifacts which provide insight into the events of the Civil War as experienced by the soldiers. Life-size dioramas depict scenes from battlefield medicine, soldiers' everyday lives, and the strategic aspects of the war. The collections range from

Florida Dept. of Commerce Div. of Tourism

military weapons and uniforms to field surgical equipment. Details:
108 S. Palafox Street, Pensacola; (904) 469-1900; open Monday
through Saturday from 10 a.m. to 4 p.m. Admission is $4 for adults, $2
for children ages 6 to 12. The museum is wheelchair accessible and has
restrooms, bookstore, and gift shop. (1–2 hours)

✯✯✯ **Gulf Islands National Seashore**—The national seashore is dotted by strips of developed beach as well as beach wilderness, along 23
miles of barrier islands bordering the Gulf of Mexico from South
Mississippi to West Florida. Although not part of the national seashore,
the Pensacola Beach area, on Santa Rosa Island, sits at its center, with
strips of the national seashore on either side. A large part of this seashore
is contained on Santa Rosa, with another large portion on Perdido Key.
Created in 1971, the national seashore preserves these unspoiled beaches
with their miles of high, wind-sculpted dunes and wide-open spaces.
Historic sites abound throughout the area. Details: Call (904) 934-2600,
or call or visit the Pensacola Convention and Visitor Information Center
at 1401 E. Gregory Street, Pensacola; (904) 434-1234 or (800) 874-1234.
(half to full day)

✯✯✯ **Historic Pensacola Village and the Colonial Archaeological
Trail**—The historic village is a complex of nineteenth-century buildings with several historic sites, including some first-rate history trails,
museums, and historic homes. Historic Pensacola Village showcases
the Charles Lavalle House at 203 E. Church Street, the Clara Barkley
Dorr House at 311 S. Adams Street, and the Julee Cottage at Zaragoza
and Barracks Streets, some of the oldest houses in the area. All were
built during the early to late nineteenth century.

Included in the historic village is the Colonial Archaeological
Trail, which leads visitors through different eras of Pensacola history
and highlights an ongoing program of excavation by local archaeologists. The trail includes evidence of the fortifications that existed
between 1752 and 1821, including the commanding officer's compound, the officer's kitchen, the garrison kitchen, and the Government
House. Both guided and self-guided tours of the village area are available and include the homes in the Seville and North Hill Historic
Districts. Don't miss the Pensacola Museum of Art housed in the Old
City Jail. Details: 407 S. Jefferson Street, Pensacola; (904) 444-8905;
open daily from 10 a.m. to 4 p.m. Admission is $5.50 for adults, $4.50
for seniors, and $2.25 for children ages 4 to 16. (1–4 hours)

★★★ **National Museum of Naval Aviation**—This is the top attraction for visitors to the area. Located on the Pensacola U.S. Naval Air Station, the museum traces the history and development of American naval aviation. Highlights include fighter aircraft from every war, the *Skylab* Command Module, actual combat flight simulators for public use, and the NC-4 *Flying Boat*, which became the first plane to cross the Atlantic in 1919. Four A-4 *Skyhawks* are suspended in formation from the ceiling in the Blue Angle Atrium. Models of aircraft carriers, Navy blimps, and a Vietnam POW camp are displayed. Included in one section of the museum is a replica of a World War II aircraft carrier island and flight deck with a working elevator. The spacecraft collection includes the Mercury Space Capsule, a Lunar Rover Vehicle, and a spacesuit used on the moon. Exhibits even cover pre–World War I aviation memorabilia. Visitors can take the controls of aircraft trainers and simulators located throughout the museum, and the Flight Adventure Deck is a hands-on activities center for children. Details: Located on the Pensacola U.S. Naval Station, 1750 Radford Boulevard, Pensacola; (904) 452-3604 or (800) 327-5002; open daily (except New Year's Day, Thanksgiving, and Christmas) from 9 a.m. to 5 p.m. Admission is free. (4-5 hours)

★★★ **Pensacola Beach**—Pensacola Beach is on Santa Rosa Island, a barrier island separating the Gulf of Mexico from Pensacola Bay. The sand here is remarkable—sugar-like, with a 99 percent quartz content. Mixed in with the island's sandy landscape are dunes and natural stands of trees and other shoreline vegetation. Much of Santa Rosa Island, including Pensacola Beach, is protected from development, and the beach area offers access to nature as well as to modest and upscale motels and single cabanas near the shoreline. Details: Beach Information Center (800) 635-4803; open 24 hours/day; public beach is free; $1-per-car toll to cross bridge to reach island. (4-6 hours)

★★★ **Perdido Key State Recreation Area**—Ranked as having one of the top 12 beaches in the U.S., Perdido Key sits across the Pensacola Bay inlet about 5 miles from the western tip of Santa Rosa Island and Fort Pickens. The beach is easily accessible by paved roads, offers plenty of room to stretch out, and features such welcome amenities as picnic shelters, showers, and restrooms. Perdido Key is a popular destination for people who appreciate the unhurried pace and quiet of the barrier island. The area also sports vacation homes, beach-oriented shops, and a handful of memorable old-time honky-tonks. Details: Gulf Beach Highway, Perdido Key; (904) 942-4660. (half to full day)

★★★ **Seaside**—If you head 60 miles east of Pensacola on U.S. 98 and then on C30A, you'll come to the small community of Seaside, once called the "down home utopia" by *Time* magazine. Known as a center for rejuvenation, Seaside offers privately owned, furnished cottages along the Gulf of Mexico for rent by individuals and families. Each of the 200 cottages within the town limits has a distinctive personality. Quiet retreat centers for executive conferences and seminars are also available. Many of Seaside's charming streets are cobblestone. The area also offers tennis, golf, deep-sea fishing, bicycle rentals, and exceptional downtown shopping. Details: Seaside Information, P.O. Box 4730, Seaside, FL 32459; cottage rental agency and info (800) 277-8696, or front desk reservations (904) 231-2222. (half to full day)

★★★ **The ZOO**—At the east end of Pensacola near Gulf Breeze is The ZOO and botanical garden. From hand-feeding giraffes to riding the Safari Line train, The ZOO was built to give children, photographers, and other visitors a close-up look at many animals, including numerous endangered species. Watch zookeepers prepare food for more than 700 animals and visit Ellie the Elephant, the 10-year-old pachyderm who plays music and paints with watercolors as part of her daily shows. Ellie's paintings fetch high prices at charity fund-raisers. The gift shop features a simulated rain forest, environmental gifts, and genuine African art. Details: 5701 Gulf Breeze Parkway, 10 miles east of Gulf Breeze; (904) 932-2229; open daily (weather permitting) from 9 a.m. to 5 p.m. during summer and until 4 p.m. in winter. Admission is $9.25 for adults, $5.25 for children, $8.25 for senior citizens. Parking is free, and there are facilities for those with disabilities. (1–2 hours)

★★ **Fort Pickens**—One of three forts built in the 1820s to guard the entrance of Pensacola Bay, Fort Pickens covers the western end of Santa Rosa Island. Popular with local as well as out-of-town visitors, the restored fort is open for free public tours and houses a museum, an auditorium, and a handy visitor center that offers up-to-date information about the Pensacola area. Popular as a place to picnic and skin dive, the park also features a campground for overnight visitors. Fort Pickens is the best-known of the three fortresses, including Fort McRee on Perdido Key, which has mostly deteriorated over time from the weather, and restored Fort Barrancas across Pensacola Bay at the Naval Air Station. Fort Pickens was held by the Union troops during the Civil War and later was the prison of Apache leader Geronimo. Details: Fort Pickens Road, 9 miles west of Pensacola; (904) 934-2622; open 9 a.m. to 5 p.m. daily from April to October, and from 8 a.m. to 4 p.m. the rest of the year. Guided tours daily at 2 p.m. Admission is $4 per vehicle. (1–5 hours)

☆☆ **Pensacola Historical Museum**—Housed in the Old Christ Church at Adams and Zaragoza Streets, the Pensacola Historical Museum was built in 1832 as an Episcopal church and used during the Civil War as a barracks, prison, hospital, and chapel by the federal forces. The museum now presents the history of the city of Pensacola, displaying such historical items as clothing, silver, bottles, Indian artifacts, glass, and geological finds. The museum has a gift shop and resource center featuring maps, photos, genealogy, manuscripts, and local history. Details: 405 Adams Street, Pensacola; (904) 444-8905; open Monday through Saturday from 9 a.m. to 4:30 p.m. Admission is $2 for adults and $1 for children. (1–2 hours)

☆☆ **Pensacola U.S. Naval Air Station**—One of the country's principal naval air stations, the Pensacola U.S. Naval Air Station is recognized as the "cradle of naval aviation" because of its role in the development of military aircraft. Visitor passes and area maps are available at the front gate; more detailed maps are offered in the aviation museum. The area also includes Fort Barrancas, built in the sixteenth century and recently refurbished. Details: Located at the south end of Navy Boulevard, Pensacola; (904) 452-2311; open daily from 9 a.m. to 5 p.m. Free to the public. Fort Barrancas is free and open daily, with tours at 11 a.m. and 2 p.m. (3-4 hours)

☆☆ **T. T. Wentworth Jr. Florida State Museum**—In the restored Pensacola City Hall, the state museum contains exhibits about the history and natural history of West Florida. Children will love the three-story museum with its eclectic collection of items ranging from shrunken heads and political mementos to Coca-Cola memorabilia. Details: 330 S. Jefferson Street, Pensacola; (904) 444-8586; open Monday through Saturday from 10 a.m. to 4 p.m. and on Sunday

from 1 to 4 p.m. Included in the admission price to Pensacola
Historical Museum. (1 hour)

⭐⭐ **Wildlife Rescue and Sanctuary**—This sanctuary provides
treatment and refuge for injured and orphaned wildlife, including
alligators, eagles, cormorants, herons, pelicans, and hawks. Short
tours are given. Details: 105 N. S Street, Pensacola; (904) 433-9453;
open Wednesday through Friday from 10 a.m. to 2 p.m. and on
Saturday from 10 a.m. to noon. Donations to the sanctuary are
accepted. (2-4 hours)

FITNESS AND RECREATION

The Pensacola area offers an ample assortment of recreation and fitness opportunities. Family outings can be an all-day affair of swimming, boating, hiking, and picnicking at one of the three forts in the
area. **Fort Pickens**, on Santa Rosa Island, is popular with divers,
boaters, campers, and picnickers. Many local boaters and picnickers
opt for **Fort McRee** on Perdido Key. **Fort Barrancas**, located at
Pensacola Naval Air Station, offers not only picnic grounds, a
wooded area, and a nature trail, but a glimpse of history as well.

Tennis enthusiasts will enjoy **Bayview Recreation Center**,
open from early morning until late evening, with six tennis courts.
The center is located at **Bayview Park**, a sprawling recreation area
on East Hill near Bayou Texar. Although Pensacola has many fishing
boats, land fishing is best achieved from either the 3-mile-long
Pensacola Bay Bridge or the **Bob Sikes Bridge**, which links Gulf
Breeze and Pensacola Beach. For the best hiking and nature trails,
head out to the woods and marshes at **Big Lagoon State Park**,
which also offers camping facilities.

The Pensacola area boasts a half-dozen good golf courses,
including **Creekside Golf Club**, 2355 W. Michigan Avenue, (904)
944-7969, open daily from 7 a.m. to dusk; **Marcus Pointe Golf
Club**, 2500 Oak Pointe Drive, (904) 484-9770, open daily from sunrise to sunset; the **Moors Golf Club**, 3220 Avalon Boulevard, (904)
995-4653, open daily from 7 a.m. to dusk; **Sonebrook Village Golf
Center**, 5555 Woodbine Road, (904) 995-0900, open daily from
8 a.m. to 9 p.m.; **Osceola Golf Club**, 300 Toanwanda Drive, (904)
456-2761; and **Perdido Bay Golf Club**, Doug Ford Drive on
Perdido Key, (904) 492-1223.

FOOD

Pensacola offers a varied assortment of restaurants, but seafood is definitely the area cuisine standout. In the city of Pensacola the **Grouper Seafood and Steak Restaurant**, 830 E. Gregory Street, (904) 438-3141, regularly gets high marks from local critics. Open from 11 a.m. to 11 p.m., the restaurant features casual dress, a children's menu, carryout, and a lounge. Considered by some area fishermen to be the best seafood restaurant, **Captain Jack's Seafood Shack**, 63 Via de Luna, (904) 934-6030, is one of the most reasonably priced of the bunch, with most meals under $10. Be sure to ask about the catch of the day. **The Oyster Bar**, 709 Navy Boulevard, (904) 455-3925, is open Monday through Saturday from 11 a.m. to 10 or 11 p.m. and features an extensive menu and a good lounge. Dress casually. **Boy On A Dolphin**, 400 Pensacola Beach Boulevard, (904) 932-7954, is open Monday through Saturday from 4 p.m. to 11 p.m. and on Sunday from 11 a.m. to 11 p.m. This restaurant is a good choice for family or business dinners. It's casual yet elegant and features a spectacular view of Santa Rosa Sound. Indoor and outdoor seating is available. **Flounder's Chowder & Ale House**, just east of the Quietwater Beach Boardwalk at 800 Quietwater Beach, (904) 932-2003, is open daily from 11 a.m. to 2 p.m. It features a children's menu, a Jamaican-style Beach Bar with excellent reggae music, and the house specialty, fresh seafood charbroiled over a flaming hardwood fire. Enjoy a great view of Santa Rosa Sound, too.

LODGING

There are many hotels and motels to choose from in the Pensacola area, most with an "average" rating, by Florida standards. The highest-rated and most expensive digs are found on Pensacola Beach, among them the **Clarion Suites Resort & Conference Center**, 20 Via de Luna Drive, (904) 932-4300, which offers 86 handsome suites for about $105 to $155 per night during the winter and $64 during the summer. The rooms include a microwave oven; an exercise room and coin-operated laundry are other amenities. Expensive but nice, the **Best Western Pensacola Beach Motel**, 16 Via de Luna Drive, (904) 934-3300, offers large, well-equipped rooms on the Gulf Beach for about $105 to $115 during the winter and $49 to $69 during the summer. The **Holiday Inn Pensacola Beach Motel**, 165 Fort Pickens Road, (904) 932-5361, has balconied rooms and four lighted tennis courts. Some rooms have a refrigerator.

GULF BREEZE

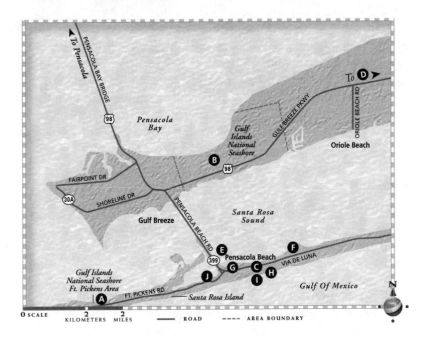

Sites

A Ft. Pickens

B Gulf Islands National Seashore

C Pensacola Beach

D The ZOO

Food

E Boy on a Dolphin

F Captain Jack's Seafood Shack

G Flounder's Chowder & Ale House

Lodging

H Best Western Pensacola Beach Motel

I Clarion Suites Resort & Conference Center

J Holiday Inn Pensacola Beach

Camping

A Ft. Pickens Campground

Note: Items with the same letter are located in the same town or area.

The average rate during winter is $100 to $140 per day, $60 to $90 during the summer. The most affordable hotels and motels are found in the city of Pensacola and include the **Executive Inn**, 6954 Pensacola Boulevard, (904) 478-4015, which offers some rooms with microwave ovens and refrigerators for about $36 to $56 during the winter, $31 to $41 during the summer. The **Bay Breeze Bed & Breakfast**, 1326 E. Jackson Street, (904) 470-0316, has four units and serves a complimentary breakfast. This B&B offers honeymoon accommodations, laundry facilities, and an exercise room rates are $55 to $75.

CAMPING

Camping near Pensacola gives travelers access to some of the most beautiful sand beaches in the world. The Gulf Islands National Seashore covers about 10,000 acres of protected beaches on the Gulf of Mexico, including the Fort Pickens area, open to the public year-round. The fort is located 9 miles west of Pensacola Beach, on SR 399. The museum at Fort Pickens describes the history of the fort and its role in protecting the entrance to Pensacola Harbor during the Civil War. The National Seashore Park offers hiking trails, bicycle paths, a boat ramp, and fishing. Swimming is available nearby on the beaches. Camping facilities at **Fort Pickens Campground**, (904) 932-2621 or (800) 280-2267, include 200 sites: 131 sites with electric, and 200 with water. The campground is 2 miles south of Gulf Breeze on SR 399; it's 7 miles west on Fort Pickens Road to the campground entrance. Rates are $12 (subject to change); electricity $2 extra. Sorry, pets are not allowed in Florida state parks.

    Perdido Bay KOA, (334) 962-2727, is located on Perdido Bay, directly on the beach at the west side of the entrance to Pensacola Bay. Take Exit 2 off I-10 to SR 297 leading to CR 292, and west across Perdido Bay bridge to U.S. 98 and Spinnaker Drive. The private park offers 93 sites, some shady and on Perdido Bay. Seven camping cabins are also available, from $25 to $40 per night, depending on the number of people in the party. The well-managed park supplies such camping needs as groceries and propane. Campers also have access to a beach, pool, boat ramp, and fishing. The park is open year-round.

    Tall Oaks Campground, (904) 749-3212, is a 5-acre, 24-site facility located off I-10, Exit 2B, 0.2 miles north on SR 297 to 9301 Pine Forest Road. Many of the park's mostly shaded sites are pull-through and full-service, with water, electric, and sewer hookups. A laundry is also available. Rates are $14 for four persons, year-round.

PANAMA CITY

As you travel down Florida's west coast, one of the first beach resort areas you'll encounter is Panama City. Nestled tightly in Florida's Panhandle, stretching along the Gulf of Mexico, the area offers simple sights and a minimum of organized activities; it's a nice, quiet place for visitors to sit back and relax. The fresh seafood here can't be beat, and the area's 27 miles of white, powdery beaches are ranked as some of the best in the nation. Depending on the time of the year, the waters off Panama City can be some of the clearest in the state. Offshore man-made diving reefs and dive shops are abundant, and there are plenty of motels, golf courses, and nature trails to choose from. The beach areas of South Walton Beach and Destin are just down the road.

The ocean here boasts an average water temperature of 72 degrees, while the average year-round air temperature is 78. Late spring and early fall are delightful times to visit Panama City. ◨

PANAMA CITY

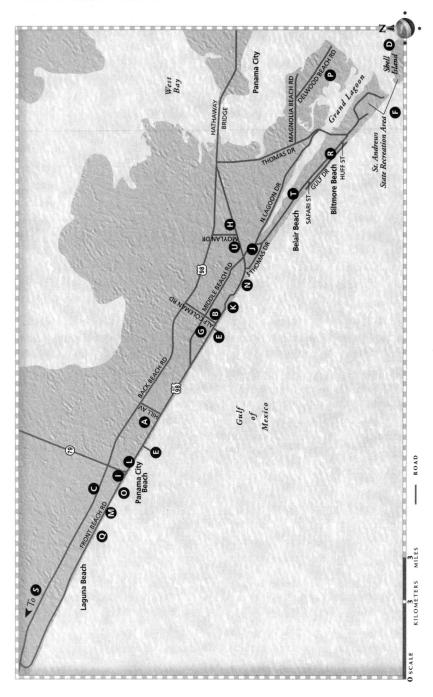

Sightseeing Highlights

(A) Gulf World Marine Park

(B) Miracle Strip Amusement Park

(C) Museum of Man in the Sea

(D) Natural and Artificial Reef Diving

(E) Panama City Fishing Piers

(F) St. Andrews State Recreation Area

(G) Shipwreck Island Water Park

(H) Zoo World Zoological & Botanical Park

Food

(I) Boar's Head

(J) Hamilton's Restaurant and Lounge

(K) Runaway Island Restaurant

(L) Sharky's Beach Club & Restaurant

Lodging

(M) Beachcomber by the Sea

(N) The Boardwalk Beach Resort

(O) Impala Motel

(P) Marriott's Bay Point Resort

(Q) Sea Witch

(R) Treasure Island Motel

Camping

(S) Holiday Travel Park

(T) Panama City Beach KOA

(U) Park Place Campground

A PERFECT DAY IN PANAMA CITY

Since Panama City's main draws are its water and beach activities, pack a big bottle of sunblock and carry a wide-brimmed hat. Spend the morning exploring the animal life, beach facilities, and nature trails at St. Andrews State Recreation Area. There's enough here to keep a family busy for several hours. Top off the morning with a little fishing from the jetties or the pier located at the east end of the park.

In the afternoon, when the sun rises and the day heats up, cool off at the Shipwreck Island Water Park or tour the shady Zoo World Zoological & Botanical Park. To get away from the heat, visit the Museum of Man in the Sea. For dinner try one of the excellent beach-front restaurants. Cap the evening with a stroll down the public pier and along the beach. Or, if you're up for something more eventful, try one of the nightclubs; go to the greyhound races at nearby Ebro Greyhound Park (located off State Highway 79, open March through September); or visit the Miracle Strip Amusement Park, buzzing with neon intensity and carnival games and rides.

SIGHTSEEING HIGHLIGHTS

✪✪✪ **Natural and Artificial Reef Diving**—The Florida Panhandle is one of the best places in the state for snorkeling and skin diving. Hundreds of reefs, both natural and artificial, lie off the coast. The area's natural reefs range in depth from 80 to 110 feet. About 50 man-made reefs, coordinated by the Panama City Marine Institute, have been constructed out of 160-foot-long and 35-foot-high bridge spans, ten barges, and the *City of Atlantis* ship. The artificial reefs range in depth from 45 to about 120 feet.

A half-dozen major ships have been wrecked off the coast, from 110-foot tugboats and a 441-foot WWII liberty ship, to the Gulf of Mexico's most famous wreck, the 465-foot *Empire Mica*. *Skin Diver* magazine has called Panama City Beach the "wreck capital of the south." Details: Information on snorkeling and diving trips, customized vacation packages, and equipment is available by calling (800) PCBEACH (800/722-3224) or visiting any full-service area dive shop.

✪✪✪ **St. Andrews State Recreation Area**—The stretch of beach associated with the St. Andrews State Recreation Area was recently highlighted on NBC's *The Today Show* and was ranked the number 1 beach in America twice in the 1990s: first in 1992, when it received the Golden Compass Award by the News Travel Network, and again in 1995 by *Condé Nast Traveler* magazine, which compared more than 600 beaches nationwide. This beach seems almost to have been designed by nature with families in mind, with inviting white sand and clear green waters.

This recreation area, situated on 1,063 acres, is known for more than its beach, though. Its pine flatlands, salt- and freshwater marshes, and nature trails are perfect for bicycling and hiking, and the ample campgrounds provide 176 camp sites, picnic shelters, a playground, and restroom and shower facilities. St. Andrews is surrounded by woodlands on one side and the beach on the other. Don't miss the boat ride to **Shell Island**, just offshore from the recreation park, for a few hours of swimming, diving, and fishing. Details: 4607 State Park Lane, Panama City; (904) 233-5140. (4–6 hours)

★★ **Gulf World Inc., Marine Park**—This marine park is one of the better ones in Florida, with a complete but simplified marine showcase offering four continuous shows daily. Stroll through the Tropical Garden, filled with parrots, flamingos, and peacocks. Take in the bottle-nosed dolphin and trained sea lion shows. Experience the walk-through shark tank. The marine park is an excellent place to take kids if it gets too hot at the beach. At the Coral Reef Theater enjoy captivating views of fish and natural coral in the amphitheater and learn about the mysteries of marine life through a scuba-diving film. Details: 15412 Front Beach Road, Panama City; (904) 234-5271; open year-round. Admission is $13.95 for adults, $7.95 for children under 12. (2 hours)

★★ **Museum of Man in the Sea**—This one-of-a-kind museum traces the history of underwater diving back to the sixteenth century. The historical displays include artifacts from the first days of scuba diving and underwater exploration as well as exhibits gleaned from shipwrecks. Exhibits show how divers have influenced marine life sciences, exploration, salvage and construction, oceanography, and underwater archaeology. Details: 17314 Back Beach Road, Panama City; (904) 235-4101; open daily from 9 a.m. to 5 p.m. Admission is $4 for adults, $2 for children age 6–16; under 6 free. (1–2 hours)

★★ **Panama City Fishing Piers**—The Panama City Beach area has three public piers, all excellent for strolling and fine for fishing. Catches may include Spanish mackerel, redfish, flounder, sea trout, bonito, and bluefish.

A boat ramp is located on Grand Lagoon near the fishing piers. The Bay County Pier, with a very charming boardwalk, is free to the public; the Dan Russell Pier, Florida's longest at 1,642 feet, charges a nominal fee. The third pier, another popular fishing spot, is at St. Andrews State Recreation Park, along with the jetties. Details: All three piers can be accessed from Front Beach Road.

✹✹ **Zoo World Zoological & Botanical Park**—Home to more than 150 animals, including rare and endangered species, the zoo is a partner in the Species Survival Plan, established in 1980 by world zoological authorities and dedicated to protecting the world's most endangered animals. Focusing on big cats, reptiles, orangutans, and other primates, the zoo also has an aviary and a petting zoo. Details: 9008 Front Beach Road, Panama City; (904) 230-1243; open year-round. Admission is $8.95 for adults, $6.95 for children age 3–12. (1 hour)

✹ **Miracle Strip Amusement Park**—The amusement park contains 30 rides, including one of the bigger (2,000-foot-long) roller coasters in the area. The park's 9 acres encompass continuous entertainment, arcades, contests, games, and special events. Souvenir shops and concessions abound. You can even find miniature golf courses within the park. Details: 12000 Front Beach Road, Panama City; (904) 234-5810; reopened spring of 1997. Call for more information and new admission prices.

✹ **Shipwreck Island Water Park**—This water park is the largest in the Florida Panhandle. Covering 6 landscaped acres, it offer enough variety to please every member of the family. There are regular rides and picnic facilities as well as tons of flowing and rushing water. Water rides include a 1,600-foot meandering course, a 35-mile-per-hour speed slide, a 370-foot white-water tube, and the Tadpole Hole for kids. Lifeguards are on duty, and umbrellas, lounge chairs, and inner tubes are free. Details: Shipwreck Island Water Park is located at 12000 Front Beach Road, Panama City Beach; (904) 234-0368; open in warm weather only. Call for admission prices and more information. (2–4 hours)

FITNESS AND RECREATION

Fitness and recreation activities in the Panama City area include golf, water sports, hiking, and annual athletic events. Four of the best golf courses open to the public include **Bay Point Country Club**, 100 Delwood Beach Road, Panama City Beach, (904) 235-6950. The country club is a semi-private par 72, divided into two courses, Club Meadows and Lagoon Legend. The club has a driving range, pro shop, and dining facility. There's no walking and tee times are required. The **Holiday Golf Club**, 100 Fairway Boulevard, Panama City Beach, (904) 234-1800, is a semi-private, par 72 course with an additional nine-hole executive par 3 course. The golf club includes a lighted driving range, golf shop, and snack bar. Walking is permitted; tee times recommended. The **Hombre**, 120 Coyote Pass, Panama City Beach, (904) 234-3673, is a semi-private par 72 course with a nine-hole par 3. The facility has a driving range, golf shop, and lunch counter. Walking is permitted, on occasion, and tee times are recommended. **Signal Hill Golf Course**, 9615 N. Thomas Drive, Panama City Beach, (904) 234-3218, is a public par 71 course with a golf shop and snack bar. Walking is permitted and tee times are recommended.

Each May the Boardwalk Beach Resort sponsors the **Annual Gulf Coast Triathlon**. Held for the last 14 years, the triathlon also acts as a qualifier for the Ironman World Championship.

St. Andrews State Recreation Area sports a nature trail that starts near Grand Lagoon at the old "Cracker" turpentine still (where turpentine is made from the sap of pine trees) and winds through pine flatwoods, sandpine scrub, and fresh- and saltwater marshes. Watch for alligators, deer, and wading birds.

FOOD

Panama City restaurants focus primarily on seafood, with a sprinkling of spicy Cajun specialties and Southern delicacies. Some of the best restaurants border the beach, including **Runaway Island Restaurant**, 6627 Thomas Drive, (904) 230-9933, a Caribbean-style eatery serving local seafood and hand-cut steaks at reasonable prices. Also hugging the beach is the **Boar's Head**, 17290 Front Beach Road, (904) 234-6628, three-time winner of *Wine Spectator's* Award of Excellence. Serving only dinner, the regular menu features seafood, steaks, and wild game.

Located between the two public piers is **Sharky's Beach Club & Restaurant**, 15201 Front Beach Road, (904) 235-2420. There's a pleasant beach access here, live music, an in-house DJ, good seafood, and dancing. Set back off the beach at Thomas Drive and North Lagoon Drive at the Grand Lagoon inlet is **Hamilton's Restaurant and Lounge**, (904) 234-1255, noted for its annual Cajun Fest in March. The menu primarily features seafood, and mesquite grilling is a house specialty. The food is above average. So are the prices.

LODGING

Panama City Beach has a wide range of hotels and motels and a good selection of resort and convention centers. Probably the nicest resort hotel and convention center is **Marriott's Bay Point Resort**, 100 Delwood Beach Road, Panama City Beach, (800) 874-7105. Luxurious compared to the regular hotels, the Marriott is a four-star resort that has been listed as one of the "top 24 golf resorts in America" by *Golf Illustrated* magazine. It has the best selection of meeting rooms and convention amenities in the Panama City area. Another excellent resort convention center is the **Boardwalk Beach Resort**, 9450 S. Thomas Drive, (800) 224-GULF, with more than 20,000 square feet of meeting space. For pleasure travelers and visiting families, the **Sea Witch**, 21905 Front Beach Road, (800) 322-4571, offers one of the better locations, accommodations, and facilities for a reasonable price. There are other equally good motels, such as **Beachcomber by the Sea,** 17101 Front Beach Road, (904) 234-6681, with its island landscaping; the family-oriented **Treasure Island Motel**, 5005 W. Gulf Drive, (904) 234-3552, with beachfront access; and the simple **Impala Motel**, 17751 Front Beach Road, (904) 234-6462, providing all the basics and a pretty beach entry.

CAMPING

Panama City Beach KOA, (904) 234-5731, covers 10 acres in the lively center of Panama Beach, with its restaurants, music, and nightlife. The well-managed campground features Kamping Kabins ($45), a grocery store, laundry facilities, phone hookups, cable TV, both a pool and a wading pool, and its own access to the beautiful beach across Thomas Drive. Propane is for sale here. Open year-round, the park has 114 sites, some for tenters. Reservations and deposits are requested. Rates range from $18.95 to $22.95 March 1 through September 7 and $13 to $17.95

September 8 through February 28. Pets are permitted. To reach the campground, follow U.S. 98 to CR 3033, 0.8 mile east to SR 392 (Thomas Drive), then 2 miles southeast to 8800 Thomas Drive and the campground (watch for the KOA sign).

If you wish to camp near the beach, try **Park Place Campground**, (904) 234-2278, a privately owned facility with 51 sites on 3 partially shaded, grassy acres located 2 miles west of Hathaway Bridge at 32407 Front Beach Road (W 98A). The park features a grocery store, recreation room, laundry facilities, and cable TV. Pets are permitted. Rates for four persons are $13 to $17 March 1 through September 15 and $13 to $17.95 September 16 through February 28.

For beachfront sites head to the **Holiday Travel Park**, (904) 837-6334, located at 5380 U.S. 98, 8.5 miles east of Destin. The 250-site park on 17 acres features a beach, pool, store, rec room, fishing, and swimming. Rates for five persons are $27 to $37 March 1 through September 15 and $15 September 16 through February 28. An extra $2.50 is charged for water and electricity. Pets are permitted.

NIGHTLIFE

Many nightclubs and beach clubs are clustered along the beachfront area. Most will take credit cards, but some don't, so ask first. Most of the following spots also feature a variety of music; some have bands, so if you're looking for a show, call ahead. **The Brig** at the Treasure Ship, 3605 Thomas Drive, (904) 234-8881, is open seasonally, offers food and dancing, and occasionally spotlights a show band. **Club La Vela**, 8813 Thomas Drive, (904) 234-3866, is also open seasonally. **The Curve**, 4130 Thomas Drive, (904) 234-1055, is open year-round and offers dancing but no food. **Salty's by the Sea**, 11073 Front Beach Road, (904) 234-1913, is open year-round and offers food and dancing. **The Spinnaker**, 8795 Thomas Drive, (904) 234-7882, open seasonally, features food and dancing. **Spud's**, 651 Clara Avenue, (904) 235-1205, is open year-round for dining and dancing. **U-turn Sunburn Beach Club**, 17283 Front Beach Road, (904) 233-6625, is open seasonally, plays all types of music except country, occasionally has a show band, and offers dancing and food.

For an alternative to the nightclub scene, **Panama City Beach** is an excellent spot for a secure night walk on the beach. While you're at it, check out the **Miracle Strip** for its carnival-like atmosphere and great family activities, including games and rides.

Scenic Route: Beach Drives

Although Panama City Beach and the surrounding county is growing rapidly, the beach area is politically managed so as not to be
overrun or spoiled by the swelling population and urban sprawl
that characterize other parts of Florida. Try a cruise down U.S.
98 south to Port St. Joe, or a drive north on Alt. U.S. 98 to **Fort
Walton Beach**. Both highways skim along the edge of the Gulf
of Mexico and make for a relaxing beach drive. **Port St. Joe**,
about an hour's drive from Panama City Beach, is listed as a historic city and was the site of the state capital until the city was
destroyed by a yellow fever epidemic and a tidal wave in 1841.
It was also the site of the first railroad and first pure thoroughbred
horseracing stable in the state.

You can also tour the **St. Andrews State Recreation
Area** by following Thomas Drive to State Road 392 and into the
park. The road follows a circular route inside the park, offering a
look at numerous vegetation and animal habitats.

BEACH DRIVES

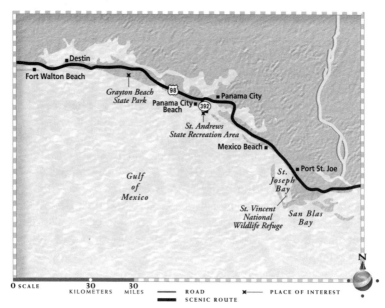

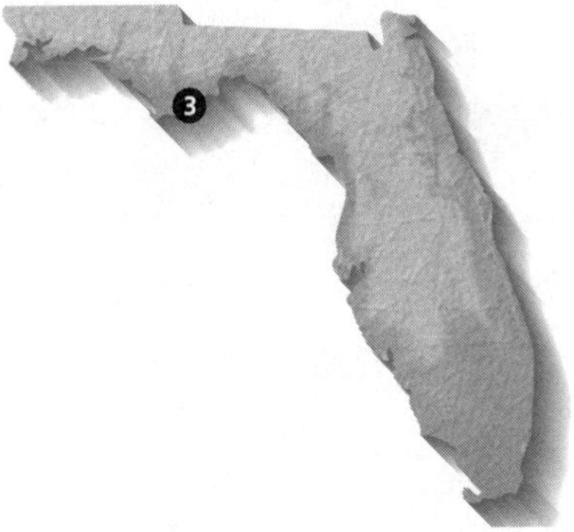

3
APALACHICOLA

Apalachicola and its neighbors, St. George Island and Eastpoint, provide visitors with some of the finest seafood catches in the state. Over 80 percent of the state's and 10 percent of the nation's total oyster crop is cultivated from the 6,000 acres of oyster beds in the Apalachicola area. Apalachicola, a Hitchiti word meaning "people residing on the other side," refers to the area's first inhabitants. Apalachicola's interesting historic district dates back to the 1830s, and the town has two waterfront parks.

Today Apalachicola hosts the state's oldest maritime festival (held in November), while Eastpoint is considered the heart of Franklin County's commercial seafood industry and the home port of many of its oyster boats. The sight of returning boats makes Eastpoint's docks a great place to tour at sundown. But it's St. George Island that offers visitors 30 miles of white beaches and acts as a barrier island enclosing Apalachicola Bay. Just west of St. George Island, Cape St. George and its lighthouse comprise a fully protected state park. To the north of Franklin County is the Apalachicola National Forest, the largest of the state's three national forests, encompassing 565,000 acres and stretching across four north Florida counties.

APALACHICOLA

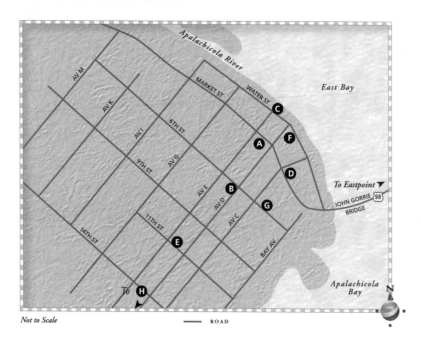

Not to Scale   —— ROAD

Sightseeing Highlights

A   Apalachicola Historic District

B   John Gorrie State Museum

Food

C   Boss Oyster

C   Caroline's River Restaurant

D   The Gibson Inn

E   Magnolia Grill

F   Roberto's

Lodging

G   Coombs House Inn

D   The Gibson Inn

C   Rainbow Inn

H   Rancho Inn

Note: Items with the same letter are located in the same town or area.

A PERFECT DAY IN THE APALACHICOLA AREA

Take a morning walk through the Apalachicola Historical District and visit some of the 50 sites of historical interest there. Spend some time at the John Gorrie State Museum. After lunch at a tasty seafood and sandwich shop on St. George Island, head over to Little St. George Island to rent a boat and relax. Sundown is the perfect time to visit the lighthouse at Cape St. George. Wrap up the evening with a late dinner at the Gibson Inn.

SIGHTSEEING HIGHLIGHTS

★★★ **Apalachicola National Forest**—Just north of Apalachicola and stretching across four county lines, the Apalachicola National Forest's varied terrain includes pine flatwoods and hardwood hammocks, swampy rivers, lakes, and two wilderness areas, Bradwell Bay and Mud Swamp-New River. The area is popular with canoeists, who paddle the forest's secluded lakes and streams as well as the canoe trails on the Sopchoppy and lower Ochlockonee Rivers. Part of the Florida National Scenic Trail passes through the forest and highlights a wide variety of plants and wildlife. One of the forest's special features is the Trout Pond, a recreational spot designed for the physically disabled that offers swimming, an interpretive trail, and a fishing pier. Details: The forest is reached by most northbound roads heading out of Apalachicola; (904) 926-3561 (district headquarters offices). (half to full day)

★★★ **John Gorrie State Museum**—Located on Gorrie Square, the John Gorrie State Museum celebrates Apalachicola's prosperity during the 1830s, when the town was the third-largest seaport on the Gulf Coast. Dr. John Gorrie was the inventor of man-made ice. The scientific foundation that led to modern refrigeration and air conditioning is the highlight of this museum, which also contains other scientific exhibits related to the area. Details: 6th Street and Avenue D, one block east of U.S. 98/319, Apalachicola; (904) 653-9347; open Thursday through Monday from 9 a.m. to 5 p.m. Admission is $1 for adults; children are free. (½ hour)

★★★ **St. George Island**—The largest of four barrier islands, St. George is situated directly across the bay from Apalachicola and offers visitors 28 miles of white beaches as well as fishing opportunities. With clear water on the Gulf side, swimming and boating are popular activities. The island has been developed for vacationers, offering some of the best dining in the area as well as two motels and other rental accommodations. **Dr. Julian G. Bruce State Park** (1,883 acres) sits on the east end of the St. George shoreline and contains a series of hiking trails and boardwalks from which to enjoy a unique estuary. Details: St. George Island is located 11 miles from Apalachicola and is connected to Eastpoint by a 4-mile bridge and causeway. (4–6 hours)

✯✯ **Apalachicola Historic District**—A walk through historic old Apalachicola reveals some fine old homes and buildings dating back to the 1830s, including stately antebellum houses and the cotton warehouses that once housed the city's prosperous cotton export. Don't miss the Trinity Episcopal Church, the Raney House, and the Chestnut Street Cemetery. Also, look for the sailing schooner *Governor Stone 1877*, a two-mast, gaff-rigged schooner built to service towns along the Gulf Coast. A 52-site tour is sponsored by the Apalachicola Bay Chamber of Commerce and the Apalachicola Area Historical Society. Details: Apalachicola Historical Society, 128 Market Street, Apalachicola; (904) 653-9419. (1–2 hours)

✯✯ **Cape St. George on Little St. George Island**—Little St. George Island sits at the west end of St. George Island, just across Bob Sikes Cut, a small pass separating the two islands. To the west, across West Pass, is the St. Vincent National Wildlife Refuge. Built in 1833, the Cape St. George Lighthouse and lighthouse-keeper's dwelling sit midpoint on the small island. The lighthouse still serves as a beacon for passing boats. The island is also home to the **Cape St. George State Reserve**, providing an opportunity for visitors to explore a remnant of Florida's original natural landscape. The island is accessible only by private boat. Details: Call the Chamber of Commerce (904) 653-9419. (4–6 hours)

✯✯ **St. Vincent National Wildlife Refuge**—Located on St. Vincent Island and accessible only by private boat, this island refuge is just across the bay from Apalachicola on the mainland and across West Pass from St. George Island. The 12,358-acre refuge provides a home to more than 270 species of wildlife, including Sambar deer, bald eagles, turkeys, and alligators. In 1990 the barrier island, which was originally purchased by the Nature Conservancy before being acquired by the

U.S. Fish and Wildlife Service, became one of several Southeastern coastal islands where endangered red wolves are bred before being released into the Southeastern environment. St. Vincent offers visitors great beaches and two camping areas. Details: On St. Vincent Island; (904) 653-8808. (1–6 hours)

★ **Fort Gadsden State Historic Site**—Located 35 miles from Apalachicola within the Apalachicola National Forest, this historic fort commemorates the site of a bloody battle in 1816 between the United States and the local inhabitants, who included an African American community comprised mostly of runaway slaves. The fort, named for Lt. James Gadsden of the Engineers Corps, no longer exists, but an open-sided, walk-around interpretive center displays six authentic miniature replicas of it and the battle sites. A picnic area is available, and earthworks mark the fort locations. Details: P.O. Box 157, Sumatra, FL 32335; (904) 670-8988; open 8 a.m. to sunset. (1–2 hours)

★ **Munson Hills Off-Road Bicycle Trail**—Also located in the Apalachicola National Forest, the bicycle trail is a 7.5-mile loop with a 4.25-mile shortcut that offers the rider a scenic and challenging ride through some of the most rolling terrain in the national forest. The trail was established by the Munson Hills Off-Road Bicycle Trail Association and is run by the U.S.D.A. Forest Service. Details: The Munson Hills Trail connects with U.S. 363 or the Woodville Highway 1.25 miles south of Tallahassee, and can be reached from Apalachicola driving east on U.S. 98 and north on U.S. 363 to Apalachicola National Forest; (904) 926-3561. (4–8 hours)

FITNESS AND RECREATION

With barrier islands acting like giant piers, the northwestern Gulf Coast of Florida is well-known for its fishing, and Apalachicola's major recreational draw is freshwater and saltwater fishing. In fact, many regular visitors keep boats berthed at local marinas year-round. Anglers can fish from the surf, from marshes, from deep-sea fishing boats, and from piers. Freshwater fishing is also productive, especially from the Apalachicola River and its tributaries, which have produced six state records for carp as well as sunshine, spotted, redeye, striped, and white bass.

Other sports and recreational activities include golf and tennis, but water sports dominate the area. Landlubbers enjoy camping and hiking the forests and marshlands of the national and state park areas, such as those found on **St. George Island, Little St. George Island,** and **St. Vincent's Island.** Fishing camps and villages can be found along the **Ochlockonee River,** the **Sopchoppy River,** the **Wakulla River, St. Marks River,** and the **Carrabelle River,** as well as along the Gulf coastal communities. Call the Apalachicola Bay Chamber of Commerce, (904) 653-9419, for more information.

FOOD

Although this area's seafood quality is excellent, the number of restaurants is limited. One of the better restaurants with a standard menu and good seafood is the **Gibson Inn,** (904) 653-2191, a restored turn-of-the-century Victorian inn offering meals in the $11 to $20 range. Located at Market Street and Avenue C, the Gibson Inn is open from 7:30 a.m. to 3 p.m., and from 6 to 9 p.m. For seafood and atmosphere try the **Rainbow Inn,** (904) 653-8139, Water Street, on the shores of the Apalachicola River in historic downtown Apalachicola. Besides enjoying marina facilities and lodging, you can dine in either the upscale **Caroline's River** Restaurant or find a complete oyster menu at **Boss Oyster.** One of the most highly rated restaurants in the area is **Magnolia Grill,** (904) 653-8000, on Highway 98 in the Crooms Transportation Plaza, downtown Apalachicola. For eclectic Italian cuisine try **Roberto's,** 15 Avenue D, (904-653-2778). Roberto's hosts the Apalachicola Wine Society, which holds wine tastings each month.

LODGING

One of the highest-rated but affordable accommodations in Apalachicola is the **Gibson Inn,** at Market Street and Avenue C, (904) 653-2191, which offers rooms ranging from $65 to $85 per night. Overlooking Apalachicola Bay, The Gibson Inn also handles conventions and meetings with more than 600 square feet of meeting space. Try the **Coombs House Inn,** 80 6th Street, (904) 653-9199, for an excellent bed and breakfast set in an elegant 1905 Victorian mansion complete with its original wood furnishings. At $89 to $110 per night, it's affordable, but make reservations well in advance. the **Rancho Inn,** (904) 653-9435, located on U.S. 98 1 mile west of Highway 240, offers very reasonable

APALACHICOLA REGION

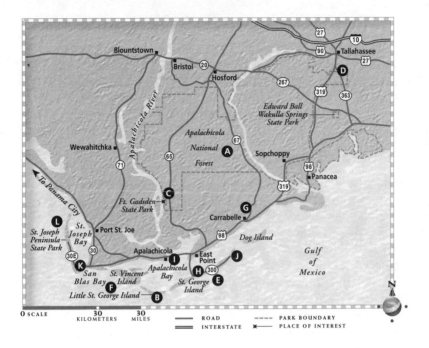

Sightseeing Highlights

Ⓐ Apalachicola National Forest

Ⓑ Cape St. George

Ⓒ Ft. Gadsden State Historic Site

Ⓓ Munson Hills Off-Road Bicycle Trail

Ⓔ St. George Island

Ⓕ St. Vincent National Wildlife Refuge

Lodging

Ⓖ Beachside Motel

Ⓗ Buccaneer Inn

Ⓗ St. George Inn

Camping

Ⓘ Apalachicola Bay RV Park and Campground

Ⓙ St. George Island State Park

Ⓚ Cape San Blas Camping Resort

Ⓛ St. Joseph Peninsula State Park

Note: Items with the same letter are located in the same town or area.

rooms for families and pets from $34 to $40 per night. For accommodations that offer complete marina facilities, try The **Rainbow Inn** on the Apalachicola River on Water Street. If you're staying overnight in nearby Carabelle, try the **Beachside Motel**, (904) 697-2759, located on Old Carabelle Beach along Highway 98 West, for simple and comfortable rooms. On St. George Island, stay at the **St. George Inn**, (904) 927-2903, or the **Buccaneer Inn**, (800) 847-2091.

CAMPING

Apalachicola Bay RV Park and Campground, (904) 670-8307, is located 1.3 miles west of Apalachicola on U.S. 98. The 7-acre park is near the bay in a quiet place with 68 open and shaded sites. A pool, playground, store, and cable TV are provided. Small pets are allowed. Rates are $13 to $15 year-round. **St. George Island State Park**, (904) 927-2111, covers more than 1,900 acres on the east end of St. George Island, which is a showplace of beautifully designed, light and airy Florida-style homes, all nestled among the Gulf beach dunes. To reach the island take Highway 300 south off U.S. 98 1.3 miles west of Eastpoint. Upon reaching the island, turn left, following Highway 300, and continue east to the park. All 60 sites have electricity and water, and Gulf swimming, nature trails, and fishing are available. The year-round rate is $8 per night. No pets are allowed in Florida state parks.

For beachfront and primitive sites, **Cape San Blas Camping Resort**, (904) 229-6800, is the place. The 44 sites may be open or shaded, and city water is provided. Facilities include flush toilets, a beach, pool, and playground. The store supplies groceries. Also available are hiking trails, canoeing, fishing, and swimming. The resort is located off U.S. 98 on CR 30. Head 7 miles south to Cape San Blas Road, then 1.5 miles west to the campground. Rates are $11 to $15. Pets are permitted.

Wilderness camping on 2,500 acres is available near Port St. Joe at the T. H. Stone Memorial, **St. Joseph Peninsula State Park**, (904) 227-1327, 20 miles southeast on CR 30E, west of U.S. 98. The park provides 119 sites, a boat ramp, marina, playground, nature trails, fishing, and canoe and bicycle rental. A park attendant is on duty at the park 24 hours a day. Rates are $15 March 1 to October 31 and $8 November 1 to February 28. Cabins are also available (call for rates).

4

TALLAHASSEE

L ocated on the edge of the Florida Panhandle, the city of Tallahassee has served as the state capital since 1824. This same area was once the capital of the Apalachee Indian Nation back in 1539, when Hernando De Soto first happened upon it. De Soto spent the winter of 1539–40 camped here, and some historians believe that Dominican priests traveling with the De Soto exploration party conducted America's very first Christmas celebration on the same hill site where the capitol building stands today. In the early 1700s Creek Indians established a town here. They called the place *Tallahassee*, which means "old town."

The area represents a unique blend of what northern Florida is all about. The capitol stands on the highest piece of land in the city, and the view from the top floor offers a fine panorama of rolling hills, flowering azaleas, dogwoods, magnolias, and hundreds of shimmering lakes, springs, and rivers, stretching all the way to the Gulf. Good beaches are within an easy one-hour drive. Tallahassee is home to Florida State University and Florida A&M University.

City attractions are diverse, ranging from historical sites and museums to family recreational spots and outdoor activities, all served up with a generous amount of Southern hospitality. Medium-sized but growing rapidly, Tallahassee offers the best blend of what's Southern and what's new in Florida. But personal clocks may need to be reset to a slower speed. Tallahassee—like many older Southern cities—can be great for the blood pressure. ◼

TALLAHASSEE

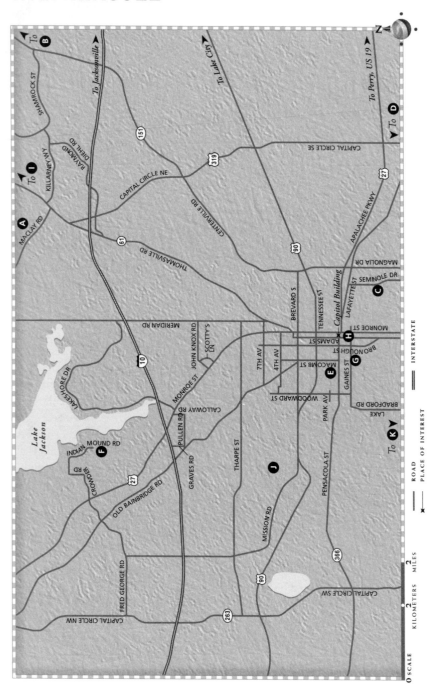

Sightseeing Highlights

A   Alfred B. Maclay State Gardens

B   Bradley's Country Store

C   De Soto Archaeological and Historical Site

D   Edward Ball Wakulla Springs State Park

E   Knott House Museum

F   Lake Jackson Mounds State Archaeological Site

G   Museum of Florida History

H   Old Capitol Building and New Capitol Building

I   Pebble Hill Plantation

J   San Luis Archaeological and Historic Site

K   Tallahassee Museum of History and Natural Science

A PERFECT DAY IN THE TALLAHASSEE AREA

Tallahassee is a lovely place for walking. Before setting out for a stroll, pick up the visitors bureau's comprehensive brochure "Touring Tallahassee: A Walking Guide to Historic Downtown." The old city is nicely planned, with oak-shaded squares, placid lakes, and antebellum homes. Wear comfortable shoes and get an early start, beginning at the New Capitol Building, which affords jaw-dropping views from the 22nd floor. Then follow the Historic Trail, touring some of the homes that are open to the public. The Knott House Museum provides an interesting glimpse into Tallahassee's past. The Megin-Monroe House is an art gallery now but once served as a Civil War field hospital.

In the afternoon take a scenic drive following the suggestions in "Canopy Roads and Country Lanes: A Driving Guide to Scenic Leon County," another brochure published by the Visitors Bureau that highlights the area's famed canopied roads, where branches of towering old trees form sun-dappled green tunnels. Stop now and then to browse through the country stores and antebellum plantations. The Tallahassee Museum of History and Natural Science includes a woodland trail through 52 acres of native Florida ecosystem. When all this exploring brings on hunger pangs, stop at the picnic area here. If time allows, visit Bradley's Country Store. Owned by the same family for generations, it's a tourist trap for sure, but a bright spot all the same. A late afternoon stop at the Alfred B. Maclay State Gardens is a must: the gardens are a masterpiece of floral architecture during the blooming season. Ready for some nightlife? It can be either stimulating or laid-back. Things tend to shut down early here, but you probably won't mind. After all, it's been a busy day!

SIGHTSEEING HIGHLIGHTS

★★★ **Alfred B. Maclay State Gardens State Park**—Originally built as the winter home of New York businessman Alfred B. Maclay, the gardens are the focal point of this 308-acre park. Enchantingly landscaped, these gardens were first planted in 1923. They feature more than 200 floral varieties, including colorful azaleas, camellias, and oriental magnolias, as well as native plants. The masterpiece is Killearn Gardens, surrounding the financier's restored home. The Maclay House is still furnished as it was in the 1920s and now serves as an information center for camellia enthusiasts. The park offers nature trails, swimming, and boating. Details: 3540 Thomasville Road, just north of I-10 on Exit 30, Tallahassee; (904) 487-4556. The gardens and house are open daily from 9 a.m. to 5 p.m. only January through April during the blooming season; the rest of the park is open year-round. In-season admission is $3.25 to $4.25 per carload and $1 for motorcycles, bicycles, and pedestrians; $3 for adults and $1.50 per child to enter the gardens and house. Admission is free the rest of the year. (1–2 hours)

★★★ **Edward Ball Wakulla Springs State Park**—This park is home to one of the world's deepest freshwater springs and the site of several 1930s Tarzan movies. The springs were originally thought to be the Fountain of Youth when they were discovered by Ponce de Leon in 1513. They've been explored to a depth of 250 feet and have the largest rate of water discharge in the state, with a daily average of 576 million gallons bubbling from more than 10,000 feet of underwater tunnels. Want to see alligators? This is the place to find them! Watch along the shore from the parking lot area, or have a real adventure and take one of the river cruises or glass-bottom boat tours. The narrated cruises offer glimpses of a variety of animals in their native habitats, while the tours provide views of fish, marine plant life, and mastodon bones. The park is popular with birdwatchers and offers hiking, bicycle and nature trails, and swimming areas. Details: 15 miles south of Tallahassee, at the junction of State Roads 61 and 267; (904) 922-3632; open from 8 a.m. to dusk; tours depart every half-hour. Admission is $3.25 to $4.25 per carload; cruises cost $4.50 for adults and $2.25 for children. (3 hours)

★★★ **San Luis Archaeological and Historic Site**—Here is an active archaeological site that was both an Apalachee Indian village and seventeenth-century Spanish mission. Spanish Franciscans served the Christian Indians who lived here, and they called the mission church San Luis de Talimali. An Apalachee village and a Spanish home have been reconstructed, and trails with interpretive displays describe the site's excavation and history, including exhibits and living-history demonstrations. The annual Heritage Festival features costumed reenactors, crafts, performers, and period foods. Details: Near the intersection of Tennessee Street and White Drive at 2020 W. Mission Road, Tallahassee; (904) 487-3711; open Monday through Friday from 9 a.m. to 4:30 p.m., Saturday from 10 a.m. to 4:30 p.m., Sundays and holidays from noon to 4:30 p.m. Admission is free; guided tours are offered daily at noon. (1–2 hours)

✮✮✮ **Tallahassee Museum of History and Natural Science**—The museum features a restored 1880s farm complex along with history and natural science exhibits. A trail winds through the 52 acres of woodlands, cypress swamps, and fields to reveal the flora and fauna of north Florida. Red wolves, Florida panthers, alligators, and other native wildlife thrive on this complex that is home to over 100 indigenous animals. Back in 1826 Tallahassee society was excited about the marriage of Catherine Gray, a great-grandniece of George Washington, to Prince Achille Murat, nephew of Napoleon Bonaparte. Their restored antebellum plantation is here, along with a one-room schoolhouse, church, gristmill, and caboose. Picnic facilities are available. Details: Lake Bradford, 6.5 miles southwest of Tallahassee, 3945 Museum Drive; (904) 576-1636; open Monday through Saturday from 9 a.m. to 5 p.m., Sunday from 12:30 to 5 p.m. Admission is $5 for adults, $4 for seniors, and $3 for children. (2 hours)

✮✮ **De Soto Archaeological and Historical Site**—This is the site of the 1539 encampment of Spanish explorer Hernando De Soto, and the location of the first Christmas observed in North America. Annual reenactments of the celebration are held in December. The oldest copper coins ever discovered in the United States were unearthed here. Details: Near downtown, off Lafayette Street at 1022 De Soto Park Drive, Tallahassee; (904) 922-6007; open daily from 8 a.m. to sunset. Admission is free. (½ hour)

✮✮ **Knott House Museum**—Built in 1843 as a private home, the stately house has been restored and fully furnished with Victorian pieces owned by the Knott family when they bought the house in 1928. Known as "The House That Rhymes," for the eccentric poems written by the mansion's matron and attached to the chairs, tables, lamps, and other household furnishings, the historic home is considered a time capsule of Tallahassee history. An eight-minute video presents the history of the house and the Knott family, after which visitors are guided on a one-hour narrated tour. Details: 301 E. Park Avenue, Tallahassee; (904) 922-2459; open Monday through Friday from 8 a.m. to 5 p.m., Saturday from 10 a.m. to 4 p.m. Admission is $7 for families, $3 for adults, and $1.50 for children. (2 hours)

✮✮ **Lake Jackson Mounds State Archaeological Site**—Six temple mounds and one burial mound are the remains of a ceremonial center that existed from A.D. 1200 to 1500. The site reveals that ancestors of the Seminole and Creek tribes lived along the banks of the Jackson River. Guided tours and interpretive programs are offered. Details: Get off U.S. 27 at Crowder Road, then head for 3600 Indian Mounds Road, Tallahassee; (904) 922-6007; open daily from 8 a.m. to sunset. Admission is free. (½–1 hour)

✰✰ **Museum of Florida History**—This museum encompasses both prehistoric and recent Florida history. The museum's mascot, Herman, a 9-foot-tall skeletal mastodon pulled from Wakulla Springs in the 1930s, oversees the exhibit on prehistoric Florida. Other historical and archeological exhibits include Spanish trade and maritime culture displays, sunken treasure from Spanish galleons, war relics from the seventeenth and eighteenth centuries, and a reconstructed steamboat visitors can explore. Special educational programs are offered too. Details: Downtown near the state capitol at 500 S. Bronough Street, Tallahassee; (904) 488-1484; open Monday through Friday from 9 a.m. to 4:30 p.m., Saturday from 10 a.m. to 4:30 p.m., Sunday and holidays noon to 4:30 p.m. Admission is free. (1–2 hours)

✰✰ **Old Capitol Building**—Built in 1845, the Old Capitol has been restored to its 1902 appearance with red-and-white-striped awnings, a stained-glass dome, a classic rotunda, the historically accurate House and Senate Chamber, and a Supreme Court and Governor's Suite. Nicely mounted interpretive exhibits illustrate Florida's political evolution, including the Bourbon era, the territorial period, and the years between statehood and Reconstruction. The Old Capitol is located adjacent to the New Capitol Building, which is also worth a visit. On the top (22nd) floor, an observatory/art gallery reveals a spectacular view of the rolling hills of the city and surrounding country all the way to the Gulf of Mexico. Self-guided tours cover the entire Old Capitol complex. Details: Downtown, adjacent to the New Capitol building at the corner of S. Monroe Street and Apalachee Parkway (U.S. 27), Tallahassee; (904) 487-1902; open Monday through Friday from 9 a.m. to 4:30 p.m., Saturday from 10 a.m. to 4:30 p.m., Sunday and holidays from noon to 4:30 p.m. Admission is free. (1 hour)

✰✰ **Pebble Hill Plantation**—This Southern plantation home from the Civil War period boasts an eclectic collection of fine art, crystal, porcelain, and antique furnishings. Visitors may wander through the pine- and magnolia-covered grounds, which feature a dog kennel and hospital, cow barn, firehouse, historic cemetery, log cabin, schoolhouse, and brick horse stables. Details: 20 miles north of Tallahassee on U.S. 319; (904) 226-2344; open Tuesday through Saturday from 10 a.m. to 5 p.m., Sunday from 1 to 5 p.m. Admission is $2 for adults and $1 for children; guided tours of the plantation house last one hour and cost $5 for adults and $2.50 for kids. (2 hours)

☆ **Bradley's Country Store**—Listed on the National Register of Historic Places, this store looks the same as it did on opening day in 1927. Still family-owned, the tin store is renowned for its Southern goods and homemade sausage, selling more than 65,000 pounds of it every year. It's still made with "Grandma Mary's time-proven seasoning." Details: Nestled on canopy-covered Centerville Road, 12 miles north of Tallahassee; (904) 893-1647; open Monday through Friday from 9 a.m. to 6 p.m., Saturday from 9 a.m. to 5 p.m. (1 hour)

FITNESS AND RECREATION

Tallahassee offers a wide and varied range of activities. Sports and fitness enthusiasts will discover venues for cycling, in-line skating, golf, tennis, or horseback riding, as well as assorted health clubs. Equestrians can head 20 miles southeast of Tallahassee to saddle up at **Natural Bridge Stables**, (904) 421-4843. Contact **Trail Head Bikes & Blades**, 4780 Woodville Highway, (904) 656-0001, to strap on those in-line skates or rent a bike and hit the 16-mile **Saint Marks Historic Railroad Trail**.

For those who can't miss a workout, Tallahassee offers a half-dozen health and fitness clubs. For the routine workout, there's **Gold's Downtown Athletic Club**, 1147 Apalachee Parkway, (904) 942-9712; the **Plantation Club**, 3870 Tall Timber Court, (904) 385-7533; or **Fitness, Etc., Inc.**, 1813 Wagon Wheel Circle E., (904) 942-9712. For the heavier workout, try **World Gym**, 2695-D Capital Circle NE, (904) 386-3161; or **CBJ Energetics**, 1420 N. Meridian Road #215, (904) 681-2699.

Three area parks have tennis courts, including **Forestmeadows Park**, 4750 N. Meridian Road, (904) 891-3920, with nine clay, six hard lighted courts, and three indoor racquetball courts; **Tom Brown Park**, 501 Easterwood Drive, (904) 891-3966, with 12 lighted tennis and 12 outdoor racquetball courts; and **Winthrop Park**, 1601 Mitchell

Avenue, (904) 891-3980, with six lighted tennis and two outdoor racquet-ball courts. If you prefer to swing clubs instead of racquets, Tallahassee has six courses, three public and three private or semi-private. **Hilman Park Golf Course**, 2737 Blairstone Road, (904) 891-3935, is open daily and offers an 18-hole par 72 municipal course with driving range, putting green, pro shop, clubhouse, and restaurant. **Jake Gaither Golf Course**, 801 Tanner Drive, (904) 891-3942, is a wooded nine-hole municipal course with carts. **Seminole Golf Course**, 2550 Pottsdamer Street, (904) 644-2582, is a public 18-hole course with a lighted driving range, locker rooms, cart and club rentals, pro shop, clubhouse, and restaurant. **Killearn Country Club**, 100 Tyron Circle, (904) 893-2186, is a private 27-hole course with guest rooms. **Players Club at Summerbrook**, 7505 Preservation Road, (904) 894-GOLF, is a semi-private 18-hole par 72 course with a driving range, putting green, restaurant, pro shop, and locker rooms. **Tartaruga Creek**, 35 miles east of Tallahassee on U.S. 221 at Highway 146, (904) 997-0036, is a rolling 18-hole European-style golf course with covered driving range, inn, restaurant, and pro shop. This semi-private course is open Tuesday through Sunday.

For family fun and entertainment, try the **Discovery Zone**, 3425 Thomasville Road, (904) 893-6050, a playground with 14,000 square feet of tunnels, tubes, and more, all designed with active youngsters in mind. Kids of all ages enjoy **Lazer Storm**, located off North Monroe Street in the Sugar Creek/Waccamaw Plaza, (904) 385-5277. It features a state-of-the-art, 3,500-square-foot interactive laser tag area.

FOOD

Two culinary delicacies are harvested in the Tallahassee area and should not be missed. The famous Apalachicola oysters and Panacea blue crabs come from the Gulf of Mexico, just 30 minutes away, and are served in many of the town's best restaurants. Don't miss the fresh fried mullet platters, either. For steak and seafood, one of the best restaurants is the **Silver Slipper**, 531 Scotty's Lane, (904) 386-9366, with dinners between $11 and $20. A Tallahassee landmark in legislative circles and a winner of eight Golden Spoon Awards, the Silver Slipper offers Greek special-ties, steaks, and fresh seafood. As the oldest family-owned restaurant in the state, it has served its steaks to five U.S. presidents.

Another of the area's best is **Andrew's Second Act**, 228 S. Adams Street, (904) 222-3444. It, too, has received the Golden Spoon

TALLAHASSEE

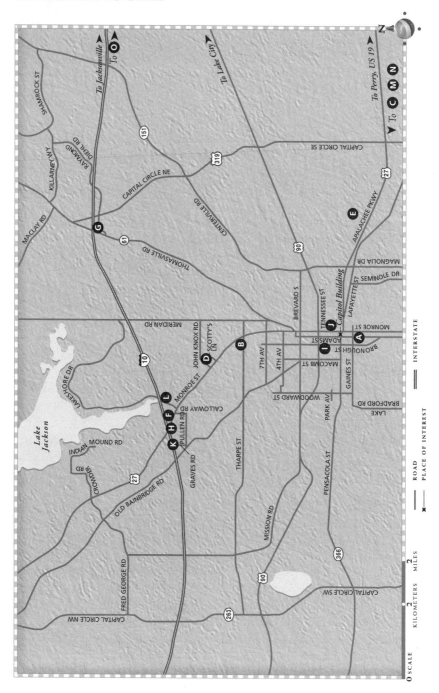

Food

A Andrew's Second Act

B Barnacle Bill's

C Posey's Restaurant

D Silver Slipper

Lodging

E Best Western Pride Inn Suites

F Cabot Lodge North

G Cabot Lodge Thomasville Road

H Comfort Inn

I The Governor's Inn

I Holiday Inn Capitol Plaza Hotel

J Radisson Hotel

K Ramada Inn Tallahassee

L Shoney's Inn

Camping

M Alligator Point Campground

N Holiday Park Campground

O Tallahassee RV Park

Note: Items with the same letter are located in the same town or area.

Award—every year since 1979. With the largest wine cellar in north
Florida, Andrew's Second Act is known for beef and fresh seafood,
with most meals between $15 and $20. It's open daily and serves
lunch Monday through Friday. **Barnacle Bill's**, 1830 N. Monroe
Street, (904) 385-8734, offers fresh grilled, steamed, or smoked
seafood. Meals range from $10 to $15, and there's an oyster bar. A
seafood restaurant in the $10-to-$15 range, **Posey's Restaurant**,
located in Panacea on Highway 98, (904) 984-5799, is popular among
the local folks. Open Tuesday through Sunday, it serves the full range
of seafood.

LODGING

Tallahassee offers more than 5,000 rooms in area hotels and motels.
The **Governor's Inn**, 209 S. Adams Street, (904) 681-6855, is a historic bed and breakfast with good rooms and service costing between
$119 and $219 per night. With just 40 guest rooms, including Jacuzzi
suites, the inn has no swimming pool or restaurant but does offer dry
cleaning. At a reasonable $50 to $75 a night, the **Cabot Lodge
North**, 2735 N. Monroe Street, (904) 386-8880, has 160 rooms and
holds as high a rating as any hotel in the area. It lacks a restaurant
but offers dry cleaning. The **Cabot Lodge Thomasville Road**, 1653
Raymond Diehl Road, (904) 386-7500, is another highly rated lodge,
with 135 moderately priced rooms, $55 to $175 per night. There's no
restaurant but there is an Executive Floor with personal computer
hookups, a Jacuzzi, and a whirlpool.

Some of the best accommodations in the area are the better-
known national chain motels and hotels, including the **Best Western
Pride Inn Suites**, 2016 Apalachee Parkway, (904) 656-6312, offering
78 rooms at $39 to $65 per night; the **Radisson Hotel**, 415 N.
Monroe Street, (904) 224-6000, 116 rooms at around $100 per night;
the **Comfort Inn**, 2727 Graves Road, (904) 562-7200, 100 rooms
from $45 to $77 per night; the **Holiday Inn Capitol Plaza Hotel**,
101 S. Adams Street, (904) 224-5000, 244 rooms from $59 to $250
per night; and the **Ramada Inn Tallahassee**, 2900 N. Monroe
Street, (904) 386-1027, 198 rooms from $49 to $85 per night.
Shoney's Inn, 2801 N. Monroe Street, (904) 386-8286, offers 115
rooms from $43 to $175 per night, and has electronic appliances and
a swimming pool.

CAMPING

Florida's capital is also famous for its huge oak trees, which wrap the city in a cool, green blanket with their wide branches. Almost all camp-grounds in and around Tallahassee have leafy cover over the sites. The **Tallahassee RV Park**, (904) 878-7641, spans 8 acres with 66 sites, most of them pull-throughs. Sites are grassy and shaded, all with electric, water, and sewer hookups. Facilities include phone hookups. The wooded setting is in a residential area at 6504 Mahan Drive. Take Exit 31A off I-10 onto U.S. 90 and head west a half-mile to Mahan Drive and the park entrance. Year-round rates are $18.

About 25 miles from Tallahassee and near the Gulf is the well-kept **Holiday Park Campground**, (904) 984-5757, located on U.S. 98 at the end of the new Panacea Bridge crossing the Ochlockonee River. The grassy, attractive campground offers some shaded and some waterfront sites under pine trees on the bay at the mouth of the river. Telephone hookups, propane, cable TV, a swimming pool, boat ramp, and dock are available. Year-round rates are $11.95 to $17.95.

The 24-acre **Alligator Point Campground**, (904) 349-2525, near Panacea, is located on CR 370, 5.5 miles toward the Gulf from U.S. 98. Directions can be confusing, because U.S. 98 jogs and heads north and south for a while before returning to its east-west orientation. With 140 sites on the Gulf (100 with electric and water), the campground offers excellent beach-walking opportunities. Its convenient location makes it a weekend favorite with Tallahassee area residents. Midweek is a more peaceful time for campers. Groceries, cable TV, swimming in the pool or at the beach, a rec room, and a playground are all available. Year-round rates are $14.95.

NIGHTLIFE

Dooley's Down Under, a club at 2900 N. Monroe Street in the Ramada Inn, (904) 386-1027, features an Outback atmosphere, a full bar, and the Comedy Zone, where professional comics perform Friday and Saturday nights. For dinner and dancing, try the **Sparta 220 Club & Grill**, 220 Monroe Street, (904) 224-9711, featuring one of Tallahassee's finer restaurants and live musical entertainment. For faster-paced dancing, **The Moon**, 1105 E. Lafayette Street, (904) 222-6666, is an upscale, high-energy dance club with country dancing on Friday nights. The **Mustard Tree**, 1415 Timberlane Road, (904) 893-TREE (893-8733), is

casual yet sophisticated, with live entertainment, many imported and
domestic beers, and a very affordable wine list that includes 15 selections
available by the glass. Don't miss **Diamond Jim's Lounge**, 531 Scotty's
Lane, (904) 386-9366, a popular place with state legislators and Florida's
movers and shakers when they're in town.

SCENIC WALKING AND DRIVING TOURS

Tallahassee lies in a region of rolling hills, oak and pine forests, and
rivers, but the city itself is best known for its lakes and beautiful gardens.
Much of Tallahassee's past has been well preserved in its public buildings
and historic homes, 124 of which are recorded on the National Register
of Historic Places. There are three historic walking tours, all within sight
of downtown. In addition, three self-guided driving tours explore the
Tallahassee area noted for canopy roads, including Miccosukee,
Centerville, Meridian, and Old Bainbridge Roads.

"Touring Tallahassee: A Walking Guide to Historic Downtown" is
offered by the Tallahassee Area Convention and Visitors Bureau, (800)
628-2866. This brochure divides the tours into three in-city groups .75
to 1.5 miles in length. **Downtown Tallahassee** highlights the New and
Old State Capitols, Florida's oldest surviving bank, and the Museum of
Florida History. The **Park Avenue Historic District** showcases the
1843 Knott House Museum, the azalea-laced City Parks dotted with
140-year-old oak trees, and the **Old City Cemetery**, which predates the
Civil War. The **Calhoun Street Historic District** tours old Calhoun
Street, once known as "Gold Dust Street," for the many wealthy residents who lived on it at the time. "Canopy Roads and County Lanes: A
Driving Guide to Scenic Leon County," published by the visitors bureau,
is available at any Tallahassee Area Visitor Information Center or featured landmark. The brochure features three leisurely tours of once-his-
toric trails and moss-draped roads. The **Native Trail** weaves along rich
archaeological sites including Apalachee Indian mounds and a 1565
Spanish mission. The **Cotton Trail** traces the history of Tallahassee
"when cotton was king" and makes stops along scenic and unpaved historic Magnolia Road, shaded by a thick canopy. Stops include Goodwood
Plantation, which once boasted the South's largest cotton crop. The
Quail Trail highlights the emergence of post–Civil War hunting estates,
including Alfred B. Maclay State Gardens, and passes under some of the
lushest canopies in the area.

5

CEDAR KEY

Cedar Key, one of Florida's most historic settlements, lies 3 miles out in the Gulf of Mexico. This small fishing village and arts colony (pop. about 700 permanent residents) can be reached from U.S. 19 by heading west on Highway 24 for about 20 miles. The road leads over a series of bridges linking together the chain of small islands called "keys." The village of Cedar Key is located on Way and Rye Keys, the highest land around, 8 feet above sea level. In fact, the village appears to be built on a hill in this low, picturesque land of grass hummocks protruding from back bay tidal flow streams. Old live oaks and weathered wooden houses line the road leading to the Gulf, and the dock area, with its expanse of blue water, is a photographer's dream. Bustling dockside activity recalls Cedar Key's long history as a fishing village. Many of those sturdy docks now house first-rate restaurants and shops. Commercial fishing for grouper, mullet, blue crab, and stone crab, and service industries such as restaurants, lounges, hotels, and shops keep Cedar Key alive.

A visit to Cedar Key is a step back in time. The town is filled with architecture of the past, such as wooden homes with porches, gables, and old tin roofs. The pace of life is slower here, and time is measured not by clocks or newspapers, but by the ebb and flow of the Gulf tides.

CEDAR KEY

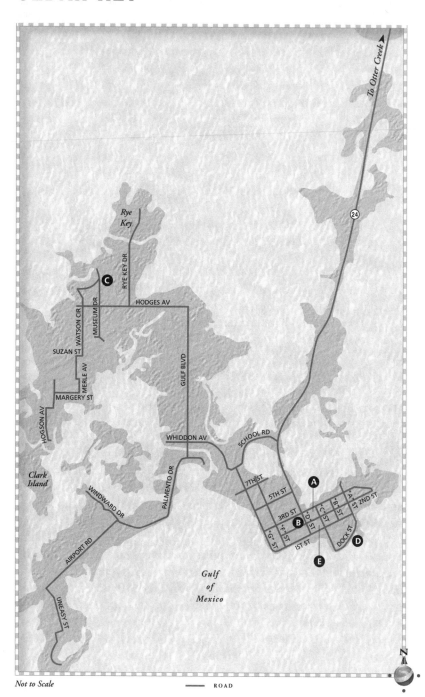

To Otter Creek

24

Rye Key

RYE KEY DR

C

WATSON CIR

MUSEUM DR

HODGES AV

SUZAN ST

MERLE AV

MARGERY ST

HOGSON AV

GULF BLVD

WHIDDON AV

SCHOOL RD

Clark Island

WINDWARD DR

PALMENTO DR

AIRPORT RD

UNEASY ST

7TH ST

5TH ST

3RD ST

1ST ST

"G" ST

"F" ST

"D" ST

"C" ST

"B" ST

"A" ST

2ND ST

DOCK ST

A

B

C

D

E

Gulf of Mexico

N

Not to Scale

ROAD

Sightseeing Highlights

Ⓐ Cedar Key Bookstore

Ⓑ Cedar Key Historical Society Museum

Ⓒ Cedar Key State Museum

Ⓓ City Docks and Boat Ramp

Ⓔ Fantasy Fashions

Ⓓ Ibis Gallery

Ⓓ Rustic Woods

Ⓓ Sweet Memories

Ⓓ The Water's Edge

Note: Items with the same letter are located in the same town or area.

A PERFECT DAY IN CEDAR KEY

Sunrise at Cedar Key can be nothing short of magical. The sun appears above the trees behind the town, gradually highlighting the islands and blue waters of the Gulf of Mexico. Perhaps it's the moisture in the air or a little fog, but the whole scene seems suspended, almost unreal. (This phenomenon might be related to the famous "green flash" seen over the sun the moment it disappears into the Gulf at sunset. Watch for that too!)

Begin your day with a quiet stroll on the City Docks to see what the early fishermen have landed—perhaps whiting, yellowtail, trout, redfish, or flounder. Sheepshead fishermen dangle fiddler crabs on hooks alongside the pilings to lure the black-and-white-striped delicacy. Have breakfast at nearby Cook's Café, then stroll through a few of the shops and galleries along the docks. Rent a bicycle and take a leisurely ride over to the Cedar Key Museum. Bring a camera—photo opportunities abound on these old streets. Check out the many varieties of Florida native trees on the museum grounds. If the afternoon weather is fine, board the Island Hopper Queen for a peaceful cruise among the islands and along the coastline.

Finish the day with a scrumptious meal at the Captain's Table Restaurant, on the docks overlooking the Gulf. It's a casual, historic place with an excellent reputation among locals and visitors alike. If stone crabs are in season, don't miss them. The cabbage palm salad with its secret dressing is a must.

SIGHTSEEING HIGHLIGHTS

★★★ **Cedar Key Bookstore**—Books of all kinds, plus a wide selection of cards and gifts, fill the shelves of this interesting downtown store. Trade a book for one you want or buy a history of the area. Details: 310 2nd Street, Cedar Key; (352) 543-9660; open Monday through Saturday from 10 a.m. to 5 p.m. and Sunday from noon to 5 p.m. (1 hour)

★★★ **Cedar Key Historical Society Museum**—The society offers brochures describing self-guided tours of the city. These are available in the downtown Cedar Key Historical Society Museum, which is housed in an interesting, circa 1870 house. Lots of rare photos, news clippings, and articles are on display, donated to the museum by members of the society and other residents interested in preserving the history of Cedar Key. Exhibits include Indian relics, antique furnishings, and mineral rock collections. Details: State Road 24 at 2nd Street, Cedar Key; (352) 543-5549; open weekdays from 11 a.m. to 4 p.m. and Saturday from 1 p.m. to 4 p.m. Admission is $1 for adults, 50 cents for children. (1 hour)

★★★ **Cedar Key Seafood Festival**—Every year in mid-October this festival attracts thousands of seafood lovers who come to the island to sample fresh delicacies while enjoying a local crafts show.

★★★ **Cedar Key Sidewalk Arts Festival**—Held annually in April, the arts festival is well worth attending. Local and visiting artists display their works in the historic downtown area. Fast becoming a prestigious event, the juried show attracts entrants from all over the country.

Crowds of art lovers flock to the wide-open waterfront area to enjoy the festival and fresh seafood in the park. Details: Call the Cedar Key Chamber of Commerce, (352) 543-5600, for more information. (1 day)

★★★ **Cedar Key State Museum**—This 19-acre museum is dedicated to the memory of long-time resident and town benefactor St. Clair Whitman. It was opened in 1962 to preserve Cedar Key's colorful history. On display is Whitman's extensive shell collection, recognized by the Florida Department of Environmental Protection as one of the most beautiful and complete ever assembled. An impressive collection of early Civil War photos chronicles the attack of federal forces on this Southern town in 1862. When the war ended, logging and commercial fishing returned prosperity to Cedar Key. Cedar from this area was rated the world's finest for the manufacture of pencils. The bronze plaque on the front lawn tributes conservationist John Muir and his history-making journal, *A Thousand-Mile Walk to the Gulf*, a journey that ended at Cedar Key in 1867. A quiet walk around the museum grounds reveals many species of Florida plants and trees, including sand and slash pine, red cedar, live oak, sabal palm, saw palmetto, yaupon, and coontie. Details: 1710 Museum Drive, Cedar Key; (352) 543-5350; open from 9 a.m. to 5 p.m. Thursday through Monday; closed Tuesday and Wednesday. Admission is $1 for adults, free for children under 6. (1–2 hours)

★★★ **City Docks and Boat Ramp**—The Cedar Key waterfront is located in the downtown area and offers private and public docking facilities. Access to the protected marina area inside the docks is limited by a bridged entrance. Boats with draft deeper than 3 feet cannot enter to the inside docks, one of which has water and electric hookups. Larger boats can use the outside docks, and the Cedar Key Public Marina is available for either docking or launching your own boat. This picturesque area is among the most-photographed and -painted subjects along Florida's west coast. Details: Launch fee for the boat ramp is $5. Boat slips are free on a first come, first served basis, with a three-night maximum stay. For further information, call the Chamber of Commerce, (352) 543-5600.

★★★ **Fantasy Fashions**—This downtown shop is a good place to find unique styles, gifts, and original clothing and jewelry. Details: Located at 3rd and D Streets, Cedar Key; (352) 543-9318; open from 9 a.m. to 4.30 p.m. (1 hour)

★★ Shops on the Dock—Several charming boutiques and eateries dot the docks. Some of the most noteworthy include **Ibis Gallery**, which showcases a unique collection of fine handicrafts ideal for home decorating or gift-giving. Details: (352) 543-6111; open daily from 10:30 a.m. to 6:30 p.m.

Handmade furniture stars at **Rustic Woods**. A set of shelves, a custom-made mailbox, or a cedar box will serve for years as a practical reminder of your visit to Cedar Key. Crafts, ceramics, dolls, T-shirts, hats, and collectibles are also sold at this interesting shop. Details: (352) 543-9400; open Monday through Friday from 10 a.m. to 6 p.m.; call for weekend hours.

Take care of that nagging sweet tooth at **Sweet Memories**, which tempts with freshly made fudge, taffy, and hand-dipped and molded chocolates. Details: (352) 371-4383; open daily from 11 a.m. to 6 p.m. and evenings Thursday, Friday, and Saturday.

Seashells and coral make the **Water's Edge** unique. The large selection of gifts and souvenirs includes cookbooks and a better-than-average selection of greeting cards. Details: (352) 543-5710; open Monday through Thursday from 10 a.m. to 6 p.m., and until 8 p.m. on Friday, Saturday, and Sunday.

FITNESS AND RECREATION

Outdoor activities, especially fishing and boating, are popular in Cedar Key. Swimming in the Gulf and walking on the sand beaches of the offshore islands can be fun additions to picnicking and exploring by boat. Boat rentals are available at **Norwood's Marina**, (352) 543-6148, at the docks on Route 24 a few blocks from downtown.

Bird-watching is excellent in the **Cedar Keys National Wildlife Refuge** on the islands off Cedar Key. The refuge includes a major seabird rookery and an 1850s lighthouse on Florida's highest coastal elevation. In the refuge and surrounding areas, ospreys nest during the spring and early summer, and salmon-colored roseate spoonbills perch in the island mangroves. Great blue heron, egret, ibis, and many other wading birds quietly work the water's edge in search of food, while overhead the graceful, forked-tailed frigate bird circles, its sharp eyes spotting small fish in the water far below. At dusk watch for raccoons coming out to find dinner on the oyster bars and marshes, where many species of shellfish and crustaceans live. Ungainly pelicans diving for fish and following fishing boats provide ongoing entertainment.

Cedar Key is small enough to explore by bike, and biking offers great views of its historic houses and wetlands. **Dock on the Bay**, (352) 543-9143, rents bicycles, as do several other places in town. If you prefer to sit back and relax while exploring the scenic islands and shoreline, take a cruise on the *Island Hopper Queen*, (352) 543-5904. Walking sightseers can rest at the **City Park and Bathing Beach** facing the Gulf, between 1st and 2nd Streets downtown. There are picnic tables, a gazebo, children's playground, restrooms, and a public bathing beach here too.

The Gulf waters off Cedar Key offer excellent sport-fishing opportunities, and there are a number of well-qualified guides ready to show visitors some choice spots. The **City Dock** is another favorite fishing locale, and a great place to watch the spectacular sunsets. For further information, call or visit the Chamber of Commerce, at C and 2nd Streets downtown, open Monday, Wednesday, and Friday from 10 a.m. to 2 p.m., (352) 543-5600.

FOOD

Seafood is the specialty in Cedar Key. Order it at one of the many restaurants in town, or buy it fresh from **Cooke's Oysters**, (352) 543-5334, on Highway 24 across from the Jiffy Food Store. Cooke's will help with food preparation too: cooking tips come free with every purchase. The many seafood choices in the shop include fresh littleneck, farm-raised clams, mullet, sheepshead, flounder, grouper, and live blue crabs. Oysters are plentiful and fresh, at around $25 per bushel.

Small plane pilots often fly into Cedar Key airport just to buy fresh seafood for dinner. While dining in one of the many excellent restaurants, be sure to sample such traditional island dishes as heart of palm salad, smoked mullet, crab cakes, stone crab claws, and soft-shell crabs. The **Captain's Table Restaurant**, (352) 543-5441, on Dock Street, is one of the most historic in Cedar Key and has great views of the Gulf. Specialties include jambalaya and stuffed flounder ($9.95 to $13.95), along with their well-known crab bisque ($4.95). Surf and turf entrées satisfy steak lovers ($18.95).

For informal dining and take-out food, try the **Clam Shack**, (352) 543-9500, which has an excellent sandwich and salad selection, with freshly made lunches to go. Snacks vary from sausage sandwiches to smoked shrimp and stuffed clams.

Meet the neighborhood egret at **Cook's Café**, (352) 543-5548,

CEDAR KEY

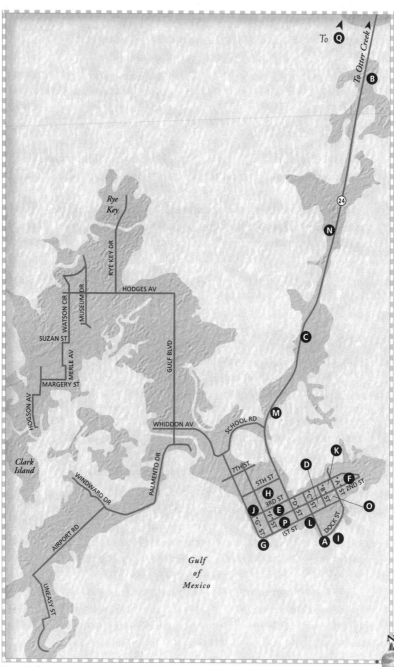

To Q

To Otter Creek

B

24

N

Rye
Key

RYE KEY DR

HODGES AV

WATSON CIR

MUSEUM DR

SUZAN ST

MERLE AV

MARGERY ST

HOGSON AV

GULF BLVD

C

M

WHIDDON AV

SCHOOL RD

Clark
Island

WINDWARD DR

PALMENTO DR

AIRPORT RD

UNEASY ST

7TH ST

5TH ST

3RD ST

D

K

F

"A" ST

2ND ST

"B" ST

"C" ST

"D" ST

O

"E" ST

H

E

J

"F" ST

P

1ST ST

L

DOCK ST

"G" ST

G

A

I

Gulf
of
Mexico

N

Not to Scale   ROAD

Food

Ⓐ Captain's Table Restaurant

Ⓑ Clam Shack

Ⓒ Cooke's Oysters

Ⓓ Cook's Café

Ⓔ The Heron

Ⓕ Island Hotel

Lodging

Ⓖ Beachfront Motel

Ⓗ Cedar Key Bed & Breakfast

Ⓘ Dockside

Ⓙ Faraway Inn

Ⓚ Island Hotel

Ⓛ Island Place

Ⓜ Mermaids Landing

Ⓝ Norwoods Marina Hotel

Ⓞ Park Place Motel

Camping

Ⓟ Cedar Key RV Park

Ⓠ Rainbow Country RV
     Campground

while enjoying a home-cooked breakfast and a good cup of coffee. The cafe offers outside seating and daily specials as well as seafood platters and burgers.

One of the most interesting buildings in town is the **Island Hotel**, built in 1859. Today it offers gourmet dining graced by lamplight, fresh flowers, and classical music in an attractive, old-fashioned dining room. Chef Jahn McCumbers, Island Hotel veteran of ten years, prepares such specialties as jambalaya, stuffed flounder, artichokes and shrimp, stone crab, and other local seafood. Entrées range from $9.95 to $18.95. Appetizers include delicious seafood-stuffed mushrooms ($6.50). Be sure to visit the Neptune Bar with its colorful murals dating from 1948.

For good homemade soup and sandwiches try **The Heron** in the historic Hale building, circa 1880. Excellent salads accompany lunch, served from 9 a.m. to 2:30 p.m. Wednesday through Sunday.

LODGING

The **Island Hotel** (1859) is Cedar Key's oldest and most famous lodging. With its pot-bellied stove and paddle fans, this place has provided a relaxing getaway for many guests, including famous entertainers and politicians. The well-built old hotel has weathered many storms and has undergone numerous restorations, but it remains one of the most authentic historic hotels in Florida. The present owners, Tom and Alison Sanders, bought the Island Hotel in January 1992. Tom, a journalist, recently completed *A Brief History of the Island Hotel, Cedar Key, Florida*, with the help of local residents, the Historical Society, and others. Sanders describes the hotel's history over the past 130 years, partially attributing its longevity to a firm foundation laid by Cedar Key pioneers.

He writes, "They mixed oyster shell, limestone and sand to pour tabby walls ten inches thick. Massive 12 inch oak beams were framed in the basement to support the wooden structure. . . . [A] recent structural survey complements the original workmanship and confirms the soundness of the building."

The famous Neptune Bar in the Island Hotel has been restored as the meeting place where Cedar Key "regulars" and visitors go to swap "fish stories." In the spring and fall the revamped courtyard becomes a beer garden featuring live entertainment.

The hotel has a reputation for romance, and many couples return year after year, celebrating anniversaries with dinner and champagne in the candlelit restaurant. (In fact, the Sanders themselves enjoyed their own first candlelit dinner and reception here after their Cedar Key wedding aboard the charter boat *Gondola*.) They both agree that there will be no changes made to destroy or even alter the hotel's unique and eccentric charm.

The hotel has ten distinctive guest rooms. To preserve the romantic and traditional ambience, there are no in-room televisions or telephones. Some rooms have feather beds, some have old-fashioned claw-foot bathtubs, and all have the original hand-cut wooden walls and floors plus access to the balcony overlooking the street. Rooms with private baths are available upon request. Air conditioning and ceiling fans are Florida touches in every room. Rates are usually $85 per night and $95 on weekends, and include a full breakfast. The hotel is open year-round. From Highway 24, on the outskirts of Cedar Key, turn left at the intersection with Main Street and drive about three blocks. The Island Hotel is on the left. For reservations, call (352) 543-5111.

The only motel on the dock is **Dockside**, (800) 868-7963. This is a place for avid fishermen, only 40 feet away from the fishing pier. Cedar Key's newest motel, Dockside is also close to restaurants and shopping. Rates begin at $55 per night. Rent a 14- to 24-foot-long boat for exploring or fishing from **Norwoods Marina Motel**, (352) 543-6167. All boating and fishing supplies—fishing licenses, tackle, bait, ice, and gas—are for sale available at the marina. The motel has efficiency rooms equipped with cable TV, full kitchens, telephones, and air conditioning.

The waterfront cottages at the **Mermaids Landing**, (352) 543-5949, can accommodate large and small groups. Rates start at $35 for an efficiency to $65 for a two-bedroom cottage with full kitchen. Pets are permitted if kept on a leash. Arrange to rent a car or bicycle if you don't want to walk the six to eight blocks from the cottages to downtown restaurants and shops; however, smoked mullet and spread made by Miss Madge is only two houses away. Also, farm-raised clams and oysters on the half shell or by the pint can be delivered to your door. Try catching blue crabs from the dock and relax watching the birds feeding in the wetlands off the dock.

The whole bay is spread out in front of the **Beachfront Motel**, (352) 543-5113, which offers a pool on the waterfront, efficiencies, and cable TV. Pets are permitted. Rates range from $44 to $51 per night. The **Island Place**, (352) 543-5307, rents one-bedroom condominiums with a small separate master bedroom. Two full-sized bunk beds are built into the wall by the kitchen. A private balcony overlooks the outer islands in the Gulf. Small boats may be beached in front of the complex or at the city marina a half-block away. Amenities include a swimming pool, sauna, and Jacuzzi. Rates range from $85 to $90 for one-bedroom units, which come with a washer/dryer.

To get away from the hustle and bustle, try the **Faraway Inn**, (352) 543-5330, built on the site of the nineteenth-century Eagle Pencil Mill. It's a mere six-block walk past historic Victorian homes to the downtown shops and restaurants. Rates begin at $40 per night. Cedar Key Park is at your doorstep in the **Park Place Motel**, (352) 543-5737, close to shopping and restaurants. All units are efficiencies with cable TV and telephones. Rates begin at $65. Bed and breakfast buffs will love the circa 1880 **Cedar Key Bed & Breakfast**, (352) 543-9000. Innkeepers Lois and Bob Davenport have restored this Victorian-style, two-story home built entirely of yellow pine. The home is shaded by live oaks and features high ceilings, paddle fans, lace curtains, and comfortable beds. It also has a separate "honeymoon cottage." Rates begin at $65.

CAMPING

Cedar Key has one RV park in town, on the water. **Cedar Key RV Park**, (352) 543-5150, overlooks the harbor and has 29 sites, each 16 feet wide with full hookups. Although few sites actually face the water, the proximity to the beach and downtown make staying here worthwhile. Call for advance reservations. Rates range from $10 to $15. Five miles east of Cedar Key on Highway 24, **Rainbow Country RV Campground**, (352) 543-6268, offers boating, saltwater fishing, and a limited grocery store. The park has 62 sites, most 20 feet wide and 25 with full hookups. Rates start at $12.

6

CRYSTAL RIVER
AND HOMOSASSA

U.S. 19, 80 miles north of Clearwater, passes through the town of Crystal River, the business hub and fishing and dive center for western Citrus County. Crystal River's downtown area is currently being revamped to include historical museums and an antique shopping center. It's now home to the Nature Coast's only regional shopping mall, the Crystal River Mall, which houses specialty shops, antique art dealers, and large department stores. Of course, there are beaches, too, and freshwater activities to please fishermen and scuba divers as well as swimmers and sunners. To enjoy Crystal River's Gulf beach, follow the Fort Island Trail west (State Road 44) to a beautiful sandy beach and park with picnic tables, volleyball court, and boat ramp—a perfect place to relax.

A wide range of lodging and restaurants is available in Crystal River and the surrounding King's Bay and Homosassa River areas. The well-equipped airport, located on the east side of U.S. 19 between Crystal River and Homosassa, makes small-plane travel possible for vacationers and business travelers

The region is well-known as a "fisherman's paradise." Local dive shops and marinas in both Crystal River and Homosassa supply equipment for fishing, boating, and diving. Experienced local guides take sports enthusiasts to favorite fishing spots on the rivers and in the Gulf of Mexico, where record-sized tarpon, often in the 150-pound range, are landed every year. ◣

CRYSTAL RIVER AND HOMOSASSA

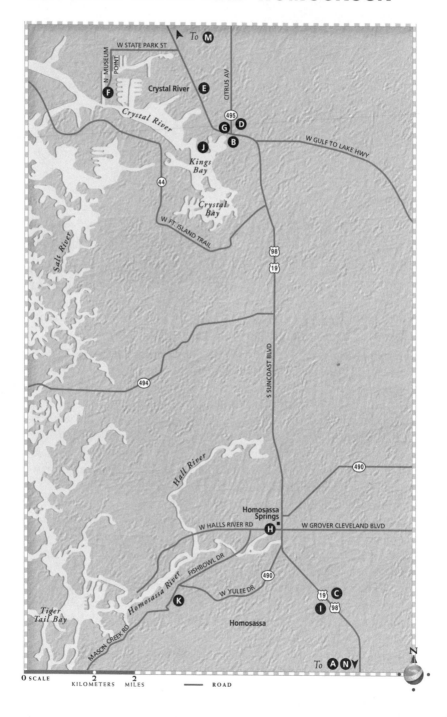

Sightseeing Highlights

A Buccaneer Bay

B Buccaneer Bay Coastal Heritage Museum

C Chazerei Antiques

D Cobblestone Alley Antiques

E Crystal River Mall

F Crystal River State Archaeological Site

G Heritage Antiques Mall

H Homosassa Springs State Wildlife Park

I Howard's Flea Market

J Manatees at King's Bay

K Old Homosassa Village

K The Olde Millhouse Gallery and Printing Museum

L Old Keg Antiques

M The Power Place

K River Works Studio and Copper Art Gallery

K Sugar Mill Gallery

N Weeki Wachee Spring

K Yulee Sugar Mill Ruins State Historic Site

Note: Items with the same letter are located in the same town or area.

A PERFECT DAY IN CRYSTAL RIVER AND HOMOSASSA

A perfect day in Crystal River and Homosassa begins aboard the first tour boat out of the Plantation Inn's marina, headed to King's Bay to watch the morning activities of the manatees. If it's early springtime, perhaps some baby manatees have joined the herd. These gentle giants graze contentedly on the sea grasses at the bottom of the bay, coming to the surface every few minutes to breathe, affording watchers a better view.

After the boat returns to the marina, drive south to Homosassa Springs State Wildlife Park to visit the manatee rehabilitation station. Here injured manatees are cared for until they can be released into the wild. There are other endangered creatures here, too, including deer, bobcats, otters, cougars, alligators, and snakes. Don't miss the "Spring of 10,000 Fish," where the visitor stands in a floating glass observatory and the fish peer inside!

The afternoon and evening follow a historical theme. After a picnic lunch and tour of the ruins at the Yulee Sugar Mill, head over to Old Homosassa Village to stroll through the shops and old buildings. Don't miss the Olde Millhouse Gallery and Printing Museum. Dine amidst antiques and the rustic charm of Barnacle Ray's Yardarm.

HISTORY

Originally inhabited by the Calusa and Seminole Indians, Homosassa and its spring are one of the oldest residential communities on the Florida Gulf Coast. Recent excavations have unearthed not only Indian burial grounds, but canoes, cooking pots, axes, and many other artifacts. David Levy Yulee founded a settlement in 1846, when he established a 5,100-acre sugar cane plantation and built the historic Yulee Sugar Mill. Later, many families escaping the aftermath of the Civil War settled on islands off the Chassahowitzka, Ozello, and Homosassa Rivers. The islands were named for the self-supporting families occupying them: Gordy Island, Shiver Bay, Loennecker Point, and Peny Creek. Many of these settlers were well-educated, and the first community building was a schoolhouse, soon followed by a church. What could not be grown in individual gardens was purchased with money made by selling fish and other seafood to customers 60 miles north in Cedar Key.

News of the Homosassa area's excellent hunting and fishing attracted famous sportsmen. They traveled by rail as far as Ocala, then switched over to horse-and-buggy for the rest of the trip to Homosassa. John Jacob Astor and Grover Cleveland were among those who came to the village for duck hunting on the river. Henry Plant fell in love with the area but died before his plans to build a great hotel were realized. A tourist hotel on Tiger Tail Island maintained 75 thoroughbred horses for the pleasure of its hunting guests, and elaborate private homes appeared along the riverfront at aptly named Fortune Point.

The 1983 centennial celebration at the well-known Homosassa Inn, located at the end of County Road 480 and the river, attracted statewide attention. The story of the grand affair is told in *Nature's Masterpiece at Homosassa*, a history of the area written by Pulitzer Prize–winning journalist W. Horace Carter, who described the hundreds of costumed residents, guests, musical groups, and dignitaries attending the celebration from all over the state. The frosting on the fun-filled day was "Peggy Player's cake, a replica of the two-story Homosassa Inn with porches, sweeping lawns, alligators and boats, . . . big enough to serve 600 people."

Nature is still in control on the Homosassa River, where the economy continues to rely on commercial fishing, guiding, and the recreational and vacation opportunities so readily available in this beautiful, bountiful, and peaceful land.

SIGHTSEEING HIGHLIGHTS

★★★ **Buccaneer Bay**—Next door to Weeki Wachee (see below) is Buccaneer Bay, where visitors can swim in the clear spring waters, then sunbathe on an immaculate white sand beach. Visitors of all ages enjoy challenging the speed timers on the river slides or floating down the spring waters featured in the new "Lazy River" tube ride. The children's area is well equipped with beach volleyball, rope swings, and a video game arcade. Details: 6172 Commercial Way, Weeki Wachee; located on U.S. 19, at State Road 50, 20 miles south of Homosassa; (800) 678-9335 or (352) 596-2062; open daily from April 4 to September 7, from 10 a.m. to 5 p.m. Admission is $10.95 adults, $9.95 children ages 3 to 10. A combination package for both Buccaneer Bay and Weeki Wachee may be used on different days and costs $17.95 for adults. (2-4 hours)

★★★ **Buccaneer Bay Coastal Heritage Museum**—This museum is filled with a variety of historical displays and artifacts, including a 1930s jail cell and a 1914 fish house facade. Details: 532 Citrus Avenue, Crystal River; (352) 795-1755; open Tuesday through Friday from 10 a.m. to 2 p.m. Donations are accepted. (1–2 hours)

★★★ **Crystal River State Archaeological Site**—This six-mound, 14-acre site is believed to have been occupied by Deptford Indians for 1,600 years, from 200 B.C. to A.D. 1400, making it one of the longest continuously occupied sites in Florida. A half-mile paved walking trail leads from the visitor center through the mound complex. Exhibits in the center include pottery and artifacts from excavations of the mounds. Park personnel are on hand to answer questions and guide visitors. Details: North of Crystal River off U.S. 19 on Museum Point; (352) 795-3817; visitor center open daily from 9 a.m. to 5 p.m.; the grounds open from 8 a.m. to sundown. Admission is $2 per vehicle at the park entrance. (2 hours)

★★★ **Heritage Antiques Mall**—Thirty-three dealers offer the largest collection of antiques in Citrus County. Details: 103 U.S. 19 N.W., Crystal River; (352) 563-5597; open every day from 9 a.m. to 5 p.m. (1–2 hours)

★★★ **Homosassa Springs State Wildlife Park**—Homosassa Springs, 8 miles south of Crystal River on U.S. 19, is known for attracting manatees. They can easily be viewed and photographed from the underwater floating observatory at the Homosassa River headwaters within this 166-acre park. In 1962 the huge 188-ton glass observatory was slipped down the ways into the 55-foot deep spring. (To avoid polluting the water with heavy grease, the ways were lubricated with banana peels.) The observatory makes manatee-watching possible for everyone, and a ramp over the spring helps people with disabilities. These curious creatures inspect visitors through observatory windows, while saltwater fishermen watch in awe as snook, redfish, sheepshead, and large schools of jacks swim past accompanied by freshwater varieties. However, nothing equals the excitement generated by the rare sight of the silver side of a big tarpon flashing past the window.

The park is one of the few along the Gulf Coast equipped with a rescue and rehabilitation center for injured manatees and other wildlife. Homosassa's first-magnitude spring produces 6 million gallons of water per hour, creating not only the wide Homosassa River, which flows 8 miles west to the Gulf, but attracting more than 40 species of fresh- and saltwater fish. Knowledgeable residents and ecologists manage the park and work carefully to preserve the natural vegetation and wildlife within its borders. Details: main park entrance located on U. S. 19, Homosassa Springs; (352) 628-5343; open daily 9a.m. to 5:30p.m. Admission is $7.95 for adults, $4.95 for children ages 3 to 12; children under 3 are free. (2–4 hours)

★★★ **Howard's Flea Market**—Covering more than 50 acres, Howard's claims to have the largest selection of antiques, collectibles, jewelry, and crafts on the Florida west coast. There's lots of good food at the concession stands. Details: on U.S. 19, 2½ miles south of Homosassa Springs; (352) 628-5343; open year-round, Saturday and Sunday from 6:30 a.m. to 4 p.m.; office hours are Thursday and Friday from 10 a.m. to 4 p.m. (4–6 hours)

★★★ **Manatees at King's Bay**—Crystal River's best-kept secret is that it's one of the few places in Florida where you can swim with the manatees. West of town, at King's Bay, swimmers are allowed in the water with the gentle "sea cows." Created by Florida's second-largest spring head, the bay is a winter haven for hundreds of manatees, well protected by a surrounding 45-acre national wildlife refuge. Many of these smart and affectionate distant relatives of the elephant live year-round in the comfortable 72-degree waters.

Manatees can be seen easily through the clear water as they pass underneath a drifting boat, feeding on vegetation growing from the spring bottom. Herbivores, they eat 10 to 15 percent of their body weight daily, and do not bite or harm humans or any other living creature. Adults can reach 17 feet in length and weigh more than 3,000 pounds. Fortunately for humans, they are very friendly and gentle, often nudging swimmers for attention, with old timers rolling over for a tummy scratch. According to the U.S. Fish and Wildlife Service, swimmers may touch a manatee only if the manatee touches the swimmer first!

An endangered species, the manatee is vulnerable to dangerous motorboat propellers, and state and national regulations are strictly enforced to ensure the animal's survival. Only about 2,500 exist in U.S. waters today, and unpreventable deaths do occur; in 1996 more than 100 died from a heavy concentration of red-tide toxins in their algae-based diets. Details: Check with your hotel or motel or the

Nature Coast Chamber of Commerce, 28 U.S. 19 N.W, in downtown Crystal River, to find reputable local guides and dive shops; (352) 795-3149. (2–4 hours)

✰✰✰ **Old Homosassa Village**—The historic buildings and shops in this village offer visitors a glimpse into the past. Old Homosassa, settled in the early nineteenth century, is one of the oldest residential communities on the Florida Gulf Coast. For generations, people interested in nature and wildlife have been drawn to the area, seeking peace and quiet, often building homes in the dense forest where "subtropical" Florida is said to begin. The village's active civic club supports various activities in the creative community and is home to many artists. For information about the history of Homosassa, visit the Old Homosassa Library downtown. Details: Turn west off U.S. 19 onto Highway 490, then take West Yulee Drive for 4 miles to Old Homosassa Village, on the banks of the river. For more information, contact the Nature Coast Chamber of Commerce, 28 U.S. 19 N.W., downtown Crystal River; (352) 795-3149.

The following three art galleries are all clustered on West Yulee Drive next to Yulee Sugar Mill Ruins State Historic Site Park in Old Homosassa Village:

The Olde Millhouse Gallery and Printing Museum—An educational experience in letterpress printing methods from the mid-1800s to the present. The gallery features examples of printing in the art field as well as original works by local artists. Artists give occasional live demonstrations. Details: 10444 W. Yulee Drive, Homosassa; (352) 628-1081; open Thursday through Saturday from 10:30 a.m. to 3 p.m. (1 hour)

Sugar Mill Gallery—Owner Jack Lambert designs custom jewelry by fashioning it from older pieces. The artist's award-winning designs are displayed with a variety of other arts and crafts. Details: 10644 W. Yulee Drive, Homosassa; (352) 628-2230; open Thursday through Saturday from 11 a.m. to 3 p.m. (1 hour)

River Works Studio and Copper Art Gallery—Original sculptures include a 7-foot copper fish, copper fountains, dried flower arrangements, fish trays, prints, and more. Custom orders are accepted. Details: 10844 W. Yulee Drive, Homosassa; (352) 628-0822; open by appointment. (1 hour)

Homosassa Arts, Crafts, and Seafood Festival—Held annually in November on Yulee Avenue in Old Homosassa, both local and visiting artists from the Southeastern states enter this juried art show, which attracts more than 40,000 buyers, browsers, art enthusiasts, and fish lovers. Details: For further information, call Betty Helms, (352) 628-0411. (1 day)

★★★ **Old Keg Antiques**—Specializing in antique furniture. Come and find a treasure for the home. Details: 2040 N. Cedarhouse Terrace, Crystal River; (352) 795-4403; open Tuesday through Saturday from 10 a.m. to 5 p.m. (1 hour)

★★★ **The Power Place**—In the Florida Power Corporation's Crystal River Energy Complex, The Power Place features energy exhibits, video presentations, and educational lectures at the visitor center. "A Celebration of Light" takes you through history to meet Benjamin Franklin, Thomas Edison, and Enrico Fermi, father of the atomic age. Visitors can test their pedal power aboard a bicycle generator, discover how much energy is needed to run a portable television and other appliances, or view a video presentation on atomic energy. Details: At the end of Power Line Street, 3.8 miles west of U.S. 19 and 2½ miles north of Crystal River; (352) 563-4490; open Monday through Friday from 9:30 a.m. to 4 p.m. Free admission. (1–2 hours)

★★★ **Weeki Wachee Spring**—The underwater spring theater has long been famous for its live "mermaids." Generations of visitors have been delighted by year-round productions viewed from the comfortable, air-conditioned indoor amphitheater through 19 four-inch-thick plate glass windows. Graceful mermaids effortlessly glide, speak, and even sing from their sparkling spring-water stage, about 16 feet underwater. Recent offerings have included *The Little Mermaid* and *Pocahontas.* The park hosts such outdoor attractions as the educational, narrated wilderness river cruise down the spring waterway to the refuge where disabled and injured birds are nursed back to health and released or given a permanent home. The waterway is lined with subtropical foliage inhabited by monkeys and other wildlife. Within the park, birds-of-prey and exotic-bird exhibits feature eagles, hawks, falcons, and owls, as well as macaws and parrots, some amazingly trained to perform in a most entertaining fashion. The forest petting zoo is a favorite with kids. Llamas, pygmy deer, and an emuari cozy up to visitors. Details: Located on U.S. 19 at State Road 50, 20 miles south of Homosassa; (352) 596-2062; open year-round, from 9:30 a.m. to

5:30 p.m. Admission is $16.95 for adults, $12.95 for children ages 3 to 10. (4–5 hours)

✵✵ **Yulee Sugar Mill Ruins State Historic Site**—The ruins of the Yulee Sugar Mill, nestled on 6 wooded acres, symbolize a historic time in the development of Homosassa and Crystal River. In 1839 David Levy Yulee came to the Homosassa area. His impressive credentials identified him as an attorney, businessman, statesman, and planter. He later became Florida's first U.S. Senator, when the territory gained statehood in 1845. Yulee established a 5,100-acre sugar cane plantation along the Homosassa River banks and built a handsome home on beautiful Tiger Tail Island off the mouth of the river. During the Civil War, Union forces burned his home and destroyed the mill and sugarcane fields, which had been supplying sugar and arms to the Confederate army. Hewn from native limestone, the partially restored mill consists of a large chimney and a shed housing the boiler and parts of the grinding machinery. Picnic tables under giant oaks are available for visitors. Yulee also left his mark on Florida by developing the "Homosassa Orange" in his citrus groves. The orange, at one time considered Florida's finest, is still enjoyed today. Details: 10470 W. Yulee Drive (Highway 490), Old Homosassa; (352) 795-3817; open from 8 a.m. to sunset. Free admission. (1 hour)

✵ **Crystal River Mall**—The Nature Coast's largest regional mall has 38 stores, including Sears, JC Penney, Belk Lindsey, Radio Shack, and Kmart. The mall should not be confused with Crystal River Plaza, located across from the airport south of town, where the anchor store is Bealls. Details: East side of U.S. 19, north Crystal River; (352) 795-2585; open daily from 10 a.m. to 9 p.m.; some stores may have different evening and Sunday hours.

Chazerei Antiques—Located across from Howard's Flea Market, Chazerei has plenty of furniture, pottery, and glass, and a fine variety of collectibles. Details: 6360 S. Suncoast Boulevard (U.S. 19), Homosassa; (352) 628-0558; open daily from 10 a.m. to 3 p.m. (1 hour)

Cobblestone Alley Antiques—Specializing in Americana and country antiques, this is a good place to find unique Christmas decorations. Details: 657 N. Citrus Avenue, Crystal River; (352) 795-0060;

open Monday through Friday from 10 a.m. to 5 p.m., Saturday from
10 a.m. to 4 p.m. (1 hour)

FITNESS AND RECREATION

Crystal River and Homosassa offer plenty of recreational and leisure-
time activities, the most popular of which tend to be water-related.
Fishing, swimming, boating, sailing, canoeing, diving, snorkeling,
and windsurfing top the list. Here, where the waters of seven spring-
fed rivers mingle with the Gulf of Mexico, record-sized tarpon
weighing upwards of 150 pounds are boated almost every year. Bass
fishermen, hoping for record catches, too, explore riverbanks,
streams, and bays. To explore the Homosassa with fish in mind, call
River Safaris, Inc., (352) 628-5222, or **MacRae's of Homosassa,
Inc.**, (352) 628-2922, both located on Cherokee Way in Old
Homosassa. Ask about the **Cobia Big Fish Tournament** held annually in June.

There's more! Ten golf courses are located less than an hour's
drive from Crystal River; right in town you'll find a championship
course at the **Plantation Inn**, (800) 632-6262.

FOOD

Seafood is abundant and delicious in the Crystal River and Homosassa
area and is often fresh off the boat. **Barnacle Ray's Yardarm** restaurant and lounge, located at the Riverside Inn Resort, 5295 S. Cherokee
Way, off West Yulee Drive on the river in Old Homosassa, (352) 628-
3327, is a historic hunting and fishing lodge. Customers enjoy the
restaurant's many antiques, as well as a river view that includes the
antics of the monkeys on "Monkey Island." Barnacle Ray's offers a
wide selection of local seafood, including fresh grouper, oysters, jumbo
shrimp, and delicious crab cakes, as well as the standards such as steak,
prime rib, and pasta. They'll even prepare box lunches and cook your
catch of the day on request.

CRYSTAL RIVER AND HOMOSASSA

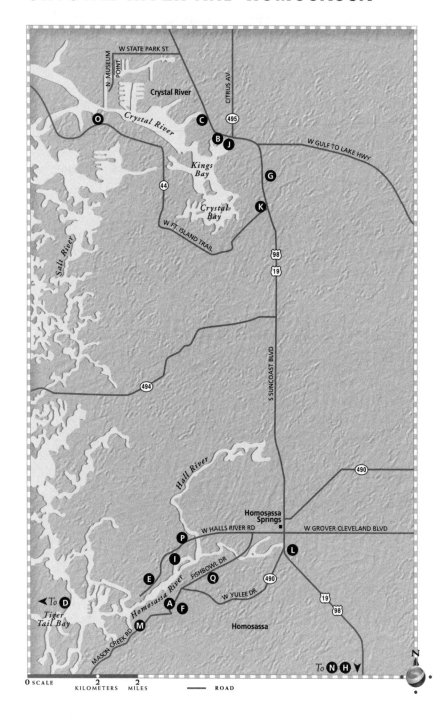

W STATE PARK ST

N. MUSEUM POINT

CITRUS AV

Crystal River

O

Crystal River

C

495

B

J

W GULF TO LAKE HWY

Kings Bay

44

G

Crystal Bay

K

W FT. ISLAND TRAIL

Salt River

98

19

494

S SUNCOAST BLVD

490

Hall River

Homosassa Springs

W HALLS RIVER RD

W GROVER CLEVELAND BLVD

P

L

I

FISHBOWL DR

E

Homosassa River

Q

490

To Tiger Tail Bay

D

W YULEE DR

A

F

19

M

98

MASON CREEK RD

Homosassa

To N H

N

0 SCALE   2   2
KILOMETERS   MILES   ROAD

Food

- **A** Barnacle Rays' Yardarm
- **B** Charlie's Fish House
- **C** Crackers
- **D** Crows Nest Restaurant
- **E** K.C. Crump's
- **F** The Old Mill Tavern
- **G** The Spinnaker
- **E** Woody's Dockside

Lodging

- **C** Best Western Crystal River Resort
- **H** Holiday Inn Weeki Wachee
- **I** The Homosassa River Retreat Fishing Resort
- **J** King's Bay Lodge
- **K** Plantation Inn
- **A** Riverside Inn Motel and Marina
- **L** Three Rivers Motel

Camping

- **M** Camp 'N' Water
- **N** Chassahowitzka Campground
- **O** Crystal Isles RV Resort
- **P** Nature's Resort
- **Q** Turtle Creek Campground

Note: Items with the same letter are located in the same town or area.

Historic **K.C. Crump's** restaurant and lounge, (352) 628-1500, built in the late 1800s, is located on Halls River Road, across the river from Barnacle Ray's. Crump's fine menu includes the delicious "Michaela," with shrimp, scallops, and crab baked in a three-cheese garlic sauce; crab cakes; shrimp scampi; fresh fish; venison stew; and, for a change, yellow-fin tuna from Key West. Downstairs, casual outdoor dining and a tiki bar are offered at **Woody's Dockside**. Hearty eaters claim that it's "The Biggest Grouper Ever" sandwich is the area's best. Crump's also owns the Crows Nest Restaurant at the mouth of the Homosassa, accessible only by boat. Launches leave from K.C. Crump's for the **Crows Nest** daily every hour from 11 a.m. to 5 p.m. for a river tour and optional lunch. Crump's also runs a water taxi on the river.

The **Old Mill Tavern**, (352) 628-2668, across from the Yulee Sugar Mill Historic Site on Yulee Drive in Old Homosassa, is the place to find Greek salad and boiled "you-peel-'em" jumbo shrimp (½ lb., $5.25; 1 lb., $10). The old-fashioned tavern posts a menu board of daily specials ($5.25–$9.75) and the soup of the day.

Bring the whole family to **The Spinnaker**, (352) 563-1184, for appetizers such as "Onion in Bloom" ($4.95), chicken wings, and stuffed mushrooms; dinner entrées including seafood, veal, chicken, and Italian fare; and a children's menu sure to make everyone happy, with spaghetti, fried shrimp, chicken fingers, and a salad bar ($2.99–$3.99). Football fans will love Happy Hour, from 4 to 7 p.m., in front of the big-screen TV in the lounge. The Spinnaker is located on the south side of town at 2035 U.S. 19 S.E.

To taste the best of local fish, try **Charlie's Fish House**, at 224 U.S. 19 N., downtown Crystal River, (352) 795-3949. On King's Bay, **Crackers** restaurant and lounge, (352) 795-3999, is convenient for guests of the Best Western Crystal River Resort.

LODGING

Lodging in Crystal River and Homosassa is clustered along U.S. 19 (Suncoast Boulevard), on King's Bay, and along both sides of the Homosassa River. It's worth the time to look for a place that makes the most of the area's unique natural surroundings. There are some quiet, beautiful resorts off the beaten path for relaxing and sunset-watching. One of the finest lodgings in Crystal River is the **Plantation Inn**, (800) 632-6262, on King's Bay off U.S. 19. Its old Southern atmosphere makes it a favorite getaway for both Florida residents and tourists. Golf is its main attraction, with a championship par 72 course and a short nine-hole course. The marina offers full-service boating and diving facilities.

Also located on King's Bay, the **Best Western Crystal River Resort**, (800) 444-1919, at 614 U.S. 19 N.W., offers a full-service marina and heated swimming pool. The resort provides guided tours, diving, and fishing trips on King's Bay and the Gulf of Mexico. Dining is easy at Crackers restaurant and lounge next door, (352) 795-3999.

Florida-style living at the **King's Bay Lodge**, (352) 795-2850, means having a natural-bottom swimming pool fed by spring water, and waterfront, air-conditioned rooms that include kitchenettes with microwaves, color cable TV, and ceiling fans. Boat docks are provided for guests, and restaurants and shopping areas are within walking distance. Room rates are $45 per day.

To really see the Homosassa River, stay in the **Riverside Inn Motel and Marina**, adjacent to Barnacle Ray's Yardarm and close to the River Safaris & Guide Centers. This area in Old Homosassa is the past and present heart of fishing and diving on the river.

One of the best places to hear fish stories is the **Homosassa River Retreat Fishing Resort**, on the Homosassa River, with new, completely furnished cottages designed for Florida living, including screened porches, lofts, and riverfront views. This is one of the area's best "fish camps." Reservations are suggested; call (352) 628-7072. Follow State Road 490-A west from U.S. 19 for 1½ miles to the resort, on the river to your left.

Convenience and economy make it hard to beat the **Three Rivers Motel**, 1 mile south of Homosassa Wildlife State Park on U.S. 19, where both rooms and efficiencies have cable TV and air conditioning. Rates start at $29 per day for a single room. For reservations, call (352) 628-6629.

For visitors to Weeki Wachee and Buccaneer Bay, the **Holiday Inn Weeki Wachee** is a good choice. Located adjacent to the spring, the hotel offers weekend packages with deals on admission to both attractions. Call (352) 596-2007 or 800-HOLIDAY for further information or reservations.

CAMPING

Campgrounds are plentiful on the Nature Coast, where outdoor activities are the main attraction. Try roughing it in luxury at **Crystal Isles RV Resort**, located on West Fort Island Trail, close to King's Bay. The park covers 30 acres with 250 sites, lots of trees, a lake, and a large recreation area with paved roads. Fishing, boating, and diving in King's Bay are accessed via the canal skirting the property. To reach the RV resort, turn west off U.S. 19 at the intersection of the Plantation Inn Country Club and drive 4 miles. Call (352) 795-3774.

The big advantage of **Turtle Creek Campground** is its boat dock on the Homosassa River. Turtle Creek is an active, family-owned park with full hookups and 15 major cable "Turtlevision" channels available at all sites. The summer rate is $15.50 for an average site. The resort features planned activities and a special rate of $160 per month for 12 months. The winter rate, from September 1 to May 1, starts at $18 per day. Call (352) 628-2928.

Nature's Resort, on Hall's River, has one of the finest river campground locations in the area. Hall's River runs into the Homosassa a few miles down from the Homosassa Wildlife State Park and spring. Although the beautiful, 97-acre gated park among the trees advertises "Stay for a day, a week, a month or longer," overnighters are advised to try down the road at a smaller campground. Boat rentals are available, and manatees are a familiar sight near the resort. From U.S. 19 drive about 4 miles west on Hall's River Road. Call (352) 628-9544 for current rates.

Try the 40-acre **Chassahowitzka Campground** for a real camping vacation on a beautiful, spring-fed river. The campground is within walking and boating distance of the 30,500-acre Chassahowitzka National Wildlife Refuge. The northern boundaries of this large refuge join the Homosassa Wildlife State Park along the Homosassa River. Some of the Nature Coast's best snorkeling and diving is found along the Chassahowitzka, said by many divers to be the clearest north of the Florida Keys. This pristine refuge is home to many species, including otters, deer, wild turkeys, black bear, alligators, and raccoons. Endangered species often spotted on boat trips are nesting bald eagles and manatees. Bring your own boat or rent one at the campground. Bass fishing is excellent in the quiet river, too shallow for large motorboats. Full hookups for self-contained vehicles are available along with separate and secluded tent sites. Rates are $14 per night with a full hookup and $10 per day for boat rental. Located west off U.S. 19 on Miss Maggie Drive (County Route 480), drive for 1.8 miles and follow the signs to the campground.

Hidden on a tree-shaded bank of the Homosassa River (just 4 miles from U.S. 19 and shopping centers) is the camping surprise

Camp 'N' Water, 11465 W. Priest Lane, Homosassa. The campground offers a nature walk, canoes, boat trips, store, swimming pool, and video game room. Choose from 74 campsites with full hookups or ten one-bedroom housekeeping park models available for rent. Sites are $15 per day and $90 per week. Unit rentals are $36.50 to $46.50 per day, two-day minimum. Rates are subject to change. The park is easy to find. Turn west off U.S. 19 onto 490-A and then left onto Fish Bowl, heading past the Yulee Sugar Mill to the fire station. Turn left on Mason Creek Road to Garcia Road, and right into the campground. Call (352) 628-2000 for reservations.

SIDE TRIP TO YANKEETOWN

Yankeetown and the Izaak Walton Lodge go hand in hand in the minds of most people who have visited this historic site on the wide Withlacoochee River. The lodge is named for Izaak Walton, who in 1653 wrote The Compleat Angler, a book promoting the advantages of serene fishing instead of violent hunting as a pastime and means of providing food. The Izaak Walton League, organized in 1922 by followers of Walton's theory, decided in 1924 to build their lodge on the

Lee Island Coast

peaceful and excellent fishing waters of the Withlacoochee. Today the lodge serves delicious fish and seafood dinners fresh from the river and Gulf waters, and has been restored to its original purpose, to accommodate guests in the delightful, old-fashioned rooms upstairs. A stroll through Yankeetown reveals elegant homes tucked away along the river. More and more of them appear each year, as nature lovers and artists escape the noise and confusion of city life. Canoe rentals and boat tours are available, making the river easy to explore.

Be sure to drive down County Road 40 near the mouth of the river, where the Elvis Presley movie Follow That Dream was filmed in 1961 on Punkin Island, beside the Bird Creek Bridge. A memorial to Elvis may soon be built on the site.

To reach the lodge from Crystal River, drive north on U.S. 19 to County Road 40 at Inglis. Turn west to 63rd Street in Yankeetown, then south on 63rd Street to the Izaak Walton Lodge. The 14-mile drive takes 15 minutes each way. Call (352) 447-2311 for reservations. The lodge is closed Monday; dinner is served Tuesday through Saturday from 5 to 9, Sunday from 3 to 8. Rates are $34 for a lodge room, $79 for an efficiency or suite, and $99 for two bedrooms.

7

TARPON SPRINGS

Back at the turn of the century, when Greek divers arrived to harvest and sell sponges from the Gulf of Mexico, Tarpon Springs became known as "The Sponge Capital" of the United States. Although the sponge industry has diminished, the colorful Greek influence is still strong in this Mediterranean-style village. Commercial fishing boats and weathered docks provide a picturesque background for more than 100 shops and 15 Greek restaurants and bakeries. Visit the sponge docks and shop, take a cruise down the Anclote River, go deep-sea fishing, see a movie about the sponge industry, or visit a saltwater aquarium.

The renovated downtown area includes Tarpon Avenue, part of the National Main Street program, with antique shops and artists' galleries. At the Cultural Center on South Pinellas Avenue, take in an art exhibit and pick up directions for a walking/bus tour of this historic area.

Several annual traditional Greek events and festivals are open to the public, preserved by the many Greek residents of Tarpon Springs (pop. 20,000). One of the most colorful is the Feast of Epiphany, which has been celebrated by the St. Nicholas Greek Orthodox Cathedral Church every January since 1903. The celebration includes a procession to Spring Bayou, where young Greek Orthodox boys dive into the chilly water to retrieve a cross and win a year of extra blessings for themselves and their families. A *glendi* (festival) follows, with Greek food, dancing, and music. More than 20,000 people attend every year. ◨

TARPON SPRINGS

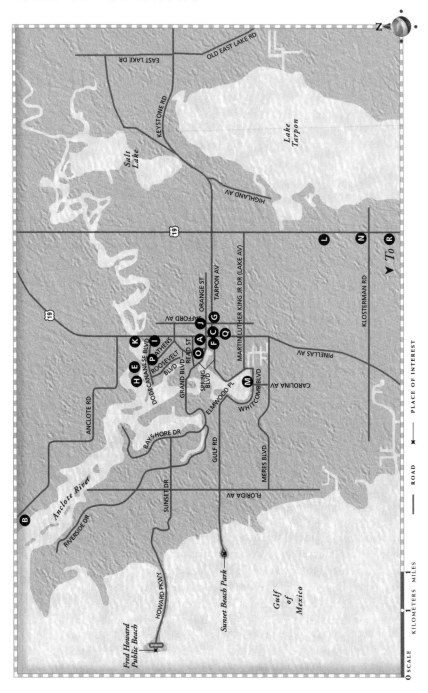

Sightseeing Highlights

A Antiques on The Main

A Carter's Antique Asylum

B Duke's Marina and Café

C Historical Society Museum

D The Inness Paintings

E St. Nicholas Boat Line

F St. Nicholas Greek Orthodox Cathedral

G Tarpon Springs Cultural Center

H Tarpon Springs Sponge Docks

Food

I Dino's Restaurant and Taverna

J La Brasserie

E Mykonos

K Pappas Restaurant

Lodging

L Days Inn Tarpon Springs

M Gulf Manor

N Holiday Inn Tarpon Springs

O Innis Manor

P Riverside Motel

Q Spring Bayou Inn

Camping

R Clearwater Tarpon Springs KOA

R Cypress Pointe Campground

Note: Items with the same letter are located in the same town or area.

A PERFECT DAY IN TARPON SPRINGS

Start the day with a walk along Dodecanese Boulevard, exploring the shops that line this busy waterfront street. They're filled with everything imaginable, from beautiful Greek pottery to inexpensive souvenirs (sponges and curios from the sea are favorites).

The smell of delicious Greek cuisine fills the air along the boulevard. Have lunch at Pappas Restaurant on the riverfront. The menu features a variety of authentic Greek dishes, including an excellent Greek salad. Try the delicious, honey-rich baklava for dessert.

Next, take an afternoon trip on an authentic sponge-fishing boat from the early 1900s. As you cruise along the river, divers demonstrate how sponges are harvested from the bottom. Dinner on one of the area's several dinner cruise ships makes a perfect ending to a colorful day in Tarpon Springs.

SIGHTSEEING HIGHLIGHTS

✭✭✭ **Duke's Marina and Café**—Private boat charters are available for fishing and sightseeing at Duke's Marina. There are cottages for rent near the marina and café, located off the Anclote River, just where it reaches the Gulf of Mexico. Details: 1029 Baillies Bluff Road, Holiday, the last fish camp on the Anclote River before it reaches the Gulf; (813) 937-9737. Rates begin at $50 per person for half-day charters. (6–8 hours)

✭✭✭ **Historical Society Museum**—The restored Atlantic Coast Line Railroad Station is now the home of the Historical Society Museum. The station's former baggage area houses the Iron Horse Acoustic Café a coffeehouse also used as a concert hall, theater, and art exhibit space. In the south end there's a wonderful 18-by-25-foot HO-gauge model railroad exhibit that includes models of Tarpon Springs historical buildings. Details: Corner of Safford and Tarpon Avenues, Tarpon Springs; (813) 934-2712; open Tuesday through Thursday, and Saturday 2–4 p.m. (1–2 hours)

✭✭✭ **St. Nicholas Boat Line**—This boat line, established in 1924, takes visitors on a half-hour round-trip cruise from the historic sponge docks marina to a diving spot down the Anclote River. The excursion includes a narration of the history of sponge diving and a sponge-harvesting demonstration by a real sponge diver dressed in the authentic large, windowed helmet and bulky dive suit used in the profession long ago. The trip is educational and fun. No reservations are necessary. Details: The cruise leaves from Dodecanese Boulevard on the sponge docks, Tarpon Springs; (813) 942-6425. Cost is $5 for adults, $2 for children ages 6 to 12, children under 6 free. (1–2 hours)

✩✩✩ **St. Nicholas Greek Orthodox Cathedral**—This historic Tarpon Springs landmark, built in 1943, is a replica of St. Sophia's in Constantinople. It is open daily to visitors and worshipers. The neo-Byzantine cathedral, adorned with a wealth of icons, is often the center of colorful pageantry and events held during Greek festivals. Details: Located at the corner of Pinellas (U.S. 19A) and Orange Streets in downtown Tarpon Springs. (1 hour)

✩✩✩ **Tarpon Springs Cultural Center**—The downtown cultural center exhibits art in its museum and hosts walking/bus tours of the city for visitors. Details: 101 S. Pinellas Avenue, Tarpon Springs; (813) 942-5605; open Monday through Friday 8 a.m. to 5 p.m., Saturday 10 a.m. to 4 p.m.; admission is free, donations appreciated.

✩✩✩ **Tarpon Springs Sponge Docks**—Shrimpers and sponge-fishing boats tie up at the docks beside Dodecanese Boulevard on the waterfront. The Riverwalk shops on the sponge docks include the Coral Sea Aquarium, where the diver hand-feeds sharks and fish in a 120,000-gallon reef tank. Also featured are the Brass Rubbing Centre and Museum Shoppe, Tarpon Treasures Gifts, and Melo's Gifts and Crafts, which sells souvenirs as well as nautical and handcrafted items. Details: Dodecanese Boulevard, Tarpon Springs; (813) 938-4404. (2 hours)

✩✩ **Antiques on The Main**—The store is part of the historical restoration of downtown Tarpon Springs. It specializes in jewelry, art and cut glass, lamps, clocks, furniture, and more. Details: 124 E. Tarpon Avenue, Tarpon Springs; (813) 937-9497; open Monday through Saturday, 10 a.m. to 5 p.m., Sunday noon to 5 p.m. (1 hour)

✩✩ **Carter's Antique Asylum**—This is the place to buy and sell antiques and collectibles. The owners also restore them. Details: 106 E. Tarpon Avenue, Tarpon Springs; (813) 942-2799; open Monday through Saturday from 10 a.m. to 5 p.m., Sunday 1 p.m. to 5 p.m. (1 hour)

★★ **The Inness Paintings**—Housed in the Unitarian Universalist Church, these 11 religious paintings by George Inness Jr., son of the American landscape artist, are the largest single collection of his works. Inness was a Tarpon Springs resident for many years and a painter of some repute in his own right, often visited here by his more famous father. Details: 230 Grand Boulevard, Tarpon Springs; (813) 937-4682; the collection is open to the public from October 1 to May 31, Tuesday through Sunday 2 p.m. to 5 p.m.; closed Monday and holidays. Admission is $1. (1 hour)

FITNESS AND RECREATION

Fishing, boating, shopping, and sightseeing are the main forms of recreation for visitors to Tarpon Springs. The 37-foot sailing yacht *Shamayem* offers snorkeling, swimming, and fishing opportunities, as well as island cruises by the hour, day, overnight, or weekend with Captain Steve "Pleasure Through Sailing" Rayow. Rates are by the hour, $10 per adult, $5 per child under 12. For further information on half-day and extended cruises, call (813) 934-6869.

Power boat rentals are available at **Fisher Marine**, (813) 934-0003, on 2,500-acre freshwater **Lake Tarpon**, on the east side of U.S. 19, across from Tarpon Springs. The 40-foot pontoon boat *M/V Helios* departs from the sponge docks for day trips of shelling, swimming, and exploring Anclote Key and its historic lighthouse. The *Helios* is also a comfortable way to explore the offshore islands and the Anclote River. One-hour sightseeing excursions are $5 per adult, $3 per child; half-day (4 hour) trips to Anclote Key are $20 per adult and $15 per child.

There are several excellent parks in the Tarpon Springs area. **Sunset Beach**, at the west end of Gulf Road, provides picnic, swimming and boat-launching areas. It also has barbecue grills, sheltered picnic tables, and public restrooms, and is open from sunrise to 10 p.m.; (813) 942-5610. **Fred Howard Park** has a mile-long causeway connecting an offshore swimming area with the mainland. This beautiful park is a 150-acre county recreation area with fishing access. Facilities include barbecue grills, sheltered pavilions, children's playgrounds, windsurfing, public restrooms, and beach showers (open from 7 a.m. to sunset; 813-937-4938). **A.L. Anderson Park**, a county-owned 128-acre park on Lake Tarpon, has picnic facilities, barbecue grills, boat access to the lake, fishing, and a nature trail (open from

7 a.m. to sunset; 813-937-5410). For further information, call the
Tarpon Springs Chamber of Commerce at (813) 937-6109.

FOOD

Greek cuisine and Greek favorites such as *pastitso*, moussaka, and baklava
are expectedly superb in Tarpon Springs. The Greek salad ($7.25 for
two) at **Pappas Restaurant**, 10 W. Dodecanese Boulevard, (813) 937-
5101, is as famous as the historic restaurant; try the blackened grouper
for a spicy seafood treat. Louis Pappas and his father arrived in Tarpon
Springs from Sparta, Greece, in 1904 and founded the restaurant in 1925
on the sponge docks, close to where it is today. Entrées range from $7.25
to $13.95.

For fun and good food, combine the live entertainment on Friday,
Saturday, and Sunday nights at **Dino's Restaurant and Taverna** with
Greek-style lamb shank cooked in a red sauce and served with rice or
pasta and vegetables ($6.95). Dino's is at 604 Athens Street, (813) 938-
9082. Authentic Greek cooking is also the order of the day at **Mykonos**,
628 Dodecanese Boulevard, (813) 934-4306. Here dinner favorites
include *kalamarakia tiganita* (lightly floured pan-fried squid, $7.45) and
specially cooked gyros (lamb on pita bread, $3.95).

For a change of pace, try Happy Hour at **La Brasserie**, 200 E.
Tarpon Avenue, (813) 942-3011. Dinners and complimentary hors d'oeu-
vres are served from 4 to 10 weekdays and from 5 to midnight on Friday
and Saturday. Onion soup is the house specialty. Live jazz is presented
Friday and Saturday from 9 p.m. to midnight.

LODGING

Tarpon Springs' lodging ranges from historic homes to modern facilities.
Holiday Inn Tarpon Springs, (813) 934-5781, offers guests all the
modern-day comforts. The café has indoor or outdoor seating, while the
palm-shaded Tiki Bar, adjacent to the pool, is ideal for vacation picture-
taking. Standard doubles range from $64.95 to $69.95, while efficiencies
begin at $73.95. Suites (from $85.95) have spacious, nicely decorated living rooms and fully equipped kitchens, with space for up to four people.
Children under 18 stay free in their parents' room. The Holiday Inn is
centrally located on U.S. 19 in Tarpon Springs.

Two bed and breakfast inns are housed in marvelous historic homes.
The circa 1880 **Innis Manor**, 34 W. Orange Street, (813) 938-2900, was

once home to American painter George Inness Jr. Originally built as a winter home and later remodeled to accommodate Inness' art students, the manor now has 27 rooms, eight baths, nine porches, and 7,800 square feet of living area. Rates range from $75 to $95. **Spring Bayou Inn**, 32 W. Tarpon Avenue, (813) 938-9333, is a large, comfortable home, within easy walking distance of picturesque Spring Bayou. Rates range from $60 for rooms with twin beds and a shared bath to $100 per night for a queen bed, private bath, and sitting room.

Conveniently located near the sponge docks, **Riverside Motel**, 7771 Roosevelt Boulevard, (813) 934-7777, makes sightseeing easy. Offering eight one-bed units with kitchens, the motel is within walking distance of restaurants and attractions in the sponge exchange. Rates are $40 to $55 per night. **Gulf Manor**, 548 Whitcom Boulevard, (813) 937-4207, boasts stately pine, live oaks with hanging moss, and flowers galore. Overlooking Whitcomb Bayou, the manor has two docks for boating and fishing. The 6-acre, privately owned estate is one of the most interesting places to stay in the heart of Tarpon Springs. In addition, Tarpon Golf Course is only a few minutes' drive away. Rates range from $48.95 for a private room to $66 per day for a large efficiency.

A convenient spot for travelers heading for central Florida and the east coast is **Days Inn Tarpon Springs**, 40050 U.S. 19 N., (813) 934-0859. The inn offers an outdoor swimming pool, playground, and free continental breakfast. In-season rates range from $55 to $60, off-season from $45 to $50.

CAMPING

Few campgrounds are located close to Tarpon Springs. However, the **Cypress Pointe Campground** on Lake Tarpon is highly rated as a recreation-vehicle resort. Cypress Pointe is located at 4600 U.S. 19, which provides access to all major roads throughout central Florida. Nearly 400 tree-shaded sites offer all the amenities for long-term camping (popular with "snow birds" who flock to Florida in the late fall), including five separate shower and restroom areas. Call (813) 938-1966 for reservations and information.

Clearwater Tarpon Springs KOA is centrally located 10 miles north of Clearwater and 2 miles south of Tarpon Springs on U.S. 19. The campground features a heated swimming pool, playground, general store, and recreation room. Special facilities are available for those with disabilities. Call (813) 937-8412 for information and current rates.

8
CLEARWATER

Clearwater, with its offshore barrier island, Clearwater Beach, was originally a harbor town with a grand bay. It now offers visitors some of the best sun, surf, and outdoor activities found anywhere in the state. In fact, *The Guinness Book of World Records* credits the region with the longest run of consecutive sunny days: 768. Built on high coastal bluffs overlooking the Gulf of Mexico, the city was chartered as a municipality in 1915, and has since grown to provide a permanent home to 104,000 citizens. Attractive natural qualities of the earlier Clearwater have been preserved and include many wetland areas.

Clearwater offers some of the best recreational opportunities in the state, with three area beaches listed in the nation's top 15, as picked by *Condé Nast Traveler* magazine. Several area parks provide great places for fishing, picnicking, bird-watching, and walking. From exploring Caladesi Island State Park, one of the few remaining undisturbed barrier islands in Florida, to following the action at any of the several area baseball spring-training camps, visitors to Clearwater can stay as busy as they want to be. Lots of folks use the town as a base camp for day trips to such attractions as Disney World, Universal Studios, and Seaworld in Orlando. ◪

CLEARWATER AREA

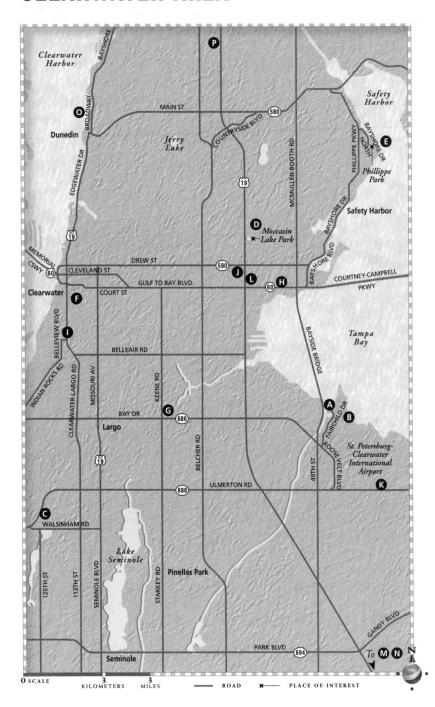

Sightseeing Highlights

Ⓐ Boatyard Village

Ⓑ Florida Military Aviation Museum

Ⓒ Heritage Village and Pinellas Historical Museum

Ⓓ Moccasin Lake Nature Park

Ⓔ Philippe Park

Food

Ⓕ O'Keef's Restaurant

Ⓖ Outback Steakhouse

Ⓗ Tio Pepe Restaurante

Lodging

Ⓘ Belleview Mido Resort Hotel

Ⓙ Clearwater Central

Ⓚ Courtyard by Marriott

Ⓛ Econolodge Clearwater

Ⓜ Renaissance Vinoy Resort

Camping

Ⓝ Bay Pines KOA

Ⓞ Dunedin Beach Campground

Ⓟ Traveltowne Travel Trailer Resort

A PERFECT DAY IN THE CLEARWATER AREA

Begin with an early morning walk along north or south Clearwater Beach. Work up a good appetite, and walk to Lenora's restaurant in the Sea Wake Inn on Clearwater Pass to watch the boats and new high bridge activity. Eat outside when it's warm and inside on cooler days. Drive to Indian Shore to see world-famous Suncoast Seabird Sanctuary, the largest wild bird hospital in North America. Stop for a close-up look at more than 40 species, which are housed and nursed in this outdoor Gulf-side zoological setting. Head back to Clearwater Beach for some boating. A Captain Memo's Pirate Cruise is always a fun option. Fishermen may prefer a half-day trip aboard one of the charter or deep-sea-fishing boats docked at the Clearwater Beach Marina. If time permits, check out the Clearwater Marine Aquarium.

When late afternoon approaches, watch the sunset from either Caladesi or Honeymoon Islands. Ferry service is available from the docks at the Clearwater Bay end of Drew Street. Pick a restaurant from the many located along the 28-mile stretch of beach communities for a leisurely dinner, then let yourself be led by the lights along the beach to some Gulf Coast nightlife.

SIGHTSEEING HIGHLIGHTS

★★★ Caladesi Island and Honeymoon Island State Parks— North of Clearwater Beach is Caladesi Island, with Honeymoon Island just north of that. Except for a little development at the side of Honey-moon Island where bridges connect it to the mainland, are among the few remaining unspoiled barrier islands in Florida. Both islands have abundant birdlife and, with more than 3 miles of white sand beach facing the Gulf, they are great places for the simple pleasures of swimming, strolling, and relaxing. To reach Honeymoon Island, drive west on Curlew Road in Dunedin, just north of Clearwater. Caladesi Island can be reached by boat; there is a marina with docking space on the bay side. Ferry service to the island departs hourly from the docks at the end of Drew Street in Clearwater and from Honeymoon Island. Details: For more information, call Caladesi Island, (813) 469-5918, or Clearwater Ferry Service, (813) 462-2628. (2–4 hours)

★★★ Clearwater Beach—Connected to the Clearwater mainland by the Garden Memorial Causeway and to Sand Key by the Clearwater Pass Bridge, wide, clean, picture-pretty Clearwater Beach is the hub of local beach activity. In 1995 *Condé Nast Traveler* magazine ranked this seashore the third-best beach in the U.S., but Clearwater Beach offers visitors much more than white, crystalline sand. With a mixture of luxury accommodations and quaint cottages, excellent attractions, and both luxurious and simple restaurants and shops, the town appeals to singles, families, students, and honeymooners alike. Much of the fun has to do with the beach and the water sports, on the Gulf. Volleyball action is notable, with permanent nets in place on the beach. In April the Pro Beach Volleyball Hall of Fame Challenge takes place here. Clearwater Beach also offers all kinds of equipment rentals and the best conditions for swimming, waterskiing, Jet Skiing, skin diving, fishing, sailing, parasailing, shelling, and tour-boating. When the water is clear enough, scuba divers can choose from more than ten artificial offshore reefs.

The Clearwater City Marina, at the junction of the beach and the Memorial Causeway, harbors a large sport-fishing fleet that take groups out for half- and full-day trips of deep-sea fishing. Smaller fishing craft can be chartered for the day as well. Sightseeing cruises also depart from the marina. Clearwater Beach makes a great starting point for exploring the coastal regions both north and south of Clearwater. Details: Greater Clearwater Chamber of Commerce, 128 N. Osceola Avenue, Clearwater; (813) 461-0011. (2–8 hours)

★★★ **Sand Key Pinellas County Park**—Drive to the southernmost tip of Clearwater Beach, then over the Clearwater Pass Bridge to the Sand Key barrier island. The entrance to the park is on the Gulf side of the road. A man-made beach park with all the amenities—parking, shower and dressing areas—Sand Key Park was ranked the 14th-best U.S. beach by *Condé Nast Traveler* magazine in 1995. A winding road curves between palm trees, and sea oats grow wild among the sand dunes. Located at the corner where the Gulf of Mexico connects with Clearwater Bay via the Clearwater Pass, Sand Key Park recalls the original natural beauty of Florida. Details: (813) 595-7677. (1–8 hours)

★★ **Clearwater Marine Aquarium**—This multipurpose facility is dedicated to the rescue, rehabilitation, and release of injured or sick marine mammals and sea turtles, and to public education and marine research. The facility, located on a man-made residential island in Clearwater Bay, is accessed by the Memorial Causeway. Large and small tanks showcase Florida's unique marine environment and sea life with educational displays and special exhibits. Displays include the Mangrove Seagrass Tank, a 55,000-gallon aquarium with as many as 100 species of Florida fish and invertebrates; the Sea-O-rama Room, which features fish replicas; and several tanks of live marine life from the Gulf of Mexico. The aquarium sponsors the Sea Turtle Program, which monitors loggerhead sea turtles nesting along Pinellas County beaches; and the Marine Animal Stranding Team, which is on call 24 hours a day to recover injured, sick, or dead whales, dolphins, and sea turtles. There are always a few rehabbed dolphins and sea turtles being readied for release back to the wild. A 1,200-gallon artificial reef tank exhibits a wide variety of animals. Details: 249 Windward Passage, Clearwater Bay; (813) 441-1790 or 447-0980; open Monday through Friday from 9 a.m. to 5 p.m.,

Saturday from 9 a.m. to 4 p.m., Sunday from 11 a.m. to 4 p.m. Admission is $5.75 for adults and $3.75 for children. (1–2 hours)

⭐⭐ **Heritage Village and Pinellas Historical Museum**—Noted for its early pioneer artifacts, this 21-acre, turn-of-the-century village and historical exhibit depicts the lifestyles of early Pinellas County pioneers. It features 22 historical buildings, including an 1852 log house, a one-room schoolhouse, a railroad depot, an operational blacksmith shop, and several authentic early-twentieth-century homes. The Pinellas Historical Museum traces the history of Pinellas County from the early Spanish period up to contemporary times, and houses exhibits depicting various themes in county and state history. Details: 11909 125th Street N., Largo; (813) 582-2123; open Tuesday through Saturday from 10 a.m. to 4 p.m., Sunday from 1 to 4 p.m. Donations accepted. (1 hour)

⭐⭐ **Moccasin Lake Nature Park**—Billed as "An Environmental and Energy Education Center," the park is situated on a 51-acre nature preserve hosting most plant and animal species native to the area. Nature trails wind through upland hardwood forests and wetlands to a 5-acre lake. The interpretive center features energy exhibits. Details: 2750 Park Trail Lane, Clearwater; (813) 462-6024; open Tuesday through Friday from 9 a.m. to 5 p.m., Saturday and Sunday from 10 a.m. to 6 p.m. Admission is $2 for adults, $1 for children. (1–2 hours)

⭐⭐ **Suncoast Seabird Sanctuary**—Situated on the coast of the Gulf of Mexico, the Suncoast Seabird Sanctuary is the largest wild bird hospital in the U.S. It is devoted to the rescue, repair, recuperation, and release of sick and injured birds. A dedicated professional staff and hundreds of volunteers have returned 15,000 birds to their natural environment. Five hundred land and sea birds live in the sanctuary compound at any one time, with an average of 20 birds arriving daily. Breeding permanently disabled birds and releasing the offspring into the wild is a goal of the Seabird Sanctuary, which is vitally aware of the interrelationships among humans, the environment, and wildlife. Educational programs are presented monthly. Details: 18328 Gulf Boulevard, Indian Shores Beach, just north of St. Pete Beach; (813) 391-6211; open daily from 9 a.m. to dusk. Guided tours and lectures are offered every Wednesday and Sunday at 2:00 p.m. Donations are requested. (1 hour)

★ **Boatyard Village**—Located on the east side of Clearwater, Boatyard Village re-creates an 1890s fishing village, right down to the old-time rickety buildings. Nestled in a cove on Tampa Bay and surrounded by mangrove-covered fishing inlets, the village is home to restaurants, shops, and a turn-of-the-century-style theater. Details: 16100 Fairchild Drive just off Roosevelt Boulevard, adjacent to the St. Petersburg/ Clearwater International Airport; (813) 531-4678. (1–2 hours)

★ **Captain Memo's Pirate Cruise**—This two-hour cruise takes place aboard a reproduction of a buccaneer pirate ship. Cruising the Gulf of Mexico aboard the *Pirate's Ransom*, visitors can interact with the entertaining pirate crew. Details: Located at the Clearwater City Marina, Dock #3, at the end of U.S. 60 on Clearwater Beach; (813) 446-2587; tours leave the docks daily at 10 a.m., 2, and 4:30 p.m.; a sunset champagne cruise is offered at 7 p.m. In the true spirit of piracy, admission is $25 for adults, $18 for seniors and kids ages 13 to 17, and $12 for children ages 2 to 12, with complimentary soft drinks, beer, and wine served. (2 hours)

★ **The Dolphin Encounter**—This unique sightseeing tour takes visitors out into the Gulf on a big, comfortable boat for a different view of the beaches. Passengers enjoy seeing dolphins feeding and frolicking in their natural environment and can feed sea birds with food provided. Details: Located at the Clearwater City Marina at the west end of U.S. 60 on Clearwater Beach; (813) 442-7433; cruises leave Tuesday through Sunday at 10 a.m., 1, 3:30, and 6:30 p.m. Admission is $10 for adults and $5.75 for children. (2 hours)

★ **Empress Cruise Lines**—Features a six-hour Gulf of Mexico cruise leaving from Clearwater Bay Marina in Clearwater. The cruise includes a gourmet buffet, casino, tropical beverages, live bands, karaoke, skeet shooting, and games. Details: 198 Seminole Street, Clearwater; (813) 895-3325; since the cruise schedule is irregular, call for times. Cost is $13 per adult, $10 per person over age 55. (6 hours)

★ **Florida Military Aviation Museum**—This open-air museum features a collection of restored military aircraft, World War II artifacts, and changing exhibits. Details: 16055 Fairchild Drive on the northwest perimeter of the St. Petersburg/Clearwater International Airport off Roosevelt Boulevard; (813) 535-9007; open Tuesday, Thursday, and

Saturday from 10 a.m. to 4 p.m., Sunday from 1 to 4 p.m. Admission is $2 for adults, $1 for children. (1 hour)

✯ **Philippe Park**—Named for Dr. Odet Philippe, the first settler on the Pinellas peninsula, who built his plantation on Tampa Bay in the 1830s, this park is set back in a peaceful woodland area and is a good place to cool off and relax. It offers visitors fishing, a boat ramp, and complete picnic facilities, including shelters and a playground. Details: 2355 Bayshore Drive in Safety Harbor, at the edge of Tampa Bay and on the eastern tip of the Clearwater area; (813) 461-0011; open until dark. (1–4 hours)

FITNESS AND RECREATION

Clearwater and the surrounding beaches offer the visitor a profusion of water sports, along with a good selection of golf and tennis venues. There are plenty of rental businesses, offering everything from bicycles and Jet Skis to kayaks and golf clubs. Some of the best outdoor activities take place along the shoreline and don't cost a thing, including beach volleyball (the city places permanent nets) and annual sandcastle-building contests.

The hottest water activity is Waverunner or Jet Ski–riding; check the local telephone book for rental locations. Catamarans may be rented just about anywhere the beach crowds gather. With ten coral- and sponge-covered artificial reefs in the area, diving is popular when the water is clear.

For a real thrill, and a view that many photographers would envy, try parasailing. **Parasail City** and **Sea Screamer** on Clearwater Beach offer an opportunity to hang beneath a parachute towed by a boat in the Gulf of Mexico. Pier fishing is a popular pastime, and significant catches are often landed from Pier 60, at the end of U.S. 60. Plenty of party boats and charter boats are available for deep-sea fishing.

For those who prefer to see the area from terra firma, try bicycling or roller-blading the **Pinellas Trail**. Built over an old railroad bed, it runs nearly the entire length of Pinellas County.

Late February through early April, Clearwater and Pinellas County become a paradise for baseball fans when spring training comes to town. The **Philadelphia Phillies** train at Jack Russell Memorial Stadium in Clearwater, while the **Toronto Blue Jays** work out in Dunedin, and the **St. Louis Cardinals** train in St. Petersburg. In all, six major league teams train within 90 minutes of Clearwater, and most spring games prove to be a gold mine for autograph hunters. Other professional sports teams in the area include the **Tampa Bay Buccaneers** football team and the **Tampa Bay Lightning** hockey team in Tampa. Baseball will also be added to the roster of home teams when the **Tampa Bay Devil Rays** play their first game in 1998 at Tropicana Field in St. Petersburg.

When it comes to golf, Clearwater and Pinellas County are rich in public and semi-private year-round courses. Some of the municipal links include **Clearwater Country Club**, 525 N. Betty Lane, Clearwater, (813) 446-9501; and the **Dunedin Country Club**, 1050 Palm Boulevard, Dunedin, (813) 446-9501. Both are 18-hole par 72 courses. The **Largo Municipal Golf Course**, 12500 131st Street N., Largo, is an 18-hole par 62 course. **Tarpon Springs Golf Course**, 1310 S. Pinellas Avenue, Tarpon Springs, is an 18-hole par 72 course. Clearwater offers the valuable free service **A Tee Times**, (800) 374-8633, which allows visitors to book times well in advance of their vacation.

Tennis is also a popular Florida sport, and the Clearwater area boasts more than 62 public tennis courts. Call the **Clearwater Parks and Recreation Department**, (813) 462-6531, for locations.

FOOD

Seafood is the unsurprising specialty of restaurants in Clearwater, especially in the beach communities. But Clearwater's eateries are remarkably varied both in menu and atmosphere. Select from elegantly decorated dining rooms or open-air patios overlooking the water. Order veal or steak or country barbecue. Try conch chowder or mussels or grouper sandwiches.

For fine dining, one of the best-known and most highly rated restaurants in the area is **The Wine Cellar**, 17307 Gulf Boulevard in North Redington Beach, (813) 360-8330, which has received international acclaim for its service as well as its American and Continental cuisine. Another well-established Clearwater Beach eatery is **Bob Heilman's Beachcomber Restaurant**, 447 Mandalay Avenue, (813) 442-4144, featuring a complete menu of seafood, ribs, beef, chicken, and lobster. For a good restaurant that's known for its veal, seafood, and mussels, try **Villa Gallace Italian Restaurant**, 109 Gulf Boulevard, Indian Rocks Beach, (813) 596-0200.

For an excellent grouper sandwich or other seafood delight served in an informal setting, drop in at **Frenchy's Mandalay Seafood Co.**,

CLEARWATER BEACH

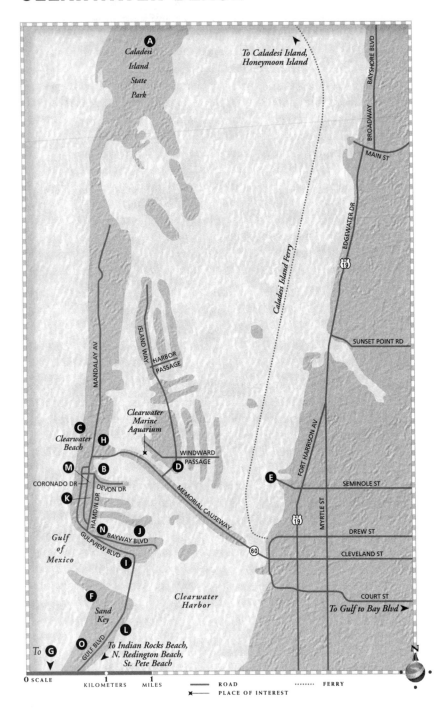

Caladesi Island State Park

To Caladesi Island, Honeymoon Island

BAYSHORE BLVD

BROADWAY

MAIN ST

EDGEWATER DR

Caladesi Island Ferry

(19)

SUNSET POINT RD

MANDALAY AV

ISLAND WAY

HARBOR PASSAGE

Clearwater Marine Aquarium

FORT HARRISON AV

WINDWARD PASSAGE

Clearwater Beach

C

H

D

E

M

B

CORONADO DR

DEVON DR

SEMINOLE ST

K

HAMDIN DR

MEMORIAL CAUSEWAY

(19)

MYRTLE ST

N

BAYWAY BLVD

J

DREW ST

Gulf of Mexico

GULFVIEW BLVD

I

60

CLEVELAND ST

Clearwater Harbor

F

COURT ST

To Gulf to Bay Blvd ➤

Sand Key

L

GULF BLVD

To G

O

To Indian Rocks Beach, N. Redington Beach, St. Pete Beach

N

O SCALE

KILOMETERS   MILES

─── ROAD   ········· FERRY

✕ PLACE OF INTEREST

Sights

A Caladesi Island and Honeymoon Island State Parks

B Captain Memo's Pirate Cruise

C Clearwater Beach

D Clearwater Marine Aquarium

B The Dolphin Encounter

E Empress Cruise Lines

F Sand Key Pinellas County Park

G Suncoast Seabird Sanctuary

Lodging

J Chart House

G Don CeSar Beach Resort

K Falcon Motel

L Radisson Suite Resort on Sand Key

M Sea Captain Motel

N Sea Stone Resort

I Sea Wake Inn

O Sheraton Sand Key

Food

H Bob Heilman's Beachcomber Restaurant

G Frog Pond Restaurant

I Lenora's

G Villa Gallace Italian Restaurant

G The Wine Cellar

Note: Items with the same letter are located in the same town or area.

435 Mandalay Avenue in Clearwater Beach, (813) 446-3607. Steak lovers enjoy the **Outback Steakhouse**, 3690 E. Bay Drive in Largo. Another area favorite is **Tio Pepe Restaurante**, 2930 Gulf to Bay Boulevard in Clearwater, (813) 799-3082, specializing in very good Spanish cuisine and featuring an award-winning wine cellar. For a quick but satisfying meal in an informal sports-bar atmosphere, try **O'Keef's Restaurant**, 1219 Ft. Harrison Avenue S. in Clearwater, (813) 442-9034. O'Keef's has the area's best hamburger menu.

A good breakfast is always important (especially before a day at one of the theme parks). Breakfast tastes extra good when served on the beach under a cool thatched roof at **Lenora's**, at the Sea Wake Inn on south Clearwater Beach, 619 Gulfview Boulevard S., (813) 443-7652. The **Frog Pond Restaurant**, 16909 Gulf Boulevard, North Redington Beach, (813) 392-4171, is another favorite breakfast spot.

LODGING

The Clearwater area has accommodations to suit just about everybody. There are luxury hotels, comfortable motels, cute cottages, and efficiency apartments. Make your reservations early!

Three area hotels steeped in history appeal to those who want the finest accommodations. These are the **Don CeSar Beach Resort**, 3400 Gulf Boulevard in St. Pete Beach, (813) 360-1881; the **Renaissance Vinoy Resort**, 501 5th Avenue N.E. in St. Petersburg, (813) 894-1000; and the **Belleview Mido Resort Hotel**, 25 Belleview Boulevard in Clearwater, (813) 442-6171. The Belleview Mido is reputed to be the largest occupied wooden structure of its type in the world. (See Chapter 9, St. Petersburg, for full descriptions of these hotels.)

Some of the best hotels and motels for the price in Clearwater include the **Clearwater Central**, 21338 U.S. 19 N., (813) 799-1565, which offers rooms from $70 to $80 in-season and $50 to $60 out of season. The **Courtyard By Marriott**, 3131 Executive Drive, just off State Road 686, (813) 572-8484, has rooms from $89 to $99 in-season and $69 to $79 out of season. For the best value in price and quality, try the **Econo Lodge Clearwater**, 21252 U.S. 19 N., (813) 799-1569, where singles and doubles go for $65 in-season and $45 out of season.

For those who want to stay on the water, there is hardly a bad place to choose. On the harbor, the **Sea Stone Resort**, 445 Hamden

Drive, (813) 441-1722, has rooms from $87 to $201 in-season and $54 to $140 out of season. On the beach, with rooms overlooking the Gulf and Clearwater Pass on south Clearwater Beach, the **Sea Wake Inn**, 691 S. Gulfview Boulevard, (813) 443-7652, offers rooms from $120 to $156 in-season, $93 to $129 out of season. If you're looking for affordability and good quality within sight of the beach or harbor, try the **Sea Captain Motel**, 40 Devon Drive, (813) 446-7550, where rooms start at $66 in-season and $46 out of season; or the **Falcon Motel**, 415 Coronado Drive, (813) 447-8714, with rooms starting at $55 in-season and $45 out of season.

For a fantasy resort on Sand Key, overlooking both the Gulf and bay, check out the **Radisson Suite Resort on Sand Key**, 1201 Gulf Boulevard, (813) 596-1100, which offers rooms from $189 to $249 in-season and $169 to $189 out of season. **Sheraton Sand Key** at 1203 Gulf Road (813-595-1611) is another fine choice. A good motel, reasonably priced and centrally located on the beach, is the **Chart House**, 850 Bayway Drive, (813) 449-8007, with rooms from $75 to $95 in-season and $65 to $85 out of season.

CAMPING

One of the Clearwater area's finest parks, **Travel Towne Travel Trailer Resort**, (813) 784-2500, is located on 18 acres on U.S. 19, 6 miles north of SR 60 and 0.5 mile south of SR 586. The 360 sites are grassy and partially shaded, and some are pull-throughs. Paved pads and rental trailers are also available. The park features a heated swimming pool, whirlpool, shuffleboard, horseshoes, and a recreational and social program for those who prefer planned activities. Only small pets are allowed. Rates are $20 March 1 to April 30 and again November 1 to February 28; $15 from May 1 to October 31.

Fishing and boating on Long Bayou is part of the fun at **Bay Pines KOA** in St. Petersburg, (813) 392-2233. One of the area's largest campgrounds, this 500-site KOA offers hot tubs, 60 cabins, and 17 boat slips for guests interested in fishing and boating. Sites are grassy or paved and feature full hookups. Rates are $27.95 April 1 to October 31 and $39.95 November 1 to March 31. Pets are permitted.

Easy access to shelling, fishing, and windsurfing is possible from **Dunedin Beach Campground**, (800) 345-7504, located at Alt. 19 north in Dunedin. Only 5 miles from Clearwater and close to the 20-mile-long Pinellas Trail, a walking and bicycling trail between

St. Petersburg and Tarpon Springs, this 233-site campground on 17 acres is ideally located. Features include a heated pool, well-kept grounds, a friendly atmosphere, and amenities such as propane, a rec room, horseshoes, and a winter recreation program. The Toronto Blue Jays play winter games nearby. Rates are $24 March 1 to May 1 and again October 1 to February 28; $18 May 2 to September 30.

AREA TOURS

The best way to see the area may be to hop in a car and cruise the 27 miles of interconnected beaches that border Pinellas County. On Clearwater Beach the drive begins on **Mandalay Boulevard** and heads south, hooking up with **Gulf Boulevard** on Sand Key and heading down to St. Pete Beach.

Cruises on the Gulf or bay provide an entertaining way to get acquainted with these barrier islands. The *Snow Queen*, (813) 461-3113, which departs Clearwater Beach Marina at noon and again before sunset, offers sightseeing with lunch, or with dinner and dancing tour aboard a triple-decker riverboat. For a three-hour tour around Clearwater Bay in a sleek cruise ship, board the triple-decker, 400-passenger *Starlite Majesty*, (813) 462-2628. Berthed at the Clearwater Beach Marina, it departs at 7 p.m. for dinner and dancing. For a longer experience, six-hour day and night cruises are offered by the *Europa Sea Kruz*, (813) 393-5110, docked at John's Pass in Madeira Beach, south of Clearwater. Included are live entertainment, a casino, and supervised children's programs. For the fastest ride in town, try the *Sea Screamer*, (813) 447-7200, at Clearwater Beach Marina. The boat offers two types of cruises each day, one a narrated, dolphin-watching cruise of Clearwater Harbor and Sand Key; and the second, a refreshing ride in the Gulf of Mexico, racing down the beach coastline. *Casablanca* Cruises, (813) 942-4452, leaves the Tarpon Springs sponge docks at noon or 7 p.m. for a three-hour lunch or dinner cruise, all of it woven around the theme of the movie *Casablanca*.

9

ST. PETERSBURG

St. Petersburg is located at the southern tip of Pinellas County, a peninsula bordered on the west by the Gulf of Mexico and the east and south by Tampa Bay. The city's 59 square miles range from sea level to 53 feet. Legend has it that in 1521, the Spanish adventurer Juan Ponce de Leon came here in search of the Fountain of Youth. More Spanish expeditions followed, and by the nineteenth century the first pioneer settlers had arrived. In 1885 the area was heralded by the American Medical Association for its health benefits, and a man named Peter Demens brought in the railroad, making St. Petersburg more accessible to folks from the North. He named the town after his birthplace in Russia, and St. Petersburg, Florida, was incorporated in 1903.

Today the city has a population of nearly a quarter million. Its beautiful downtown waterfront is the site of its most renowned landmark, the Pier. A string of barrier islands form the famous beaches to the west of St. Petersburg.

The year-round average temperature is 73.5 degrees, typically with 360 sunny days a year. The warm summer months, June through September, see afternoon rain showers. Spring is the most popular time to visit, when a host of concerts and events—including performances by the Florida Orchestra, the annual Festival of States, a celebration called *Artworks!*, and musical adaptations of Shakespeare plays—bring residents and visitors together in a festive outdoor atmosphere. ∎

ST. PETERSBURG

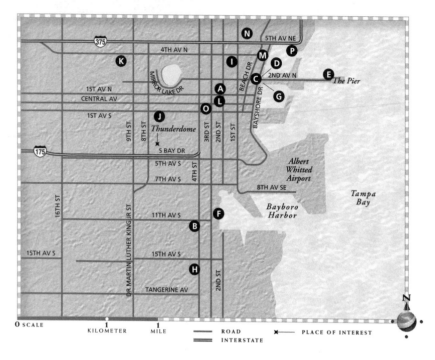

Sightseeing Highlights

A Florida International Museum

B Great Explorations, the Hands-On Museum

C Museum of Fine Arts

D Museum of History

E The Pier

F The Salvador Dali Museum

Food

G Apropos

H Basta's Fine Italian Cuisine

I Bay Gables Tea Room/Garden

E Cha Cha Coconuts

E Columbia Restaurant of St. Petersburg

J Ferg's Sports Bar & Grill

K Fourth Street Shrimp Store

L Garden Restaurant

Lodging

M Gray's Lantern Lane

N Mansion House

O Orleans Bishop

P Renaissance Vinoy

Note: Items with the same letter are located in the same town or area.

A PERFECT DAY IN ST. PETERSBURG

Leave your beachfront hotel early for a sunrise walk on the beach. Then take the short drive across the Treasure Island Causeway to downtown St. Petersburg. You'll visit three museums today: the Salvador Dali Museum, the Fine Arts Museum, and the current cultural exhibit at the Florida International Museum. Hop aboard the free trolley connecting these major attractions in one continuous loop. Lunch at the Columbia Restaurant at the Pier or dine al fresco in the courtyard of the Garden Restaurant on Central Avenue. Take a leisurely walk around the Jannus Landing area across from the International Museum to see what's old and what's new in the eclectic mix of eateries and stores.

On your way back toward the beach, stop for a peek into the multistoried Gas Plant Antique Arcade (1246 Central Avenue, 813/895-0368). Wind up at John's Pass (between Treasure Island and Madeira Beach) for a sunset cruise from Hubbard's Marina and a seafood dinner along the boardwalk, where the shops and restaurants stay open late.

SIGHTSEEING HIGHLIGHTS

★★★ **The Florida International Museum**—This converted building, once a large department store, is now the cultural focal point of the area, housing limited-engagement exhibits of significant historical value from around the world. A gift shop and informal café on the premises. Details: Located in the heart of downtown at 100 2nd Street N., St. Petersburg; (813) 821-1448 or (800) 777-9882; open daily from 9 a.m. to 6 p.m. during an exhibit. Admission to the first three collections is under $15; reservations for specific times are recommended. (1–2 hours)

★★★ **Fort De Soto Park**—Camping, fishing, boating, and bathing are the most popular pastimes at this five-island, 900-acre park. The county park service offers most modern amenities. Two fishing piers, a bait store, and the remains of an early bunker fort to be explored. Details: Reach the park from I-275 S., Pinellas Bayway Exit (80 cent total tolls) at Tierra Verde; (813) 866-2484; open dawn to dusk; free admission. (1–5 hours)

★★★ **The Pier**—St. Petersburg's most famous landmark, the Pier is shaped like an inverted, five-story pyramid and has an aquarium on the second level. There are two parking lots ($3 weekends; $2 weekdays) on the approach and a free shuttle ride if you decide not to walk to the end. Within the building itself you'll find a visitor's information booth, galleries, specialty shops, boutiques, a food court, and three restaurants. From November to April MGM's historic *HMS Bounty* is docked for tours. Sightseeing boats also leave from the Pier, and there is a bait house if you want to wet a line. Details: 800 2nd Avenue, on the waterfront, St. Petersburg; (813) 821-6164; open seven days a week, from 10 a.m. on weekdays and Saturday and from 11 a.m. on Sundays; call for information about scheduled entertainment events. (1–3 hours)

★★★ **The Salvador Dali Museum**—This museum is home to the world's largest collection of the surrealist painter's works. This amazing collection was accumulated by A. Reynolds and Eleanor R. Morse. Docents conduct guided tours, providing details and anecdotes about the paintings and Dali's life and influences. A gift shop sells an array of Dali merchandise. Details: Located at 1000 3rd Street S., St. Petersburg; (813) 823-3767; open Monday through Saturday from 9:30 a.m. to 5:30 p.m., Sunday from noon to 5:30 p.m.; closed Thanksgiving and Christmas Day. Admission is $8 for adults, $4 for students, $7 for seniors, children under age 10 free. (1–2 hours)

★★ **Gizella Kopsick Palm Arboretum**—Named after its primary benefactor, this arboretum, or tree farm, allows visitors to study many exotic and native Florida palms in one convenient setting. Details: Entrance is on North Shore Drive at the foot of 10th Avenue N.E., near downtown St. Petersburg. Call the St. Petersburg Department of Leisure Service, (813) 893-7335, for tour information and times; open dawn to dusk; free admission. (1 hour)

★★ **Great Explorations, the Hands-On Museum**—Special hands-on demonstrations, shows, and workshops for all ages put the fun back into science. This user-friendly museum even has a pitch-dark touch tunnel and experiments with lights and sounds to challenge the senses. Details: 1120 4th Street S., St. Petersburg; (813) 821-8885; open Monday through Saturday from 10 a.m. to 5 p.m., Sunday from noon to 5 p.m.; closed major holidays. Admission is $6 for adults, $5.50 for seniors over age 65, $5 for children ages 4 to 17. (1–2 hours)

★★ John's Pass Village and Boardwalk—This scenic harbor is full of commercial and charter fishing boats, as well as motor- and sailboats,Jet Skis, and parasails. There are also plenty of charming shops, restaurants, and art galleries. You can enjoy an annual fresh seafood feast, along with a craft show and musical events during the John's Pass Seafood Festival, usually the last weekend in October. (1–3 hours)

★★ Museum of Fine Arts—Representative works by Fragonard, Vigee-Lebrum, Monet, Morisot, Renoir, Cézanne, Gauguin, and Georgia O'Keeffe are among the museum's permanent collection. Here you'll find an entire gallery of Steuben crystal, a tribal arts gallery, period rooms, and selected works from the largest collection of photographs in the Southeast. Details: Located on the downtown waterfront at 255 Beach Drive N.E., St. Petersburg; (813) 896-2667; open Tuesday through Saturday from 10 a.m. to 5 p.m., Sunday from 1 to 5 p.m.; closed Monday, Christmas Day, and New Year's Day. Admission is $5 for adults, $3 for seniors over age 64, $2 for students, children under 7 free. (2–3 hours)

★★ Museum of History—See the story of St. Petersburg in the museum's collection of artifacts and interactive displays. A Flight One Gallery celebrates the birth of the world's first scheduled airline service, which began at this site in 1914. Details: Located on the approach to the Pier, 335 2nd Avenue N.E., St. Petersburg; (813) 894-1052; open Monday through Saturday from 10 a.m. to 5 p.m., Sunday from 1 to 5 p.m.; closed major holidays. Admission is $4 for adults, $3.50 for seniors over age 61, $1.50 for children ages 7 to 17. (1–2 hours)

★★ Sunken Gardens—One of St. Petersburg's longest-running tourist attractions, Sunken Gardens is a botanical garden of native and exotic plants This place is actually below sea level at its central point—hence the name. Bird shows, alligator wrestling, and an antique mall are the newest additions to this old favorite. Details: Just north of downtown at 1825 4th Street N., St. Petersburg; (813) 896-3186; open 365 days a year, from 9:30 a.m. to 5 p.m. Admission is $14 for adults, $8 for children ages 3 to 11. (2-4 hours)

★ Boyd Hill Natural Trail—This 245-acre park is owned and operated by the City of St. Petersburg and features more than 3 miles of trails and boardwalks, leading visitors through several Florida ecosystems. Details: At the south end of Lake Maggiore, 1101 Country Club Way S., St. Petersburg; (813) 893-7326; open daily from 9 a.m. to 5 p.m., with extended hours April to October; closed Thanksgiving and Christmas Day. Nominal admission fee. (1–3 hours)

✯ **Holocaust Memorial Museum and Educational Center**—This unique museum offers an opportunity to understand the causes of the Holocaust and the generations of people it affected. There are changing exhibitions including art, photographs, and historical documentation. Details: In Madeira Beach at 5001 113th Street (Duhme Road); call for hours, (813) 392-4678. Admission charged; students free. (1–2 hours)

✯ **Sawgrass Lake Park**—Within earshot but completely out of reach of busy I-275 are 400 acres of natural parkland encompassing two lakes. This site features a nature trail boardwalk where trees and wildlife (including alligators) can be studied. Details: Accessible only from 62nd Avenue N. at 25th Street, St. Petersburg; (813) 527-3814. Free admission. (1 hour)

✯ **Skyway Bridge**—It is well worth the drive just to experience the bridge—a tribute to human ingenuity and engineering genius—connecting St. Petersburg and Manatee County 431 feet above the waters of Tampa Bay. Details: Take I-275 southbound from St. Petersburg. There is a $1 toll and a turnaround lane before the toll booth at the opposite side.

Bill Jackson's Shop For Adventure—This is no ordinary sporting goods store. The complex has a pistol range, a simulated ski slope, and a 100,000-gallon diving tank in which to practice your skills. You can also get lessons or instruction and rent in-line skating equipment for the Pinellas Trail. Details: On its own lake, at 9501 U.S. 19 N., Pinellas Park; (813) 576-4169; open Monday through Friday from 10 a.m. to 9 p.m., Saturday from 9:30 a.m. to 6 p.m., Sunday from 11 a.m. to 5 p.m. (1–2 hours)

Orange Blossom Groves—Growers and shippers of Florida oranges and grapefruits for more than 40 years, this popular market welcomes visitors during the winter season, when the sweet smell of citrus fills the air. There is a gift shop, and free samples of orange juice are offered. Details: 5800 Seminole Boulevard in Seminole; (813) 392-1277; open late October to early May, Monday through Saturday from 8 a.m. to 5:30 p.m., Sunday from 10 a.m. to 5 p.m. (1 hour)

FITNESS AND RECREATION

Keeping fit while visiting St. Petersburg is not difficult. Swimming, sailing, canoeing, kayaking, Jet Skiing, parasailing, and waterskiing are part of everyday life here.

Walking, hiking, biking, and in-line skating are enjoyed by thousands, especially in the **North Shore** area of downtown St. Petersburg, around **the Pier**, or on the well-maintained trail at **Ft. De Soto Park.** Another popular spot is the 47-mile **Pinellas Trail**, which was converted from an unused railroad corridor. It begins in St. Petersburg and winds northward through Pinellas County towns and cities, ending in Tarpon Springs. The trail includes mile markers, water fountains, and benches. Mile-by-mile trail maps are available from the county. Before your visit, contact the Pinellas County Planning Department, 14 S. Ft. Harrison Avenue, Clearwater, FL 34616; (813) 464-3347.

Championship golf courses and tennis courts are open year-round, but tee times must be reserved in advance during the busy winter months; call (813) 733-0900 or (800) 374-8633.

FOOD

One of St. Petersburg's most romantic spots for lunch, dinner, or Sunday brunch is **Apropos**, overlooking the St. Petersburg waterfront, just west of the Pier on 2nd Avenue N.E. at Bayshore Drive, (813) 823-8934. With entrées from $8.95 to $16.95, this chic eatery is a favorite with locals because of its bistro-like atmosphere, downtown convenience, and chicken tarragon salad.

Take the elevator in the Pier up to the rooftop for Happy Hour at **Cha Cha Coconuts**, (813) 822-6655. Its casual, affordable menu (meals range from $4.50 to $10) is complemented by live bands after sunset. Also at the Pier is the **Columbia Restaurant of St. Petersburg**, (813) 822-8000, run by the same people who own the original Spanish favorite in Tampa's historic Ybor City. Prices are medium to high, and reservations are recommended.

SOUTHERN PINELLAS COUNTY

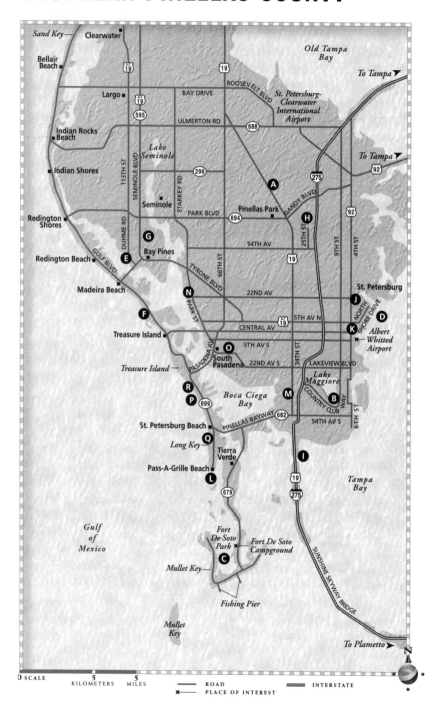

Sightseeing Highlights

A Bill Jackson's Shop for Adventure

B Boyd Hill Nature Trail

C Ft. DeSoto Park

D Gizella Kopsick Palm Arboretus

E Holocaust Memorial Museum and Education Center

F John's Pass Village and Boardwalk

G Orange Blossom Groves

H Sawgrass Lake Park

I Skyway Bridge

J Sunken Gardens

Food

K El Cap

L Hurricane Seafood Restaurant

M Leverock's Seafood House

N Saffron's Caribbean

O Ted's Famous Smoked Fish

Lodging

P Alden Beach Resort

Q Don CeSar Beach Resort & Spa

R Howard Johnson's Resort Inn

R Radisson Sandpiper Beach Resort

P The Tradewinds Resort

Camping

C Ft. DeSoto Park

Note: Items with the same letter are located in the same town or area.

Along downtown St. Petersburg's eclectic Jannus Landing block, just south of the International Museum, are several good restaurants. The **Garden Restaurant**, 217 Central Avenue, (813) 896-3800, is a Mediterranean-style bistro with indoor and outdoor tables; entrées range from $8 to $12. If you're in the mood for lace curtains and other frills, try the **Bay Gables Tea Room and Garden**, 136 4th Avenue N.E., (813) 822-0044, connected to the bed and breakfast of the same name. This is a popular lunch spot for women, with meals in the $6 to $12 range. For upscale Italian food, dine at **Bastas Fine Italian Cuisine**, near the Salvador Dali Museum at 1625 4th Street S., (813) 894-7880. The best selections are usually not on the menu but are offered by the attentive wait staff; entrée prices are medium to high.

Curry dishes, authentic jerk chicken, fresh pumpkin soup, and steamed fresh vegetables—all with spices to satisfy the true island connoisseur—are the specialties at **Saffron's Caribbean**, in the Jungle area of St. Petersburg at 1700 Park Street N., (813) 522-1234. Fill up at the buffet lunch or enjoy an island-style dinner for $8 to $14. Two local sports bars are worth at least one meal each. **El Cap**, 3500 4th Street N., (813) 521-1314, serves salami a la Bonfile (named after owner Frank Bonfile), wings, and chili ($3 to $5), in a setting bursting with baseball memorabilia. **Ferg's Sports Bar & Grill**, across the street from Tropicana Field on 1st Avenue South, (813) 822-4562, is standing-room-only after an event in the big orange sports dome. Try the On Deck circle of appetizers, which includes 50 wings, or the half-pound Dome Burger ($3.95 to $6.25).

Seafood lovers find plenty of happy choices. **Leverock's Seafood House** is locally owned and consistently good. Choose from several waterfront locations, including one at the Maximo Marina, 4801 37th Street S.; (813) 864-3883. Another great pick for fresh seafood prepared quickly and inexpensively is the **Fourth Street Shrimp Store**, 1006 4th Street N.; (813) 822-0325. Whole mullet and mackerel are smoked over red oak and served with German potato salad and a thick slice of sweet onion at **Ted Peter's Famous Smoked Fish**, 1350 Pasadena Avenue S., (813) 381-7931. It's famous for its huge burgers, too, served in a very casual setting, both indoors and out. For the end of a perfect day, the **Hurricane Seafood Restaurant**, in the Key West–style building on Pass-A-Grille at St. Pete Beach, (813) 360-4875, offers a multistory view of the area's famous sunsets along with a festive sampling of seafood entrées ($4 to $16). The best bet at lunchtime is their grouper sandwich.

LODGING

St. Petersburg is so close to the Gulf of Mexico beaches (which are actually a string of barrier islands west of the peninsula) that, from a vacation standpoint, the city can be considered a part of that resort area. Four million visitors come here each year, and there are literally hundreds of motels, hotels, and resorts to accommodate them. You'll find many of the major chains here, such as **Best Western** (800) 344-5999, **Days Inn** (800) 544-4222, **Holiday Inn** (800) 465-4329, and **Quality Inn** (800) 370-5399, but privately owned or "mom-and-pop" operations offer splendid accommodations as well.

Gulf Boulevard is the primary road that connects the beach communities where most of the hotels are located. St. Pete Beach, the largest of those islands, has one of the most famous and luxurious resorts: the **Don CeSar Beach Resort & Spa**, 3400 Gulf Boulevard, (813) 360-1881 or (800) 282-1116. The Don is often referred to as "the big pink castle" because of its imposing size, salmon color, and Mediterranean and Moorish architectural style. Built in 1928, the resort is listed on the National Register of Historic Places and is a member of Historic Hotels of America. It has hosted such famous guests as F. Scott Fitzgerald, Babe Ruth, and Lou Gehrig. In more recent years, such luminaries as Robert De Niro, Elton John, Rod Stewart, George Bush, Jimmy Carter, and President Clinton have stayed here. A $15 million restoration enhanced the property's 275 guest rooms, which now include 43 spacious suites and two luxury penthouses. Palatial elegance combines with impeccable service and room amenities like voice mail, a mini-bar, and complimentary morning newspapers. With five seasonal price changes, rates range from $165 per night for a standard room to $1,600 for a penthouse.

Just 1½miles north of the Don is the **Alden Beach Resort**, 5900 Gulf Boulevard; (813) 360-7081, (800) 237-2530, or, in Florida, (800) 262-3464. The Alden offers 140 units, from standard guest rooms to luxury suites with fully equipped electric kitchens. The resort's courtyard-style layout creates a private setting for the two heated pools and whirlpools. There are lighted tennis courts, a cookout deck, basketball court, shuffleboard, playground, and a game room, making it an ideal family destination. A coin laundry and covered parking round out the extensive list of amenities.

The **Tradewinds Resort**, 5500 Gulf Boulevard, (800) 345-6461, provides luxurious surroundings with winding walkways, waterways, gondolas, and swans. There are four restaurants, pools, tennis courts, croquet, a fitness center and sauna, a salon, whirlpools, and supervised children's activities. The only enclosed pool on the beach is at the **Radisson Sandpiper Beach Resort**, 6000 Gulf Boulevard, (813) 360-5551 or (800) 237-0707, another Fortune Hotel. The Sandpiper offers suites with full kitchens and private bedrooms among its guest room choices. Recreation includes an air-conditioned sports court, volleyball, exercise room, and daily children's activities.

The newly renovated **Howard Johnson Resort Inn** is located at 6100 Gulf Boulevard, (813) 360-7041 or (800) 231-1419. It has added 18 suites for a completely new fifth story featuring one-, two-, and three-room combinations with full and mini-kitchens, sitting areas, and in-room hot tubs.

Full-scale luxury can be found away from the beach as well. The **Renaissance Vinoy Resort**, in downtown St. Petersburg at 501 5th Avenue N.E., (813) 894-1000 or (800) 468-3571, has a private marina, 18-hole golf course, 14-court tennis complex, complete health club, spa services, and croquet courts. Overlooking the beautiful waterfront, this celebrated landmark is on the National Register of Historic Places and is a member of the Historic Hotels of America. There are 258 richly appointed guest rooms in the restored original building and 102 guest rooms in a new, connected seven-story tower. All first-floor rooms in the tower have outdoor patio spas, while the rest have private balconies. There are also 20 suites with executive amenities, each including three telephones, a stocked refreshment center, hair dryer, bathrobes, and two televisions. Depending on the season, a standard room costs $129 to $205 per night; a suite, $385 to $1,800 per night.

Downtown St. Petersburg has also seen a renaissance in bed and breakfast accommodations in lovely restored homes with polished wood floors, quaint Victorian furnishings, and fresh coats of colorful paint. They are all within walking distance of museums and the Pier. Among them is the **Mansion House**, 105 5th Avenue N.E., (813) 821-9391 or (800) 274-7520, built in 1904. This B&B offers robes for guests among the personal touches, along with a complimentary full breakfast. Owner Robert Ray also captains a 23-foot sport cruiser, the *Aussie Spirit*, and invites guests for half- or full-day cruises during their stay.

The **Orleans Bishop**, 256 1st Avenue N., is directly across from the Florida International Museum in the historic Jannus Landing block of downtown; (813) 894-4312 or (800) 676-4848. This two-story

1912 hotel, reminiscent of New Orleans with its wrought-iron trim and mahogany-paneled stairway, pampers guests with a European-style breakfast served on the veranda, in the grand lobby, or in the privacy of your room. Bicycles are available for guest's use.

While not a bed and breakfast, **Gray's Lantern Lane**, 340 Beach Drive N.E., (813) 896-1080 or (800) 880-7600, offers suite accommodations on a weekly or seasonal basis. The renovated 1922 Spanish-style building affords a view of St. Petersburg's downtown waterfront. Each unit has been immaculately outfitted to preserve the charm of its original high ceilings and tall casement windows, and includes a small refrigerator. Gray's is located next to the P. Buckley Moss Art Gallery.

Mid-range and economy motels can be found along stretches of U.S. 19, near interstate exits, and at the southern tip of St. Petersburg, headed toward the Sunshine Skyway Bridge. Another cluster of accommodations is located on Route 688 (Ulmerton Road), about 10 miles east of the Gulf beaches and near the Howard Frankland Bridge (I-275), the Tampa International Airport, and the St. Petersburg/Clearwater Airport. These motels cater to the business traveler as well as to families.

When reserving a room, remember that there are several rate structures. It costs more to face the Gulf of Mexico than it does for a poolside room or one without a view. Even-numbered addresses along Gulf Boulevard are the hotels on the beach side of the road, facing the Gulf of Mexico. Because of the area's warm winters, the season for the highest rates is usually from February through April. Using a reservation service is sometimes helpful; call (800) 345-6710 for the St. Petersburg/Clearwater area.

CAMPING

One of the best campgrounds around is **Fort De Soto Campground**, with 235 sites in Fort De Soto Park on the Pinellas Bayway in St. Petersburg, (813) 866-2662. Almost all sites are directly on the water, either under the giant oaks in the older section, or under the palms and flowering shrubs in the newer sections. Facilities include beaches, swimming, boat ramp, playground, recreation room, fishing, and a bike trail to the Gulf beaches. Pinellas County residents only are allowed to make reservations up to one month in advance. All other campers should call ahead to ask about available sites in the popular park. Fees are $16.50 per night (subject to change). Call for further information and reservations.

NIGHTLIFE

Large halls, medium-size venues, and small nightclubs have rejuvenated the music and entertainment scene in St. Petersburg, which once was so conservative that the city was said to roll up its sidewalks after 9 p.m. Things are different now. Drawing the big names on the concert circuit are **Tropicana Field** and the **Bayfront Center Arena**. The Bayfront includes the intimate **Mahaffey Theatre**, which boasts a calendar of more popular, mainstream musical performances. Call the **Entertainment St. Petersburg Hotline**, (813) 825-3333, for current event listings.

Among the smaller venues, **Jannus Landing**, downtown, and the **State Theatre**, 687 Central Avenue, are St. Petersburg's answer to bands seeking an audience as much as audiences seeking entertainment. At Jannus it's punk, folk, rock, hardcore, ska, and a full view of the nighttime sky, all contained in a one-block courtyard behind the shops and restaurants of Central and 1st Avenue North.

Jazz lovers can stay downtown after dark and hear their favorite tunes at **The Garden**, 217 Central Avenue, 813/896-3800; or at the **Renaissance Vinoy**, 501 5th Avenue N.E., (813) 894-1000. **Apropos**, 30 2nd Avenue N.E., (813) 823-8934, turns into a quiet jazz club on the weekends, with entertainment starting at 7 p.m. For jazz on the beach, the **Hurricane**, on Pass-a-Grille, (813) 360-4875, has a regular crowd.

Nightlife on the beaches is mostly a come-as-you-are selection of beach bars with thatched roofs behind the hotels that line Gulf Boulevard. If you don't care about toasting sunsets, go to the hotels or head back into town in search of the blues! The blues spots in St. Petersburg are the **Ringside Café**, 2742 4th Street N., (813) 894-8465; **Dave's Aqua Lounge**, near the Gandy Bridge, (813) 576-1091; or the **Silver King Tavern**, (813) 821-6470, near the Dome.

The DJ party during Happy Hour at the **Big Catch**, Central Avenue and 1st Street N.E. (813) 821-6444, moves from the patio inside during the later weekend hours, as local rock and alternative bands provide the jams. **Cha Cha Coconuts**, atop the Pier, (813) 822-6655, has live music most nights provided by a rotating stable of cover bands that play pop music from and rock to reggae and blues.

Because everyone's taste in nightlife differs, check out local offerings with the aid of two newspapers, available free in racks around the area. The *St. Petersburg Times* distributes a tabloid-size insert called "Weekend," and the *Weekly Planet* puts out a free Thursday publication that lists happenings by date and type of entertainment.

PARI-MUTUELS AND GAMBLING CRUISES

You can bet on the races year-round at **Derby Lane**, on Gandy Boulevard in St. Petersburg. The live, championship greyhound-racing season begins in early January and runs through June, but simulcast wagering is provided on thoroughbreds, harness, and jai alai (billed as "the world's fastest ballgame") at this picturesque track. It also has one of the best restaurants in the area, **The Derby Club**, (813) 576-1361.

The challenges of dice, cards, and roulette, and the sound of slot machines can fill the hours aboard either of two cruises that sails from John's Pass into international Gulf waters. Board the *Crown Empress*, of the Empress Cruise Lines, (813) 895-DEAL or (800) 486-8600, or sail the *FunKruz*, (813) 393-5110 or (800) 688-PLAY. Each ship sails days and evenings, seven days a week; meals are provided.

10

TAMPA

One of Florida's largest cities, Tampa (pop. 282,848) is located halfway down the Florida Gulf Coast at the head of Tampa Bay, near the mouth of the Hillsborough River. New attractions, cruise lines, and sports facilities make Tampa a great place to visit. The art museums and performing arts centers, excellent restaurants, and lodgings varying from luxurious to inexpensive, make a vacation in Tampa fun for the whole family. Millions of people visit each year, and most of them head for the 335-acre Busch Gardens or to the newly developed Garrison Seaport Center, anchored by the $84-million Florida Aquarium.

Tampa is also an industrial and shipping port, the nearest deep water American port to the Panama Canal. Tons of bananas and other tropical fruits are shipped here from South America each year. Exports include phosphate, lumber, and canned fruit. Another important industry is the production of asphalt and concrete, while fishing and shrimping add seafood processing to the growing economy.

The town's modest beginnings as a fishing village and military outpost belied the future in store for the quiet settlement. During the late 1800s, following the arrival of Henry Plant, Tampa rapidly developed as an industrial center and port city. Plant invested heavily in Port Tampa, and built the Tampa Bay Hotel (now the University of Tampa) in 1891. The posh resort hotel introduced the rich and famous to Tampa's warm climate just as the cigar industry, headquartered in historic Ybor City, was beginning. ◧

TAMPA

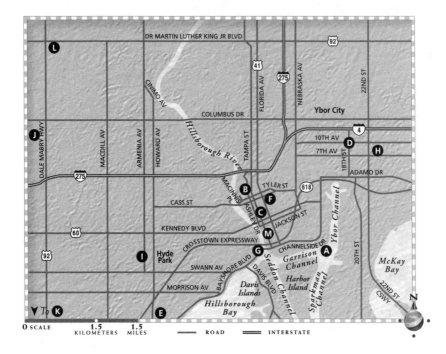

Sightseeing Highlights

Ⓐ Florida Aquarium

Ⓐ Starlite Princess Riverboat

Ⓑ Tampa Bay Performing Arts Center

Ⓒ Tampa Museum of Art

Ⓓ Ybor City National Historic Landmark District

Ⓓ Ybor State Museum

Food

Ⓔ Bern's Steak House

Ⓕ Cafe Firenze

Ⓖ Carlino's Regional Cooking

Ⓗ Columbia Restaurant

Ⓘ Infohaus

Lodging

Ⓙ Days Inn

Ⓚ HoJo Inn Tampa

Ⓛ Holiday Inn

Ⓜ Riverside

Note: Items with the same letter are located in the same town or area.

A PERFECT DAY IN TAMPA

Summertime down South and the livin' is easy. Pick a lazy day and pack a small cooler with soft drinks and sandwiches. Head for Hillsborough State Park with a friend and rent a canoe for the morning. Paddle quietly down the Hillsborough River, watching for turtles sunning themselves on logs and listening to the finches as they flit through the oak trees along the banks.

After lunch, visit the Florida Aquarium to see what's new, and find a souvenir present to mail home. Watch the playful otters for a while and then look for the beautiful roseate spoonbills perched high above in the mangroves. Plans to go snorkeling in the Florida Keys will most likely follow your visit to the fascinating coral reef exhibit. End the day with a dinner cruise on the *Starlite Princess*, watching the sunset on Tampa Bay.

SIGHTSEEING HIGHLIGHTS

★★★ **Busch Gardens**—This 225-acre family entertainment park is packed with thrilling rides, live entertainment, animal exhibits, shops, restaurants, and games, all presented in eight themed sections designed to capture the spirit of turn-of-the-century Africa. Busch Gardens ranks among the top zoos in the country, with more than 3,400 animals, and is one of the most popular attractions on Florida's west coast. One of the favorite park rides is Kumba, the largest and fastest roller coaster in the Southeast, attaining speeds of more than 60 mph on nearly 4,000 feet of track and reaching a height of 143 feet.

The park recently completed its biggest expansion ever with the "Egypt" addition, which includes an informative Egyptian museum and sand dig area for would-be archaeologists. The new addition also features the largest inverted steel roller coaster in the world, named Montu. Open year-round, Bush Gardens provides free dog kennels and food for the family pooch. Details: Located 8 miles northeast of downtown Tampa; take Exit 54 off I-75 and follow the signs; (813) 987-5082; open daily from 9:30 a.m. to 6 p.m. Admission is $36.15 for ages 10 and older, $29.75 for children ages 3 to 9; children under 3 free. (4–5 hours)

★★★ **The Florida Aquarium**—The Florida Peninsula is flanked by the Atlantic Ocean on the east and the Gulf of Mexico on the west. At

447 miles long and seldom more than 150 miles wide, there's 1,350 miles of shoreline and an amazing 8,426 miles of tidal area to explore. The Florida Aquarium, opened in 1995 at a cost of $84 million, tells the story of this unique subtropical environment. Living within the three-story, 152,000-square-foot facility are more than 4,300 native aquatic animals and plants, each in its own simulated natural environment.

Hands-on and natural exhibits lead the visitor through the aquarium. Displays include "Florida Bays and Beaches"; the fresh- and salt-water environments of "Florida Wetlands," featuring a cypress swamp, underwater mangrove roots, fish, and a river complete with otters; and "Coral Reefs," home to many varieties of colorful tropical fish. Wading birds, roseate spoonbills, and egrets live peacefully in the high palms and palmettos, as terns and gulls search for food in the waves on the beach exhibits. Details: Located along the downtown Tampa waterfront; take Exit 25 off 1-75 and follow the signs to Channelside Drive; (813) 273-4000; open daily from 10 a.m. to 5 p.m. Admission is $13.95 for adults, $12.55 for seniors, $6.95 for children ages 3 to 12; children under 3 free. (3 hours)

☆☆☆ **Lowrey Park Zoological Garden**—One of the top zoos of its size in North America, this 24-acre facility features exotic creatures from around the world. The Manatee Aquatic Center is one of only three manatee hospitals and rehabilitation centers in Florida. Manatees are huge, harmless aquatic animals sometimes reaching 13 feet in length and weighing as much as 3,000 pounds. Found in warm southern waters, they're often called "sea cows." These "gentle giants" feed on the vegetation found in Florida's spring-fed rivers. The zoo also includes habitats for primates, including chimpanzees and woolly monkeys. The Florida Wildlife Center provides habitats for native alligators, panthers, bears, and red wolves. Details: Take Exit 31 off I-75 N to North Sky Avenue, and then to North Boulevard, where you'll see the zoo; call (813) 935-8352 for hours. Admission is $7.50 for ages 12 to 49, $6.50 for seniors ages 50 and older, $3.55 for children ages 3 to 11, children under 3 are free. (3 hours)

☆☆☆ **Museum of Science and Industry**—MOSI is one of the largest science centers in the Southeast. The four-story, contemporary structure has more than 200,000 square feet of air-conditioned exhibition space, including the Saunders Planetarium, which features daily presentations. The most recent expansion of the museum, completed in July 1995, added MOSIMAX, Florida's first IMAX dome theater. Movies are projected with a 180-degree fisheye lens onto an 85-foot-high domed screen. Viewers see everything from lifelike erupting volcanoes to the Amazon rain forest, all in larger-than-life detail. The museum also maintains "The Back Woods," a 40-acre wilderness area with more than 3 miles of nature trails to explore. Details: 4801 E. Fowler Avenue, 3 miles east on SR 582 from I-275; (813) 967-6300; open daily from 9 a.m.; closing time varies. Admission is $11 for adults, $10 for seniors over age 59, $9 for college students, $8 for children ages 2 to 12. (3–4 hours)

★★★ *Starlite Princess* **Riverboat**—This authentic paddlewheel riverboat, new in 1996, sports Victorian decor with crystal chandeliers, brass and wood accents, large picture windows, and elegant, plush dining room seating. Dinner is prepared on board and served at your table. The menu offers both fish and beef entrées, including delicious seafood alfredo, filet mignon, and chicken marsala. The boat has an outdoor covered lounge and a top-level observation deck for open-air sightseeing and sunset-watching on Tampa Bay. Details: The *Starlite Princess'* home port is Garrison Seaport Center in downtown Tampa, adjacent to the Florida Aquarium on Channelside Drive; (800) 444-4814. Breakfast cruises (meal optional): Departs Tuesday through Friday at 9 a.m.; fares are $7.50 for adults, $5 for children ages 3 to 12. Luncheon cruises: Tuesday through Saturday from 11:30 a.m. to 1:30 p.m.; fares are $9.50 for adults, $6.50 for children ages 3 to 12. Ecological cruises: Call for times; fares are $7.50 for adults, $5 for children. Dinner/dance cruises: Tuesday through Saturday ($12.50) and Sunday ($15). Reservations required for Sunday cruise. Jazz cruise: Sunday at 1 p.m.; fares are $11.75 for adults, $8.50 for children. (4–5 hours)

★★★ **Ybor City National Historic Landmark District**—Ybor City (pronounced EE-bore) was named for Don Vicente Martinez Ybor, a Spanish cigar manufacturer who moved his hand-rolled cigar industry from Key West to Tampa in 1886. The first cigar factory opened the next year, encouraging more Spanish cigar makers to move factories and workers to Tampa. The Spanish, Italian, German, and Cuban workers who settled here created a vigorous, Latin-flavored multicultural community. Nearly 12,000 people filled more than 200 factories, making Ybor City the "Cigar Capital of the World," until Fidel

Castro's ascension to power in the late 1950s led to the embargo on Cuban tobacco. Pay a visit to the **Ybor State Museum**, 1818 9th Avenue, three blocks south of the I-4 exit, for an overview of the history of the cigar industry.

Now designated as one of three landmark districts in Florida, Ybor City is a mixture of historic buildings, artisan galleries, shops, and nightclubs. Many of the late-nineteenth-century buildings used in the industry have been restored as interesting shops, art galleries, and cultural attractions. Lively entertainment, Latin music, and a festive atmosphere make Ybor a favorite weekend night spot. Visitors wander in and out of the various shops and bars, enjoying the musical mix of blues, jazz, rock, and sometimes dueling pianos. Take time for lunch or dinner in Ybor City at one of the excellent ethnic restaurants featuring Cuban sandwiches, Spanish bean soup, Sicilian pizzas, and Cajun, Creole, and other cuisines. Details: Ybor Chamber of Commerce, 1800 E. 9th Avenue, Tampa, FL 33605; (813) 246-3712. (3–4 hours)

✹✹ **Adventure Island**—This 36-acre outdoor water theme park features water play areas as well as a championship volleyball complex. The park offers outdoor cafés, picnic and sunbathing areas, a game arcade, and gift shops. Paradise Lagoon, surrounded by palms and a cascading waterfall, is peaceful and relaxing, with dressing room facilities available. Details: 4500 Bougainvillea Avenue, ¼-mile northeast of Busch Gardens; (813) 987-5053; open daily in March from 10 a.m. to 5 p.m.; hours extended during summer months; open weekends only mid-September through late October. Admission is $22.30 for adults, $20.15 for children. Call for summer admission fees and hours. (3 hours)

✹✹ **Tampa Museum of Art**—The museum specializes in twentieth-century American art and features a large collection of Greek, Roman, and Etruscan work. The museum has been designated a Major Cultural Institution by the state of Florida and is accredited by the American Association of Museums. Details: 600 N. Ashley Drive; (813) 274-8130; open Tuesday through Saturday from 10 a.m. to 5 p.m., Sunday from 1 to 5 p.m. Guided tours available Wednesday, Saturday, and Sunday at 1 p.m.; call in advance. Admission is $3.50 for adults, $3 for seniors, $2.50 for students with ID, $2 for children ages 6 to 18. (1 hour)

Tampa Bay Performing Arts Center—This is the largest performing arts center in the Southeast. With its 2,500-seat Festival Hall, 1,000-

seat Playhouse, the 300-seat Jaeb Theater, and the 100-seat Off Center
Theater, the Tampa Bay Performing Arts Center has enabled the city to
present Broadway musicals such as *Sunset Boulevard* (with a hydraulically
powered grand staircase on stage), *Carousel, Man of La Mancha, Miss
Saigon,* and others. The Off Center Theater nurtures new artists with
performances by local theater groups, poets, and dancers. The arts center
was awarded the 1995 Regional Designation Award in the Arts by the
Atlanta Committee for the Olympic Games Cultural Olympiad, honoring excellence and innovation in artistic and cultural programs throughout the South. Backstage tours available on request. Details: 1010 N.
MacInnes Place, Tampa; take Exit 25 off I-75 (Ashley Street), turn right
on Tylor Street, and drive 3½ blocks to the Center. For tickets and information, call (813) 229-7827.

FITNESS AND RECREATION

Florida's outdoor lifestyle makes exercising easy. The 6-mile sidewalk
along **Bayshore Boulevard** is an interesting walking area, with Hyde
Park's historic houses on one side and the busy waters of Tampa Bay on
the other. Outdoor tennis courts can be found in almost all communities,
and excellent golf courses open to the public are easy to find. The
University of South Florida golf course on Fletcher Avenue and 46th
Street, (813) 682-6933, boasts a championship layout and fully equipped
pro shop. Special group rates are available.

Swimming, shelling, and fishing are favorite activities on the
Tampa Bay area's many saltwater beaches. Cross one of the big
bridges (Howard Frankland, Gandy, or Courtney Campbell) over to
the St. Petersburg side of the bay to reach the beaches. Bath houses
are available at all county and state parks. **Sand Key Park** (20 miles
west of Tampa, on the Gulf and immediately south of Clearwater
Beach) and **Dunedin Beach** both have excellent showering and
changing facilities and are well-maintained. Lifeguards are on duty at
Clearwater Beach and Sand Key Park daily from 9 a.m. to 4:30 p.m.
If you prefer fresh water, paddle a canoe on the picturesque
Hillsborough River. The **Bent Davis Public Beach**, on the
Courtney Campbell Causeway (Highway 60), is at the head of Tampa
Bay. It is open daily from dawn to dusk. Lifeguards are on duty dur-
ing summer months only.

There are many indoor fitness centers in the Tampa Bay area.
These usually have pools, exercise equipment, and sauna facilities.
Check the local telephone book for one near your hotel.

GREATER TAMPA

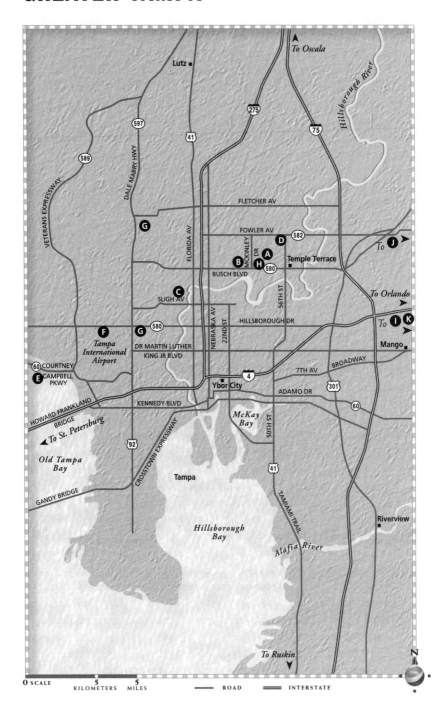

To Oscala

Hillsborough River

Lutz ■

275

597

41

75

589

VETERANS EXPRESSWAY

DALE MABRY HWY

FLETCHER AV

FOWLER AV

FLORIDA AV

G

582

To **J**

D

A

MCKINLEY DR

B

H

580

Temple Terrace

BUSCH BLVD

56TH ST

To Orlando

C

SLIGH AV

NEBRASKA AV

22ND ST

HILLSBOROUGH DR

To **I** **K**

F

G

580

Mango ■

Tampa
International
Airport

DR MARTIN LUTHER
KING JR BLVD

7TH AV

BROADWAY

60 COURTNEY

E CAMPBELL
PKWY

4

Ybor City

ADAMO DR

301

HOWARD FRANKLAND
BRIDGE

KENNEDY BLVD

50TH ST

60

To St. Petersburg

McKay
Bay

Old Tampa
Bay

92

Tampa

41

GANDY BRIDGE

CROSSTOWN EXPRESSWAY

Hillsborough
Bay

TAMIAMI TRAIL

Riverview

Alafia River

To Ruskin

N

O SCALE
5
5
KILOMETERS   MILES
ROAD
INTERSTATE

Sights

Ⓐ Adventure Island

Ⓑ Busch Gardens

Ⓒ Lowrey Park
Zoological Garden

Ⓓ Museum of Science
and Industry

Food

Ⓔ Armani's

Ⓕ CK's

Ⓖ Crabby Tom's (2 locations)

Lodging

Ⓗ Friendship Inn

Ⓗ Howard Johnson Maingate

Camping

Ⓘ Green Acres Campground
& RV Park

Ⓙ Happy Traveler RV Park
and Campground

Ⓚ KOA Tampa East

Note: Items with the same letter are located in the same town or area.

FOOD

The **Columbia Restaurant,** (813) 248-4961, offers traditional Spanish cuisine at its best. Don't miss the black bean soup and delicious flan. Among the many dinner favorites are paella, a mixture of rice and chicken, pork, and seafood, for $18.95 and fresh Florida red snapper for $16.95. The historic restaurant dates back to 1905, and today has been enlarged to cover a full city block in Ybor City. All 11 dining rooms are beautifully decorated Spanish-style, with hand-painted ceramic tiles and colorful furnishings. Columbia has been honored with several national awards, and there are now five additional Columbia Restaurants in nearby Florida cities including Clearwater and Sarasota.

   Café Firenze, 719 N. Franklin Street, (813) 228-9200, features classic Italian cuisine, music, and dancing. **Bern's Steak House,** located at 1208 S. Howard Avenue in Hyde Park near Bayshore Drive, (813) 251-2421, is Tampa's oldest steakhouse. Named first in steakhouses across the nation, Bern's serves well-aged prime beef accompanied by vegetables grown by the owner. The restaurant features an excellent wine list and there is a dining treat for everyone. **Carlino's Regional Cooking,** also located on the beautiful Bayshore waterfront, (813) 254-2323, offers excellent American-style cooking, including meatloaf and

Charles Hornbrook

Golden Gate Pasta loaded with mussels, shrimp, and scallops. **Infohaus**, 2502 Azeele St., (813) 878-2233, features gourmet coffee, desserts, and eight computers connected to the Internet. More can be learned about this innovative cybercafé by contacting its Web site at www.haus.net. Infohaus teaches introductory classes on the Internet and marketing.

Hotels combining lodging and good food include **CK's**, revolving at the top of the Tampa Airport Marriott Hotel, at Tampa International Airport (813) 878-6500; and **Armani's Restaurant**, on the 14th floor of the Hyatt Regency Westshore Hotel, (813) 281-9165, overlooking Tampa Bay on the Courtney Campbell Causeway.

Seafood lovers have many local choices. **Crabby Tom's**, 14404 North Dale Mabry, (813) 961-3499 specializes in serving large portions of king, snow, stone, and Dungeness crabs. Excellent crab cakes and many kinds of seafood, fish, and lobster range from $3.95 to $12.95.

LODGING

Where you choose to stay in the Tampa Bay area depends on what you want to do. Most national hotel and motel chains are represented in the area. Off-season rates are much lower than those in January, February, and March. Higher rates usually apply the week following Christmas and around Easter. It's best to inquire before making reservations. Local chambers of commerce also have listings of excellent smaller motels difficult to find unless you know the area.

Riverside, a Quality Hotel, 200 N. Ashley, (813) 223-2222, is located in the heart of Tampa on the Hillsborough River, only a few minutes from the Florida Aquarium and ten minutes from Busch Gardens. Within walking distance of Busch Gardens is **Howard Johnson Maingate**, 4139 E. Busch Boulevard, (813) 988-9191, with a swimming pool and all the perks. Also within walking distance of Busch Gardens is **Friendship Inn**, 2500 E. Busch Boulevard, (813) 933-3958. **Holiday Inn** is close to Houlihan Stadium on Dale Mabry Highway, (813) 877-6061. **Days Inn**, 2522 N. Dale Mabry Highway, (813) 877-6181, offers a complimentary continental breakfast and airport transportation. **HoJo Inn Tampa**, 3314 S. Dale Mabry Highway, (813) 832-4656, has efficiencies and is reasonably close to Busch Gardens. Waterfront accommodations can be found in Clearwater Beach and St. Petersburg. Bed and breakfasts are less plentiful, but there are a few. Call Gulf Beaches on Sand Key Chamber of Commerce, (800) 944-1847, for listings.

CAMPING

Green Acres Campground & RV Park, east of Tampa off I-4 on Exit 9, ⅛mile south on McIntosh Road, (813) 659-0002, is conveniently located for Tampa sightseeing. It's approximately 15 minutes from Busch Gardens and the Florida Aquarium, and 45 minutes from the Gulf beaches at the end of Highway 60 on Clearwater Beach. **Happy Traveler RV Park and Campground**, off I-75 on Exit 54, ¾ mile east on Fowler Avenue, (813) 986-3094, offers grassy sites under large oak trees, a friendly atmosphere, and full trailer hookups. **KOA Tampa East**, off I-4 on Exit 9, ½-mile south on McIntosh Road and ⅒ mile west on U.S. 92, (813) 659-2202, has a well-stocked camp store and clean restrooms. The park has lots of room for bike riding, and some pleasant tree-shaded picnic tables.

11
SARASOTA

Sarasota is a unique combination of beach community and cosmopolitan culture, with a healthy sprinkling of the arts. The downtown cultural area is enthusiastically supported by the city and its 50,000 residents. Clustered along the shores of Sarasota Bay, within a short walking distance of Van Wezel Performing Arts Hall, are Marie Selby Public Library, the West Coast Symphony Hall, and the Visitor Information Center next to the Historical Society on U.S. 41. It's a short walk to historic Palm Avenue, home to Sarasota's most prominent families in the early 1900s, now lined with art galleries.

This productive cultural arts community thrives against a background of white sand beaches on the offshore islands of Longboat Key, Lido Key, St. Armands Key, and Siesta Key. The Keys are home to many of the area's finest hotels and motels, as well as the upscale St. Armands Circle shopping area, on St. Armands Key.

Sarasota began as a cattle-ranching area following the end of the Seminole Indian wars in the mid-1800s. In December 1885 Scottish families arrived from Glasgow after investing in this "land of plenty" sight unseen, only to be greeted by tree stumps and fresh snow. Many returned home, but a few decided to stay.

Janet Snyder Matthews' book *Sarasota Over My Shoulder* is a great resource for those interested in the history of the area. In it she describes the influence of the few hardy Scots who remained, such as the determined John Hamilton Gillespie, who designed Florida's first nine-hole golf course in Sarasota in 1886. ◼

SARASOTA

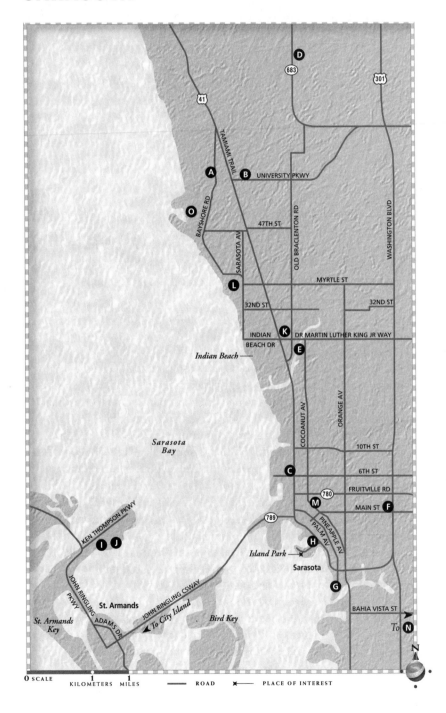

Sightseeing Highlights

(A) Asolo Center for the Performing Arts

(B) Belim's Cars and Music of Yesterday

(C) Florida West Coast Symphony

(D) The Gulf Coast World of Science

(E) Jazz Club of Sarasota

(F) The Main Bookshop

(G) Marie Selby Botanical Gardens

(H) *Marina Jack II*

(I) Mote Marine Aquarium

(J) Pelican Man's Bird Sanctuary

(A) The Ringling Museum of Art Complex

(K) Ringling School of Art and Design

(L) Sarasota Jungle Gardens

(M) Sarasota Opera Association

Food

(M) Golden Apple Dinner Theater

(N) Yoder's

Lodging

(O) Sarasota Bayfront Holiday Inn

Note: Items with the same letter are located in the same town or area.

A PERFECT DAY IN SARASOTA

Breakfast on the hotel terrace overlooking the Gulf, then drive to St. Armands Key, a few miles south. This pretty little key is the ultimate "shop 'til you drop" destination. Upscale shops and trendy restaurants prevail amid lush tropical plantings, antique statuary, and intriguing courtyards and patio restaurants. Seek out that perfect, casual Florida outfit while finding trinkets and treasures. On to the Columbia Restaurant on St. Armands Circle for hearty Spanish black bean soup over a bowl of rice topped with chopped sweet onions. Next, explore the museums and antique shops on Adams Road before listening to the great sounds at the Jazz Club. Look for regularly scheduled monthly concerts or the more informal "jazz jams."

SIGHTSEEING HIGHLIGHTS

★★★ **Florida West Coast Symphony**—This prestigious orchestra hosts a variety of internationally known guest artists. The orchestra has a strong youth orchestra program and a pops series. The symphony's annual Sarasota Music Festival, held in June, is the highlight of the season. Details: 709 N. Tamiami Trail, Sarasota; (941) 953-4252. Ticket prices for masterworks concerts range from $12 to $34; call for Sarasota Music Festival ticket prices.

★★★ **The Main Bookshop**—One of Florida's largest bookstores, the Main Bookshop occupies a historic four-story building downtown and has an inventory of more than 400,000 hardcover titles. Lounge areas and good coffee make book-hunting fun. Look for remainder and overstock books, usually selling at 10 to 30 percent of their original prices. Details: 1962 Main Street, west of U.S. 301, Sarasota; (941) 366-7653; open seven days a week from 9 a.m. to 11 p.m. (1–4 hours)

★★★ **Marie Selby Botanical Gardens**—Spread across 16 acres overlooking Sarasota Bay, the Marie Selby Botanical Gardens are famous for more than 6,000 orchids and 15 specialized garden areas. The Museum of Botany and the Arts is located within the gardens, including seven greenhouses filled with the botanical research and micropropagation and plant identification educational program of Selby's research staff. Details: 811 S. Palm Avenue, Sarasota; (941) 366-5730; open from 10 a.m. to 5 p.m. every day except Christmas. Admission is

$7 for adults, $3 for kids ages 6 to 11; kids 5 and under free. (2–4 hours)

✯✯✯ **Mote Marine Aquarium**—Rays, tropical fish, and other marine life are on exhibit here with special emphasis given to shark research. While the aquarium is interesting to most everybody, children especially will love the 30-foot "touch tank," where they can handle horseshoe crabs, rays, guitar fish, sea urchins, and whelks. Details: Located on City Island, just south of Longboat Key; (941) 388-2451; open daily from 10 a.m. to 5 p.m. Admission is $6 for adults, $4 for children ages 4 to 17, kids under 4 free. (2–3 hours)

✯✯✯ **The Ringling Museum of Art Complex**—John Ringling (1866–1936), original partner in the famous Ringling Bros. and Barnum & Bailey Circus, remains an important influence on Sarasota. Ringling and his wife, Mable, wintered here and built a huge estate overlooking Sarasota Bay. Ringling aided in the area's development when he moved the circus' winter headquarters to the city in 1927. (Although the circus now resides in Michigan, performances are given in the Sarasota area each year.)

Ringling bequeathed his art collection and Sarasota Bay estate to the people of Florida in 1936. The complex includes the John and Mable Ringling Museum of Art; the Ringling's mansion, C'ad'zan; the Circus Galleries; and the historic Asolo Theatre.

The **John and Mable Ringling Museum of Art**, known as the state art museum of Florida, is one of Sarasota's most famous attractions, with museums, elegant gardens, and a mansion carefully preserved and open to the public. The collection, which originally included 625 paintings, has grown through gifts and donations over the years to become one of the most famous art collections in the world. European and American art displayed includes a rare group of seventeenth-century Baroque paintings, unusual works from the Middle Ages and Renaissance, and a growing collection of contemporary works. Stroll through 22 galleries at your own pace, taking time to enjoy the original paintings by Rubens, Van Dyck, Velázquez, Frans Hals, Poussin, Veronese, and Tiepolo, along with American prints, drawings, and photographs. Tapestries, sculpture, and jewelry delight visitors. The art museum itself is housed in a pink Italian Renaissance villa with fountains, friezes, vaults, and columns. Marble loggias surround a courtyard displaying Greek and Roman statues.

Don't miss Mable Ringling's beautiful rose garden among the trees and well-groomed lawns facing the bay.

The original **Asolo Theatre** building is an eighteenth-century Italian Court playhouse. The interior features three tiers of extraordinary rococo boxes arranged in a horseshoe shape. It was all dismantled piece by piece at a castle in Asolo, Italy, then shipped to Sarasota in 1950, when it was painstakingly put back together behind the art museum. Since the opening of the new Asolo Center for the Performing Arts (see below) in 1990, the original Asolo has been used as a meeting place at the Ringling Museum Complex.

The **Circus Museum** features brightly painted wagons and sparkling costumes, calliopes, posters, and other circus memorabilia. In the Ringmaster section you'll see the Barlow Animated Miniature Circus, a scale model of the Ringling Bros. and Barnum & Bailey Circus of the 1930s, including the famous midget Tom Thumb.

The estate includes the Ringling residence, **C'ad'zan** (or "House of John"), a mansion of ornate Venetian gothic architectural style—a terra cotta palace of stained glass, whimsical carvings, hand-painted ceilings, marble terraces, antiques, and personal mementos of the Ringling family. Tours of the mansion can be arranged in advance.

Details: The Ringling Complex is located at 5401 Bayshore Road, Sarasota; (941) 359-5700. From Interstate 75, take Exit 40 and go west 7 miles to Sarasota Bay. The museum is open daily except Thanksgiving, Christmas, and New Year's Day. The Banyan Café, nestled among the huge banyan trees, serves lunch and snacks. Picnic areas are available by the bay. Admission to the entire complex is free to children under age 13; call for adult admission fee. (4–6 hours)

✰✰✰ **Ringling School of Art and Design**—Young people from around the world come to this school to develop their talents in both the fine and commercial arts. Tutors are leaders in their fields. Details: 2700 N. Tamiami Trail, Sarasota; (941) 351-5100; gallery (941) 359-7563. (1 hour)

✰✰✰ **Sarasota Jungle Gardens**—See banana trees, thousands of palms, hibiscus, ferns, roses, gardenias, ixoras, allamanda, and other flowering plants on the trails that wind through Sarasota Jungle Gardens' 10 lush acres. Keep an eye out for monkeys, leopards, alligators, emus, otters, iguanas, and flamingos. The Jungle Bird Circus features four daily shows of performing cockatoos and macaws. In the Petting Zoo and Kiddie

Jungle, children can play on the iguana slide, ride the tiger swings, climb the haunted tree, and dare to pass by the lifelike gorilla. Have a picture taken in the Posing Area with a real parrot on your arm. These formal gardens are beautifully manicured and often used for weddings. Details: 3701 Bayshore Road, two blocks off U.S. 41, Sarasota; (941) 355-5305; open from 9 a.m. to 5 p.m. daily except Christmas. Admission is $9 for adults, $5 for children, and $7 for seniors 62 and older. (3–4 hours)

★★★ **Sarasota Opera**—The Sarasota Opera Association presents four operas in February and March and occasional concerts. The State of Florida has honored this association for its high quality of artistic production and performance. Details: 61 N. Pineapple Avenue, Serosity; (941) 953-7030 or (941) 366-8450.

★★ **Belim's Cars and Music of Yesterday**—See 50 fully restored antique autos including Rolls Royces and Pierce Arrows, while music from the Gay Nineties and the Roaring Twenties plays on more than 1,200 music boxes in the Great Music Hall. Antique games and machines in the penny arcade are favorites for all ages. Details: Located at U.S. 41 and University Road, one block south of Sarasota Bradenton Airport; (941) 355-6228; open daily from 9:30 a.m. to 5:30 p.m. Admission is $8 for adults, $4 for children. (1–2 hours)

★★ **The Gulf Coast World of Science**—Great fun and an education for all children (who must be accompanied by an adult), this hands-on museum explores the principles of science. Children will have the opportunity to dig fossils, stand inside a giant bubble, pet a snake or turtle, watch bees make honey, and hear themselves create echoes. A unique gift shop specializes in "thingamajigs and whatcha macallits." Details: Located in Airport Mall, 8251 15th Street E. (old 301), Sarasota; (941) 359-9975; open Tuesday through Saturday, from 10 a.m. to 5 p.m. Sunday 1 to 5 p.m. Admission is $3 for adults, $1.50 for children 2-18. Free parking. (1–3 hours)

★★ **Jazz Club of Sarasota**—The club's major event, the Sarasota Jazz Festival, brings together musicians from all over the country. Dedicated to performing, preserving, promoting, and spreading the word of this original American art form, the club presents monthly jazz jams, concerts, and programs. Call for schedule. Details: 290 Coconut Avenue, Serosity; (941) 366-1552.

★★ *Marina Jack II*—This 100-foot sternwheeler, modeled after the shallow-draught steamers that navigated Sarasota Bay in the 1890s, takes visitors around the bay for dinner/sightseeing cruises. Sightseeing highlights include mangrove islands, beautiful sea birds, and historic landmarks. Oak paneling, carpeting, brass accents, fresh flowers, and excellent food, make the ship especially relaxing, and live music is played during dinner cruises. Details: Docked next to the Marina Jack Restaurant at Island Park in the downtown marina, off U.S. 41, Sarasota; call (941) 366-9255 for reservations; cruises offered Wednesday through Saturday from 7 to 9 p.m., and on Sunday from 6 to 8 p.m. (3–4 hours)

★★ **Pelican Man's Bird Sanctuary**—A must-see for bird lovers! Dale Shields first created this nonprofit rescue and rehabilitation service in his home. In 1988 the city of Sarasota granted the sanctuary a 20-year lease on a plot of land on City Island at a cost of $1 a year. The sanctuary is a haven for birds recovering from injuries and a permanent home for those that cannot survive in the wild. In 1995, more than 7,000 birds were rescued, 60 percent of which were released back into the wild. Native and migratory birds from other parts of the world are here too. Details: Next to Mote Marine on City Island, just south of Longboat Key; (941) 388-4444; open daily from 10 a.m. to 5 p.m.; closed New Year's Day, Independence Day, Easter, Thanksgiving, and Christmas Day. Admission is free; donations accepted. (1 hour)

★ **Asolo Center for the Performing Arts**—Opened in 1990, the center houses both the 500-seat Mertz Conservatory Theater and a smaller, 161-seat theater. The magnificent, detailed interior decor came from Dunfermline, Scotland. Recent productions at the center include *The Life and Adventures of Nicholas Nickelby*, *Much Ado about Nothing*, *Room Service*, and Tennessee Williams' *Summer and Smoke*. The Sarasota Ballet performs October to April. Details: 5555 N. Tamiami Trail (U.S. 41), Sarasota; (941) 351-9010 or (800) 361-8388; free tours given Tuesday through Saturday from 10 a.m. to 1 p.m. Ticket prices range from $10 to $35.

FITNESS AND RECREATION

The Sarasota/Bradenton area is justly famous for its beaches and is considered a swimmer's paradise. Golf courses, tennis courts, windsurfing, and all kinds of boating and fishing opportunities are readily available. Increasing numbers of people stride to good health on the sidewalks and beaches. Walking provides a great opportunity to talk to people who live in Florida. Don't hesitate to ask residents about the best and closest places to play golf or tennis. Most have been transplanted from Northern states and are more than happy to tell you about what they have found in their areas.

America's very first golfing links were built in Sarasota in 1886 by Scotland's Col. John Gillespie. Today the Sarasota/Bradenton area has more than 200 golf courses. One of the best, **Bobby Jones Golf Club**, (941) 365-3948, is Sarasota's only municipal golf facility, with 45 holes of excellent golf. Play the challenging American course (18 holes, par 71) or the British course (18 holes, par 72) for fun and competition. The nine-hole, par 30 Gillespie Executive is for fun. Breakfast and lunch are available at the Tavern on the Green Restaurant and Lounge at the course. Call anytime, day or night, up to three days in advance to reserve your tee time electronically. The courses are located in Sarasota at 1000 Azinger Way.

In the heart of Sarasota, **Forest Lakes Golf Club**, (941) 922-1312, is known as the "Town Golf Club." The 6,450-yard course weaves through Forest Lakes Country Club Estates. Watch for famous faces among the players on this par 71 course. Tee times may be reserved up to three days in advance throughout the year. For lessons, equipment, golf clothing, or to practice, call the course.

For players who never get enough golf in one day, the most interesting course might be the **Foxfire Golf Club**, 7200 Proctor Road, (941) 921-775?, with 27 holes and no distracting housing developments. Don't miss the Foxfire's Double Eagle Restaurant for a good home-style meal after the game.

One of the most beautiful and manicured of area courses is **Misty Creek Country Club**, (941) 921-5258, surrounded by a wildlife preserve with bald eagles, wild turkeys, and deer. This exciting 18-hole course has a links-style layout, meaning no parallel holes to distract your game. Misty Creek is located 3½ miles east of I-75, off Bee Ridge Road in Sarasota. For further information and tee times, call the course.

The **G.T. Bray Park** in Bradenton is an enormous sports complex, donated by long-time resident G.T. Bray. Open to the public and beautifully maintained, it offers tennis courts and an aquatic center with lifeguards. Two championship par 72 golf courses are only 2 miles away and well-maintained by Manatee County. Baseball, soccer, and football fields are also here. Address: 5504 33rd Avenue W., Bradenton; Activities Center, (941) 742-5973; **Manatee Golf Courses**, (941) 792-6773. Reservations are advised.

Canoe Outposts, (800) 229-1371 or (813) 634-2228, provides excellent opportunities for exploring the beautiful Florida rivers. Boat rentals of all kinds are offered at beach marinas, including **Bradenton Beach Marina**, (941) 778-2288; the **Cortez Fleet**, in Bradenton, (941) 794-1223; and **Cannon's Marina**, on Longboat Key, (941) 383-1311. The Cortez Fleet also offers chartered cruises and deep-water fishing. Be brave and try **Mr. CB's Parasailing**, (941) 346-5052, on Siesta Key in Sarasota. Mr. CB's uses U.S.C.G.-licensed captains and promises "soft, dry take-offs and landings." He also rents Waverunners. Parasailing is a popular sport on the Gulf Coast, where the warm waters and gently sloping beaches make it easy. Scuba divers enjoy **Florida Down Under**'s specially designed dive boats. Divers are required to have C-cards. For further information, call (941) 922-3483.

FOOD

Seafood is the obvious top choice of entrée on Florida's west coast menus. **Crab Trap** restaurants serve excellently prepared fresh seafood and rightfully deserve the Golden Spoon Award awarded by *Florida Trend* magazine to the top 100 restaurants in the state. Be sure to try the stone crab claws in season (fall and winter) and the Baltimore Street Cakes as an appetizer. **Crab Trap I** is on U.S. 19 just south of Terra Ciea Bay Bridge and north of the junction of U.S. 19 and 41, (941) 722-6255. Prices range from $36.50 for lobster to $11.95 for Florida catfish. **Crab Trap II**, located behind the Welcome Station at the junction of I-75 and Route 301, (941) 729-7777, is a good stopping place after shopping in the huge Outlet Center in Ellenton. Try the crabmeat quesadilla ($7.95) before enjoying the Clearwater Chesapeake crab cake entrée ($15.95). Seafood is also a specialty at Shells, 3200 E. Bay Drive on Holmes Beach, (941) 778-5997, for those who prefer casual dining on the beach. Entrées range from fried clams ($4.95) and delicious chicken pasta ($6.95) to 12-ounce grilled grouper ($13.95).

Try to visit **The Summerhouse**, on Siesta Key in Sarasota, (941) 349-1100, a gourmet restaurant known not only for excellent cuisine, but also for its romantic atmosphere. Dinner is served every night from 6 p.m. in the Tropical Garden dining room. Choose grilled salmon for

$14.50 or roast prime rib for $24. Be sure to sample the macadamia nut shrimp appetizer, $7.50. A lighter menu is offered in the Treetop Lounge. For a change of pace, try the **Golden Apple Dinner Theatre**, 25 N. Pineapple Avenue in Sarasota, (941) 366-5454. Both matinees and evening performances follow an attractive and generous buffet. Call for schedule and reservations.

Watch an unforgettable sunset over the Gulf of Mexico from the **Pier Restaurant**, on Bradenton Beach at the end of historic Memorial Pier, (941) 748-8087. Restoration of the pier's original Spanish-style restaurant by the Don Miller Corporation in 1974 preserved its historic atmosphere. The restaurant serves a variety of seafood and excellent prime rib (around $12.95). **Yoder's**, 3434 Bahia Vista Street in Sarasota, (941) 955-7771, is sure to please anyone who loves Amish home-cooking. Specialties (around $5.95) include delicious homemade pies, Cobb salad, turkey, roast beef, meatloaf, and chopped veal and tenderloin Hot Manhattans with mashed potatoes and stock gravy.

LODGING

Almost any kind of lodging can be found in the Sarasota area. Most major hotel and motel chains have facilities here. Before leaving home check the current rates by calling the 800 numbers for Hilton, Sheraton, Days Inn, Motel 6, and others. Specify Florida west coast locations, as rates vary across the state. Also try Florida chambers of commerce for listings of available local lodging. Many residents lease their condominiums and apartments for one or more months during peak tourist times, especially January, February, and March.

The **Sarasota Bayfront Holiday Inn**, in downtown Sarasota on the Tamiami Trail, (941) 365-1900, offers special rates during the year. Lodging on the beaches can be more expensive but not always. The **Ramada Inn**, on Siesta Key, (941) 921-7812, offers special rates, as does the **Siesta Beach Resort**, (941) 349-3211. Rates depend on the season and services offered.

Top-dollar motels include the **Holiday Inn/Helotomy Longboat Key**, (941) 383-3771, on the Gulf of Mexico, with spacious rooms and family suites. It has a private beach, outdoor pool, tennis, and sailing, plus the Helotomy, with an indoor pool and games. Also on Longboat Key, the **Colony Beach and Tennis Court**, (941) 383-6464, offers 234 one- and two-bedroom villas with full kitchens. The award-winning Crest Dining Room overlooks the

SARASOTA REGION

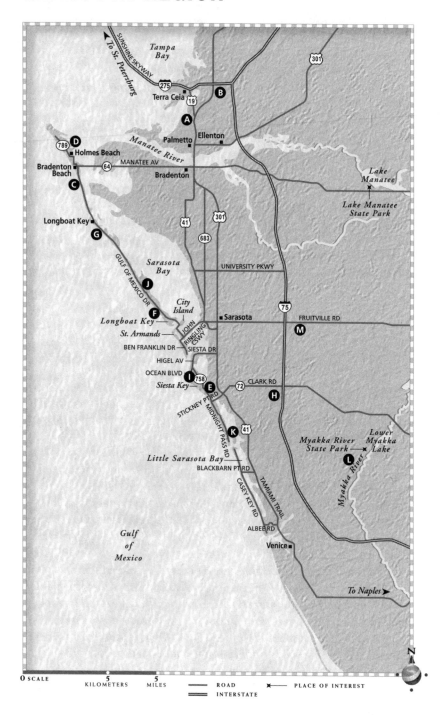

Tampa
Bay

To St. Petersburg

SUNSHINE SKYWAY

275

Terra Ceia

19

B

A

301

Palmetto   Ellenton

Manatee River

D

789

Holmes Beach

Bradenton
Beach

MANATEE AV

64   MANATEE AV

C

Bradenton

Lake
Manatee

Lake Manatee
State Park

Longboat Key

G

41

301

683

GULF OF MEXICO DR

Sarasota
Bay

UNIVERSITY PKWY

J

75

City
Island

Longboat Key

F

Sarasota

FRUITVILLE RD

St. Armands

JOHN RINGLING CSWY

BEN FRANKLIN DR   SIESTA DR

M

HIGEL AV

OCEAN BLVD

Siesta Key

I   758

E

CLARK RD

72

H

STICKNEY PT RD

MIDNIGHT PASS RD

K   41

Myakka River
State Park

Lower
Myakka
Lake

Little Sarasota Bay

BLACKBARN PT RD

L

Myakka River

CASEY KEY RD

TAMIAMI TRAIL

Gulf
of
Mexico

ALBEE RD

Venice

To Naples

N

0 SCALE   5   5
KILOMETERS   MILES   ──── ROAD   ✕ PLACE OF INTEREST
═══ INTERSTATE

Food

Ⓐ Crab Trap I

Ⓑ Crab Trap II

Ⓒ The Pier Restaurant

Ⓓ Shells

Ⓔ The Summerhouse

Lodging

Ⓕ Colony Beach

Ⓖ Holiday Inn/Helotomy
Longboat Key

Ⓗ Ramada Inn

Ⓘ Siesta Beach Resort

Ⓙ Wicker Inn

Camping

Ⓚ Gulf Beach Campground

Ⓛ Myakka River State Park

Ⓜ Sun-N-Fun RV Resort

pools and Gulf beach. The fitness center/spa and 21 tennis courts plus a children's program are also included. For atmosphere try the **Wicker Inn**, on Longboat Key, (941) 383-5562, with suites and a pool directly on the beach.

CAMPING

The **Sun-N-Fun RV Resort**, located 1 mile east of I-75, at Exit 39 at 7125 Fruitville Road, Sarasota, (800) 843-2421, is centrally located and offers all the amenities, including heavily wooded sites with hookups, tile bath houses, and lots of recreational facilities. The **Gulf Beach Campground**, on Midnight Pass Road, on Siesta Key in Sarasota, (941) 349-3839, is right on the Gulf of Mexico and offers 48 full-hookup sites, plus saltwater swimming and fishing. The owner will park your vehicle if you desire, as the sites lining the tree-shaded sandy beach road are 20 feet wide, though quite deep. RVers begin arriving in the late fall, and many stay until April, with a standing reservation from year to year in a favorite park. Specialized campground books are available in bookstores and from travel agents. Whenever possible, make reservations well ahead. Visitor centers have free Florida campground and RV parks information.

State parks offer many camping choices. No pets are allowed in their campgrounds but are permitted on a leash in the rest of the park. One of the best is **Myakka River State Park**, on Upper Myakka Lake, 14 miles east of U.S. 41 on State Road 72, (941) 361-6511. From I-75, take Exit 37 and head 9 miles east on State Road 72. Originally developed by the Civilian Conservation Corps in the 1930s, the 28,875-acre park is named for the Myakka River, which flows for 12 miles through the park. Reservations and passes for campgrounds are obtained at the entrance. There's a wildlife museum here too. Reservations are advised. **Myakka Wildlife Tours**, (941) 365-0100, provides informative, guided tours by large air boat and land train through the surrounding park wilderness. Alligators, great blue herons, cranes, egrets, and many other types of wading birds and waterfowl are plentiful in the protected environment. Land tours often provide sightings of deer, wild turkey, bald eagles, and other wild animals. The main tour office is in Sarasota. Call for reservations and further information.

12

THE GULF ISLANDS: SANIBEL, CAPTIVA, BOCA GRANDE, AND PINE ISLAND

The southwest shore of Florida's west coast is made to order for everyone who has ever dreamed of running away. The beautiful offshore islands, with their lush tropical foliage and white sand beaches, provide an unexpected sense of freedom. You'll feel it the minute you cross over the bridge or step off the boat. Somehow, the world drifts away—you relax, take a deep breath, and decide you never want to leave.

From the coast's "Old Florida" fishing villages to the tropical pleasures of exclusive Sanibel and Captiva Islands, from the traditional flair of Boca Grande on Gaspirilla Island to the agricultural palm farms of Pine Island, the serenity and natural beauty in this area is easily accessible from the mainland by causeways and bridges. Isolated islands such as Cayo Costa and Cabbage Key have no traffic lights because there is no traffic—the only way to get to these islands is by boat. ◼

THE GULF ISLANDS

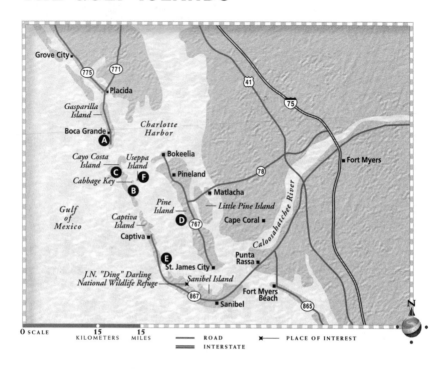

Sightseeing Highlights

A Boca Grande

B Cabbage Key

C Cayo Costa

D Pine Island

E Sanibel and Captiva

F Useppa

A PERFECT DAY IN THE ISLANDS

Watch the sun rise over the bay and enjoy breakfast (waffles and coffee) at the famous Lighthouse Restaurant on Sanibel Island, then go shelling on the west side of Captiva Island. Catch the 10:30 a.m. *Lady Chadwick* cruise fom the Plantation Inn dock to Useppa Island, where you can visit privately-owned Key West-style homes and the historic Collier Inn. The pink path down the middle of Useppa leads to an Indian mound, where you can almost feel the presence of the Calusa Indian people, who buried their pottery, tools, and weapons here. Get back aboard the *Lady Chadwick* for a short ride across the bay and have lunch at the Cabbage Key Restaurant, Bar, and Inn. From there, it's a relaxing hour and fifteen minute cruise back to the Planation Inn. Later, catch an evening show at the Old Schoolhouse Playhouse.

SIGHTSEEING HIGHLIGHTS

★★★ **Boca Grande**—Located on Gasparilla Island off the Florida Gulf Coast between Sarasota and Fort Myers, Boca Grande is considered by many residents and visitors to be the most romantic, nostalgic, unspoiled island town in southwest Florida. The village hides its wealth under a royal palm and enjoys life without the glitz.

Boca Grande's first inhabitants were the Calusa Indians, who first lived on Useppa Island around 5,000 B.C. and inhabited Gasparilla Island by A.D. 800 or 900. Charlotte Harbor was the center of the Calusa Empire, where thousands of people lived in hundreds of fishing villages on the mainland and nearby Gulf islands. Nine Indian mounds, filled with pottery shards, fish hooks, and arrowheads, have been discovered on Gasparilla Island, and more than 200 additional sites, some over 20 feet high, are located on nearby islands.

The treasure of legendary pirate José Gaspar remains buried on Gasparilla Island, named in his honor. In the early 1900s, the world discovered the famous spring and early summer tarpon run through Boca Grande pass, and the village of Boca Grande became a mecca for fishermen and a favorite vacation spot for the country's rich and famous. Well-known visitors to the island included the DuPonts, Vanderbilts, and Colliers (all of whom stayed at Mrs. Potter Palmer's Useppa Inn on nearby Useppa Island while building their own beautiful cottages on the Gulf shore at Boca Grande). One of the first hotels, the magnificent Key West–style Gasparilla Inn—completed just in time for the 1912–13 tarpon season—treated guests to elegance, gourmet cooking, and wide porches with white wicker furniture. It continues this tradition today, while offering a much more informal lifestyle than that of the early 1900s.

Carefully restored buildings still mark the center of this laid-back fishing village. A walk around town, past cottages, homes, and elegant estates tucked discreetly behind hedges and walls, takes about two hours. There are some nifty shops in the historic downtown buildings, and many art galleries and gift shops offer shoppers a wide variety of desirable items. The shops are listed with the Chamber of Commerce, and descriptive ads can be found in local publications such as the *Visitor's Guide*, published by the *Boca Beacon*, the village's weekly newspaper.

Fishermen and millionaires share the same lifestyle in Boca Grande, all in tune with the simple beauty around them. Sophistication comes in many forms, and life on Gasparilla Island is loved by all who live here. Many residents and visitors join together and work hard to keep this unincorporated village, under the umbrella of Charlotte and Lee Counties, exactly the way it is: quiet. Although the Gasparilla Fishery moved across the bay to Placida when the railroad left and the 1.9-mile causeway was built in 1957, many of the original families remain today as third, fourth and even fifth generations, earning a living by providing local guiding, fishing, and sightseeing services to visitors—especially the tarpon-fishing enthusiasts.

Fishing for tarpon in Boca Grande Pass beneath a full moon has to be one of life's greatest experiences. In April, schools of tarpon start rolling in to Boca Grande Pass for an annual get-together that attracts fishermen from around the world. **"The World's Richest Tarpon Tournament"** is sponsored annually by the Boca Grande Chamber of Commerce in early July, and tops off the tarpon-fishing season. The tournament donates money for the local school scholarship fund. The 1996 purse in this famous all-release tournament was $165,000, including donations and gifts. The number of competing boats is limited to 60, and 59 of the 60 fishing boats entered in 1996 (one withdrew) caught and released 40 fish in two days. Of these, eight were weighed, the winner tipping the scales at 138 pounds and worth $100,000 to the proud angler. Entrance fee is $3,500 plus tax per boat. Contact the Boca Grande Chamber of Commerce for more details. Registration begins in March (check for the current date with the chamber) and, for spectators, it's worth the trip just to watch the first-class boats and rigging, and to enjoy the excitement. Boca Grande does this up right! Details: Write or call for the Chamber's information packet, in which realtors list all available lodging on the island. Chamber of Commerce, P.O. Box 704, Boca Grande, FL 33921, in the Courtyard building at the north end of the island; (941) 964-0568.

★★★ **Cabbage Key**—Within sight of Useppa, Cabbage Key is a landmark among the islands. Actually built on top of an ancient Calusa Indian shell mound, the island reflects the adventurous spirit of its owner, the late novelist and playwright Mary Roberts Rinehart. Rinehart's home, built in 1938, is now the Cabbage Key Restaurant, Bar, and Inn—it's a prime spot for seafood and for celebrity-spotting. Reservations are a must. Details: Contact Cabbage Key, P.O. Box 200, Pineland, FL 33945, (941) 283-2278, for more information.

★★★ **Cayo Costa**—Located just south of Gasparilla Island and Boca Grande Pass is Cayo Costa State Park. With 2,225 acres, the park is one of the largest undeveloped barrier islands remaining in Florida and is considered one of the gems of the park system. Accessible only by boat, with docks on both the bay and Gulf sides, the park includes 12 rustic cabins available by reservation, as well as sites for tent camping. Details: For rates and reservations to any of the state parks, contact Barrier Island GEO Park Headquarters, located in the historic lighthouse on the south end of Boca Grande; (941) 964-0375. Visitors are welcome to visit the headquarters and tour the lighthouse.

★★★ **Pine Island**—Pine Island (pop. 8,128 permanent; 12,400 winteronly) is the largest island on the west coast of Florida. Considered by many residents as the last frontier—the last fragment of Old Florida—and sheltered to the west by the famous barrier islands of Sanibel, Captiva, and Cayo Costa, the island remains largely untouched by developers because it has no significant beaches. The waters of Pine Island Sound, between Pine Island and the Gulf islands, provide a sheltered route for the Intracoastal Waterway and some of the Florida west coast's best in-shore fishing grounds for snook, redfish, trout, mangrove snapper, drum, tarpon, and shark.

Pine Island is one of the most peaceful islands in the bay, perhaps because it is largely zoned for agriculture. The palm tree nurseries include the elegant, subtropical royal palms. The fruit tree orchards, which blend beautifully with the deep green long-needle pines, yield mangos, guavas, citrus, and other exotic fruits. An annual spring event appropriately named **Mangomania** and sponsored by the Greater Pine Island Chamber of Commerce, (941) 283-0336, features many varieties of fruit and other products raised on the island. The lush displays are a total surprise to many of the visitors attending the affair. Call the chamber for current dates—it's well worth seeing—and tasting.

Before reaching the island, drivers should stop at the Greater Pine Island Chamber of Commerce. The personnel are exceptionally knowledgeable and well-supplied with maps and information about camping, restaurants, and lodging. Several communities are part of the Pine Island area. **Matlacha** preserves the charm of an old fishing village—in fact, the boardwalk and lodgings are built over the water in places. The Matlacha drawbridge, where people fish round-the-clock, is known as "the fishingest bridge in the world." **Pine Island Center**, where Pine Island Road ends at Stringfellow Road, is the hub of island activities. The shopping center, community swimming pool, tennis courts, ballfields, schools, museum, and library are clustered around the intersection of Pine Island and Stringfellow Roads.

Pineland, north on Stringfellow, is the site of Calusa Indian mounds and artifacts. It is also the location of the island's smallest and oldest (circa 1927) post office. A portion of the daily mail is picked up and delivered by a mail boat that services the many islands isolated from the mainland.

St. James City, on the south end of Pine Island, is the most developed area and home to more than half the population. Fishing is the livelihood here, and many residents live on canals that lead to the bays and Gulf of Mexico.

Driving north on Stringfellow Road 17 miles through the center of the island emphasizes the island's active agricultural and palm nursery businesses. Tall, thick stands of long-needle pine make a beautiful, lush background for the rows of young palm trees that thrive in the well-cultivated fields stretching through the middle of the island. Palms are shipped throughout the state.

Stringfellow Road runs the length of the island, from St. James City in the south to the fishing village of **Bokeelia** in the north. Old-time Florida houses and narrow streets crisscross the north end of the island. There are, however, new additions to Bokeelia. Beautifully designed newer homes with tin roofs and natural siding blend well with the existing mixture of old and new. No doubt about it—Pine Island has been "discovered." People seeking peace, quiet, and some kind of escape are here, and no wonder. There's a magnificent view of Boca Grande, just 10 miles away. The bay itself is dotted with sailboats and powerboats, some carrying passengers along water routes to and from Key West–style homes on isolated islands not connected to the mainland. Details: Pine Island Road (State Road 78) is the only land route to the island. Contact the Greater Pine Island Chamber of Commerce, located on the highway before Matlacha; (941) 283-0888.

★★★ **Sanibel and Captiva**—Although they are connected to the mainland by the Sanibel Causeway, Sanibel and Captiva Islands manage to retain their island identity. Some of the best shelling beaches in the whole world are here, and superb offshore fishing waters make these islands two of the Florida Gulf Coast's major attractions.

Seashells have always influenced the lives of people on Sanibel and Captiva. Anne Morrow Lindbergh wrote the lovely and meaningful *A Gift from the Sea* while living in a rustic cabin on Captiva, and by the time the small ferry boat began bringing cars to the islands in 1928, there were already famous shelling destinations for vacationers. More than 275 kinds of collectible shells wash up in thick piles on the Gulf beaches. To experience the history and lore of seashells, visit the new Bailey-Matthews Shell Museum on Sanibel, where local shells and rare specimens from deep Florida waters are displayed with beauties from around the world. Details: 3075 Sanibel–Captiva Road (known locally as "San–Cap Road"), Sanibel; (941) 395-2233; open daily from 10 a.m. to 4 p.m.

The **Bailey-Matthews Shell Museum** is close to the island's main source of wildlife information—the 5,000-acre **J. N. "Ding" Darling National Wildlife Refuge**. There's plenty of time to see the shell museum and the wildlife refuge both on the same day. Tram rides are available to tour the refuge by land; canoes are used to follow the water trails winding through the shallows and mangroves. The sanctuary is home to beautiful egrets and other long-legged wading birds, including the rare roseate spoonbills. Even manatees find bottom-grazing excellent in the mangroves. An observation tower allows overviews of the park and a chance to watch feeding egrets, bald eagles, red-shouldered hawks, and ospreys. Wildlife is best seen during the early morning and late afternoon hours. Bicyclists will enjoy pedaling through the wilderness area. Details: 1 Wildlife Drive, Sanibel; (941) 472-1100; wildlife refuge gates open at 7:30 a.m. and close about a half-hour before sunset.

Admission is $4 per vehicle, $1 for walkers and bicyclists. The visitor center is open daily from 9 a.m. to 4 p.m. Call to confirm hours, as they change depending on the season.

Bicycling allows close contact with nature, making it a favorite form of transportation on the islands; bikes can be rented at most lodgings and many shops. Riders are rewarded with more than 30 miles of safe and well-tended bicycle paths, which are also open to hikers and rollerbladers. Bicycle paths end at **Blind Pass**, where **Captiva Island** begins. Captiva bikers enjoy the winding 5-mile ride along Captiva Drive through the spectacular tunnel of thick Australian pines, past old-fashioned cottages and the historic **Captiva Library** and **Post Office**. The road ends at the gated entrance to **South Seas Plantation**, where you are free to roam the gateway shops and Captiva History House. Details: 5400 Sanibel–Captiva Road, Captiva; (800) 282-3402 or (941) 472-5111. Room rates range from $165 to $290; cottages range from $290 to $330.

Fishing and boating continue to be mainstays in the island's lifestyle. Excellent deep-sea and shallow-water fishing are possible because of the concerned community's efforts to preserve the natural environment.

Visitors are always welcome to share the magnificent fishing and wildlife resources of Sanibel and Captiva and the neighboring islands. But the people who call these islands home really love them too, and it shows. Strictly enforced rules state that no live shelling, garbage or pollution is allowed. Explore and enjoy, but leave it the way it was meant to be. New construction is always a matter of concern here, and it's carefully controlled, but even so, some old-time residents have moved away . . . to the islands without bridges.

Shelling excursions and diving expeditions are readily available. They're usually excellent and offered by expert resident boaters from the islands. Traveling to neighboring Boca Grande, Useppa, Cabbage Key, and Pine Island on one of several excursion boats connecting the islands is fun.

Fishing is made easy on the shallow grass flats or in the Gulf of Mexico; numerous half-and full-day charters are available. Experienced captains and fishing guides know how to catch many varieties, including cobia, flounder, grouper, mackerel, pompano, snook, and tarpon. If you are an experienced boater, you may prefer to rent your own craft. For fishermen without a boat, the Sanibel–Captiva bridge, as well as the pier at the base of the historic Captiva lighthouse, built in 1884, are popular spots for surf casting 24 hours a day.

After crossing the causeway to Sanibel from the mainland, look to the right. The Sanibel–Captiva Islands Chamber of Commerce is tucked back in the trees in a pretty island-style house. Stop here to get the maps and information you will need on the islands. The friendly personnel will help visitors locate the various lodgings, shops, and attractions. Some of these places are so well hidden among the pines that they'd be otherwise hard to locate. Details: 1159 Causeway Road, Sanibel; (941) 472-1080; open Monday through Saturday from 10 a.m. to 7 p.m., Sunday from 10 a.m. to 5 p.m.

Sanibel has two main roads: Periwinkle Way, the main business route, and Gulf Drive, which follows the beaches. Gulf Drive, divided into west, middle, and east sections, is lined with accommodations on the beach facing the Gulf. **Gulf Side City Park** welcomes visitors on Middle Gulf Drive. Historic **Sanibel Lighthouse** (Point Ybel Light) marks the eastern tip of the island. From this point, you can see the causeway and Fort Myers Beach across the bay. With the exception of beach shelling, most of the island's beautiful natural attractions are found on this sheltered side of the island, including the **J. N. "Ding" Darling Wildlife Refuge, Sanibel–Captiva Conservation Center**, the **Bailey-Matthews Shell Museum**, and the **Care and Rehabilitation of Wildlife (C.R.O.W.)**. Details: C.R.O.W. is located on Sanibel–Captiva (San-Cap) Road; (941) 472-3644.

Sometimes called "The Islands of the Arts," this area is rich in artistic talent. The museums and art galleries are filled with works of both nationally known and local artists. Theatrical productions sparkle with a professional touch at the **Olde Schoolhouse Theatre**, 1905 Periwinkle Way, (941) 472-6862, and at **Pirate Playhouse**, 2200 Periwinkle Way, (941) 472-0006. Explore the museum and new library on Dunlop Road to discover the history of this unique destination.

Dining is informal, Florida-style, sometimes in shorts and never in a tie. Even so, it's best to check to see if jackets are required for gentlemen at some of the gourmet restaurants. Although seafood is the specialty on the islands, the many restaurants range from fast-food to gourmet French. Residents are happy to recommend favorite restaurants, many with beautiful views overlooking the Gulf and its magnificent sunsets.

★★★ **Useppa**—Due east of Cayo Costa Island (across Boca Grande Pass from Gasparilla Island) is historic Useppa Island. Famous for privately owned, old fashioned Key West–style cottages with big porches and airy rooms, as well as the historic **Collier Inn**, Useppa welcomes visitors. The interesting Calusa Indian excavation site can be reached by following the famous pink path running down the center of the island. The island is private, but visitors are welcome to come via tour boat to the island for lunch and sightseeing. Details: For more information and reservations, contact Useppa Island Club, P.O. Box 640, Bokeelia, FL 33922; (941) 283-1061.

FITNESS AND RECREATION

The islands are probably best viewed from the water. The many island ferries available include the 49-foot *Tropic Star*, (941) 283-0015, out of Four Winds Marina at Bokeelia, on the north end of Pine Island, east of Sanibel and Captiva. The *Tropic Star* cruises to Cabbage Key, Cayo Costa, and other islands, leaves the marina at 9:30 a.m. and returns at 4 p.m. Snacks and drinks are available, and passengers may bring a picnic, or stop at Cabbage Key for lunch. The rates are reasonable ($19 for adults, $10 for children ages 3 to 12).

Also cruising among the islands is Captiva Cruises' *Lady Chadwick*, departing 10:30 a.m. to 3:30 p.m. from the Plantation Inn dock on Captiva Island for trips to Useppa Island and Cabbage Key. Since cruising time is about one hour and 15 minutes, passengers spend over two hours on Cabbage Key or Useppa. The cost for adults is $27.50; children, $15. Cruises to Boca Grande and Cayo Costa are recent additions to the *Lady Chadwick* destinations.

To explore the waters around Boca Grande, try the Pass Marina at South Dock, where the *Caliban* ferry departs at 10:30 daily for Cayo Costa, Cabbage Key, and Useppa. The *O.K. Bayou* ferry offers a sunset cruise ($9.50 per person) timed just right for a visit to the white pelican refuge. See the big, beautiful pelicans along with handsome white ibis and other birds. The Pass Marina also houses **Sundog Charters**; the **Doodlers' Deck Restaurant,** serving fresh steamed shrimp and great burgers; and a ships store and service marina, all located at the historic phosphate dock on the south end of Gasparilla Island. For information about Pass Marina, call the Chamber of Commerce, (941) 964-0568. **Millers Marina**, (941) 964-0511, on Harbor Drive in Boca Grande, has been the hangout for tarpon fishermen as long as anyone can remember and has rightfully earned its title as the "Home of the World's Greatest Tarpon Fishing

(W.G.T.F.)." **Daily Island Charters** cruises to Cayo Costa, Cabbage Key, and Pine Island depart from the marina. The active marina also rents boats, golf carts, Waverunners, bikes, parasailing boards, and fishing charter boats.

There are plenty of shelling cruises available, especially on Sanibel and Captiva Islands. A native of Florida, **Captain Joe Burnsed** offers half-day trips just for shelling—no fishing license is required, all equipment is provided, and a cooler with ice is on-board. Four hours costs $40, and three hours, $30. Additional trips are also available; call (941) 472-8658 or (941) 472-6516 for more information.

Check with fishermen and marina owners for the names of reputable sport-fishing guides. For boat rentals, call **Captain Rubs' Boat Rental** at Whiden's Marina in Boca Grande, (941) 964-2898. The third- and fourth-generation fishing guides who operate the **Knight Brothers Charters**, (800) 551-FISH or (941) 964-2484, in Boca Grande, are some of the area's most experienced.

Shelling, picnicking, and sightseeing with a trip to Cabbage Key for lunch can be fun by small boat. For powerboat rentals on Sanibel try the **Boat House,** in Sanibel Marina, (941) 472-2531. To see wildlife and sea birds, try kayaking or canoeing and exploring the

Lee Island Coast

THE GULF ISLANDS

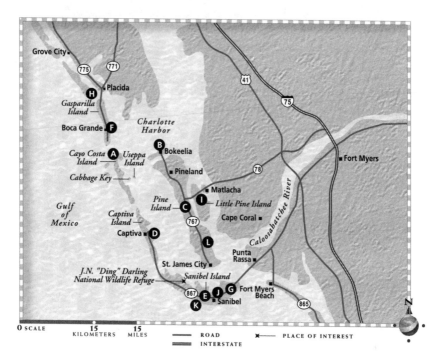

Food

A Cabbage Key Restaurant, Bar and Inn

B Capt'n Con's Fish House

C D'Aleo's

D The Green Flash

E Harbor House Restaurant

F Lighthouse Hole

G Lighthouse Restaurant

F Loons on a Limb

E McT's Shrimp House and Tavern

D The Mucky Duck

G Pink Elephant

H Uncle Henry's

Note: Items with the same letter are located in the same town or area.

J. N. "Ding" Darling National Wildlife Refuge on the Sanibel– Captiva Road. **Wildside Adventures**, (941) 395-2925, will deliver the kayak to your door. **Canoe Adventures**, (941) 472-5218, offers guided canoe trips through the refuge, down Sanibel River, and around the Buck Key areas.

Fly fishing on the flats and tarpon fishing are favorite sports on the islands. The **Sanibel Fly Shop**, 2340 Periwinkle Way on Sanibel Island, (941) 472-8485, has all the best equipment for fly-fishing enthusiasts. Saltwater fishing licenses are also available at the shop. The ultimate sport-fishing adventure could be aboard the *Jeanne Louise*, a 30-foot sleek sport-fishing boat equipped with twin diesels, long-range radio, a marlin tower, and Captain Chuck Skinner, one of the island's most experienced guides. For information and reservations call (941) 472-4898.

Details: There is a $3 toll to cross the Sanibel Causeway; the typical ferry fare is $9 for a car with a trailer.

FOOD

Seafood comes naturally to all the islands. One of the best seafood restaurants on Sanibel (and there are many of them) is the **Harbor House Restaurant**, 1244 Periwinkle Drive, (941) 472-1242. Be sure to try a side order of conch fritters with your favorite fish entrée, and top off the dinner with a slice of the delicious Key lime pie. An authentic English pub, the **Mucky Duck**, on Andy Rosy Lane, (941) 472-3434, offers atmosphere and an excellent selection of wine, English ale, and beer—just the place for lunch. Try Florida's favorite grouper sandwich with a hearty English beer or come later for the excellent dinner selections. Open Monday through Saturday; closed Sunday. Be sure to try the **Green Flash**, 15183 Captiva Drive, (941) 472-3337, located on the historic site of "Timmy's Nook" on Captiva. The famous restaurant offers seafood entrées "fresh off the fin" and a delicious Timmy's Nook Burger at noon. A popular place for breakfast is the historic **Lighthouse Restaurant**, 222 Harbor Drive, (941) 964-0511, on the east end of Sanibel. Lunch is also served. For early-bird dinners, all-you-can-eat shrimp, and a special children's menu, try the casual **McT's Shrimp House and Tavern**, 1265 Periwinkle Drive, (941) 472-3161, open seven days a week.

Boca Grande's famous **Pink Elephant**, at the corner of 5th and Bayou, (941) 964-0100, first opened in 1949 and is remembered by old-time tarpon-fishing fans as the place for dinner and fun. A major renovation in 1980 kept the original concrete pillars framing the well-stocked bar, where come-as-you-are revelers meet for lunch and dinner. The upstairs main dining room has a beautiful view of the bayou and offers outside dining as well as cozy booths. Fresh seafood and prime steaks are a specialty, as are Italian dishes.

Visit **Loons On A Limb**, located at the corner of 3rd and E. Railroad Streets in downtown Boca Grande, (941) 964-0155, for casual, old-fashioned breakfasts from eggs Benedict to grits. The blackboard lists an excellent selection of homemade soups, salads, appetizers, entrées, and desserts. Fresh local seafood and American and ethnic cuisines are specialties for dinner from 6 to 9 p.m. For great steaks as well as fabulous fresh seafood, try **Uncle Henry's**, in the courtyard at 5800 Gasparilla Road in Boca Grande, (941) 964-2300. Perched above Miller's Marina at 222 Harbor Drive in Boca Grande, the **Lighthouse Hole**, (941) 964-0511, offers a great view of the marina, Gasparilla Cabbage Key Restaurant and Lounge, and Charlotte Harbor. Dinners feature fresh seafood—Wednesday's special is all-you-can-eat fresh shrimp, while Friday's is all-you-can-eat fresh fish.

Visit Bokeelia, on the north end of Pine Island, to find the best in seafood at **Capt'n Con's Fish House**, 8421 Main Street, (941) 283-4300. Grouper and deviled crab are always daily specials at $5.95 and $7.95. Hungry for Italian cooking? Try **D'Aleo's Italian American Restaurant and Lounge** (941-283-2000) on Pine Island Center, ¼ mile south of the intersection of Pine Island and Stringfellow Roads.

Caught on the water at sunset with an appetite? Cruise over to **Cabbage Key Restaurant and Lounge**, (941) 283-2278, for dinner (from $15.95 to $19.95) and maybe a room at the inn. Reservations are recommended at this popular spot.

LODGING

Lodging of all kinds is available on these popular islands. Historic **Boca Grande** has three large hotels welcoming guests with gracious decor and all the expected amenities. Island lodging listings are available only through real estate offices. Call the Boca Grande Chamber of Commerce, (941) 964-0568, for real estate listings.

On Gasparilla Island, the private **Boca Grande Club**, 5000 Gasparilla Road, (941) 964-2211, has a limited number of individual homes and condominiums to rent through their club program. The club covers 62 acres of pristine beach facing west on the Gulf of

THE GULF ISLANDS

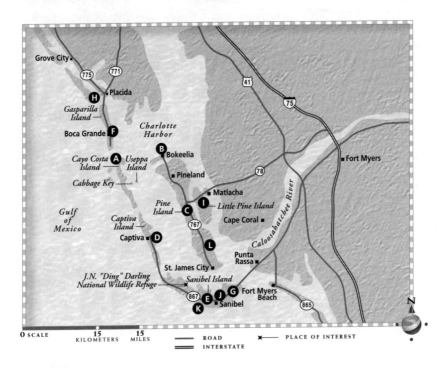

Lodging

B Beachhouse Motel

I Bridge Water Inn

F Boca Grande Club

A Cabbage Key Restaurant, Bar, and Inn

E Driftwood Inn

F Gasparilla Inn and Cottages

F Inlet Hotel

J Sanibel Inn

K Sanibel Island Best Western Beach Resort

G Sanibel Lighthouse Inn

H Uncle Henry's Motel and Restaurant

Camping

L Pine Island KOA

B Tropic Isle Campground, RV Park, and Apartments

Note: Items with the same letter are located in the same town or area.

Mexico. **The Clubhouse** restaurant features excellent cuisine. There are eight tennis courts (four clay and lighted), a tennis pro, bicycle rentals, kayaks, housekeeping service, a children's playground, and a basketball court. Rates range from $342 to $508 for a double, meals included.

Uncle Henry's Motel and Restaurant, 5800 Gasparilla Road, (941) 964-2300, on the north end of Gasparilla Island, is billed as "the biggest little boatel in Boca Grande." Reservations can be made at the marina, and boaters are free to arrange docking by calling ahead on Channel 16. The motel offers 18 rooms and suites with beautiful views and a pool, all near the Chamber of Commerce, grocery stores, and shops.

One of the most elegant and old-fashioned lodgings on Gasparilla Island is the **Gasparilla Inn and Cottages**, (941) 964-2201. The historic inn (referred to locally as "The Inn") is a tradition in this area, with roots set deep in the early 1900's, when it was built to house the rich and famous who were fast discovering the laid-back benefits of the island and the excitement of tarpon fishing in Boca Grande Pass. Now a more relaxed atmosphere greets guests at The Inn. The white wicker chairs are still on the porches, and the freshwater pool is surrounded by a deck with umbrella-topped tables, next to the enclosed dining room, providing an ideal setting for the famous Beach Club lunches. The Gasparilla Golf Club's 18-hole, 6,395-yard course is adjacent to The Inn; guests staying at The Inn may call (941) 964-2344.

The new, soft yellow color of the **Inlet Hotel**, 1171 11th Street E., Boca Grande, (941) 964-2294, reflects an extensive refurbishing that includes a new privacy wall on the street side. The Inlet is located on the sheltered waters of Boca Grande Bayou and has a new swimming pool.

Sanibel and Captiva offer every possible kind of accommodation. Along Sanibel's Gulf beach, Gulf Drive is lined with beautiful lodgings of all sizes. One of the most interesting is the **Sanibel Lighthouse Inn**, 210 Periwinkle Way, (941) 472-0939, at the historic lighthouse end of the island. The inn features one-bedroom apartments with full kitchens on the beach near the fishing pier and lighthouse. A variety of accommodations are offered at the **Sanibel Island Best Western Beach Resort**, 3287 W. Gulf Drive, (941) 472-1700, with hotel rooms, junior suites with a full kitchen, and one- and two-bedroom suites available for larger families. The **Sanibel Inn**, 937 E. Gulf Drive, (941) 472-3181, has a large swimming pool, and, like all the resorts along

East, Central, and West Gulf Drives, fronts a wide sandy beach. One block away from the Gulf beaches, the **Driftwood Inn Cottages**, 711 Donax Street, (941) 395-8874, offer reasonably priced accommodations. The one-bedroom cottage is $59 per night, while the two-bedroom cottage apartment on Donax Street has more room for families at $89 per night.

Pine Island lodgings begin with the **Bridge Water Inn**, 4331 Pine Island Road, (941) 283-2423, in historic Matlacha, the first of the Pine Island communities reached by travelers heading across the bridge to Pine Island proper. The inn is located along the base of "the world's fishingest bridge," allowing fishing right from the rooms, with boat docking at the door! The surrounding Matlacha Pass Aquatic Preserve is an excellent place for sea kayaking and wildlife watching. The **Beachhouse Motel**, on Bocilla Lane in Bokeelia, (941) 283-4303, is ideally situated for views across the bay to the surrounding islands, including Boca Grande Pass. Walk among the old and new to see beautiful homes with tin roofs and natural siding designed to match the pines and weathered surroundings.

Cabbage Key is best known for the **Cabbage Key Restaurant, Bar and Inn**. Its six double rooms rent for about $65 per night.

Florida Department of Commerce division of Tourism

Cottages go for $145, except for one that accommodates up to eight people, which rents for $200. Contact Cabbage Key, P.O. Box 200, Pineland, FL 33945, (941) 283-2278, for more information.

CAMPING

Campers on Pine Island can rest easy in the clean, friendly **Pine Island KOA,** (941) 283-2415, on Stringfellow Road near James City at the south end of the road. The campground offers bus and cruise boat trips, 371 full hookup sites, and a large heated pool and sauna. You can jog or bike along the 1½ mile road, play horseshoes, or fish in the lakes. Log cabins are available—bring along bedding and cooking gear. **Tropic Isle Campground, RV Park, and Apartments**, is located at 15175 N.W. Stringfellow Road in Bokeelia. Travelers are welcome in this large, well-maintained park among the pines. Nearby is **Alden Pines Country Club and Golf Course**, 14261 Clubhouse Drive. Call (941) 283-2179 for tee times.

13
FORT MYERS

Drive into Fort Myers on I-75 or U.S. 41, crossing more than a mile of bridges spanning the Caloosahatchee River. One of Florida's most important waterways, the river connects the state's east and west coasts. Meandering west from Lake Okeechobee for 75 miles, it passes historic downtown Fort Myers on its way to the Gulf.

The river forms a beautiful backdrop for the historical districts in this subtropical city, which is home to more than 45,000 year-round residents and to more than 70 varieties of palms and flowering shrubs. McGregor Boulevard is lined with stately royal palms, many 60 feet tall, planted by Thomas Edison more than 100 years ago. During the 1880s, Edison (1837–1931) built his 14-acre winter estate, laboratory, and botanical garden on McGregor Boulevard beside the Caloosahatchee River. His interest in horticulture helped Fort Myers become known as "The City of Palms."

The waterfront is also an important part of the Fort Myers' lifestyle. The City Yacht Basin bustles with boating activity, both private and commercial. Yachts crossing the state via the Intracoastal Waterway usually stop at the marina here before heading to the east coast or north along the Gulf of Mexico. Windsurfing sailboards and large sailboats can always be seen on the Gulf waters. Sightseeing tour boats leave several times a day, carrying tourists around the harbor and to offshore islands such as Sanibel and Captiva. It's water, water everywhere in Fort Myers. ◼

FORT MYERS

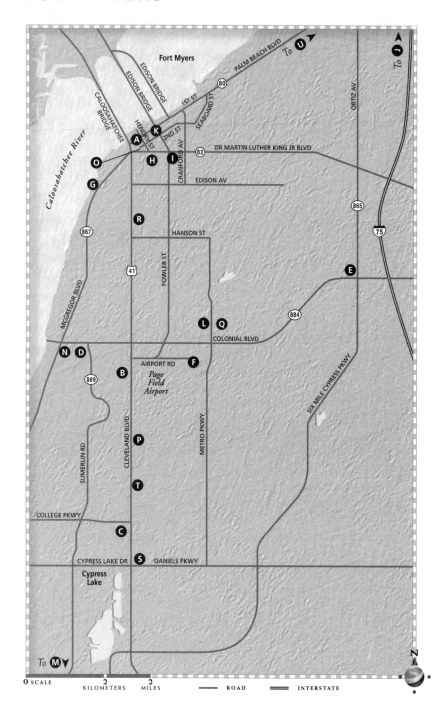

Sightseeing Highlights

Ⓐ Arcade Theater

Ⓑ Balloon Odyssey

Ⓒ Barbara B. Mann Performing Arts Hall

Ⓓ Broadway Palm Dinner Theater

Ⓔ Calusa Nature Center & Planetarium

Ⓕ Classic Flight Biplane Rides

Ⓖ Edison and Ford Winter Estates

Ⓗ Fort Myers Historical Museum

Ⓘ Imaginarium

Ⓙ Manatee Tours

Ⓚ Murphy–Burroughs House

Ⓛ Seminole Gulf Railway Excursions

Food

Ⓜ Ballenger's Seafood Restaurant

Ⓝ Capriccio's Cucina Aburzzese

Ⓞ The French Connection

Ⓟ The Mill Bakery Eatery and Brewery

Ⓚ Veranda

Lodging

Ⓠ Courtyard by Marriott

Ⓡ Holiday Inn Central

Ⓢ Holiday Inn Fort Meyers Airport

Ⓐ Holiday Inn Sunspree

Ⓣ Radisson Inn Fort Meyers

Camping

Ⓤ Orange Harbor Mobile Home and RV Park

Note: Items with the same letter are located in the same town or area.

A PERFECT DAY IN FORT MYERS

Begin the day with a stroll down the new Riverwalk to Centennial Park, where old-fashioned park benches are perfectly placed for people-watching. Boating activities in the nearby yacht basin are fun to observe, too, and there's a clear view of the busy city shuffleboard courts across the park. Walk three blocks back to the downtown historic section of old Fort Myers, past the Hall of 50 States, to explore the cluster of antique and gift shops at 1st and Hendry Streets. The Hendry Street Trading Company, Eclectics, Finders Keepers, Laura's Aura, and Old Times Antiques are all open for business from 10 or 11 a.m. until 5 or 5:30 p.m., Monday through Saturday.

After lunch at Shooters Waterfront Café in the Holiday Inn on the banks of the Caloosahatchee River, it's time for a swim from Fort Myers beach—all 8 glistening white miles of it. Maybe it's a good day to rent a windsurfer or a fast little Hobie Cat for a quick spin. Look around for a sand-sculpting contest. A fine way to end this perfect day is with dinner on the waterfront at the Channel Mark on San Carlos Boulevard.

SIGHTSEEING HIGHLIGHTS

★★ **Arcade Theatre**—The historic theater building in downtown Fort Myers is authentically renovated and offers theater, music, and dance performances. The lobby's historic artifacts are a must-see for acting buffs. Details: 2267 1st Street, Fort Myers; (941) 338-2244 or box office (941) 338-2244. Call for ticket prices and performance schedules. (2–3 hours)

★★★ **Balloon Odyssey**—A balloon flight is an excellent way to see the lay of the land. The flight is followed by a champagne breakfast. Details: 5100 S. Cleveland Avenue, Fort Myers; (941) 458-5750. Price is $35 to $50, weather permitting. (2–3 hours)

★★★ **Barbara B. Mann Performing Arts Hall**—The wide variety of programs offered here include ice shows and Broadway productions. The Southwest Florida Symphony Orchestra and Chorus also perform in the hall. New elevators and additional lobby space have greatly improved the facility. Details: Located on the Edison Community College campus at the southwest corner of Summerlin Road and

College Parkway, Fort Myers; for schedules call (941) 481-4849. Ticket prices range from $35 to $65. (2–4 hours)

★★ Broadway Palm Dinner Theatre—Broadway entertainment follows both matinee and evening buffets which feature a salad bar, dessert tables, and specialty drinks. Details: 1380 Colonial Boulevard, Royal Palm Square, Fort Myers; (941) 278-4422. Tickets cost $28 for matinees and the Sunday evening show, $31 for Tuesday through Friday shows, and $34 for the Saturday evening show. Matinees at 1:15, evening performances Tuesday through Sunday at 6:30; closed Monday. (2–3 hours)

★★★ Calusa Nature Center and Planetarium—Follow the boardwalk winding through the cypress forest and wetlands. Wildlife includes alligators, colorful birds, snakes, and tropical vegetation. Many varieties of palms are growing here, and sometimes it's possible to visit with injured wildlife here for treatment and, the staff hopes, release. Details: Corner of Colonial Boulevard and Ortiz Avenue (exit 22 off I-75), Fort Myers; (941) 275-3183; open daily from 9.30 a.m. to 7 p.m. Admission is $3 for adults, $2 for children ages 3 to 11. (2 hours)

★★★ Classic Flight Biplane Rides—Fly over the bays and barrier islands to see dolphins and other marine life in their natural habitat. Biplane rides offer an excellent view of the Fort Myers waterfront. This is one of several such flights available in the area. Details: On U.S. 41 at Airport Road, Fort Myers; call (941) 939-7411 for rates and schedule. (2–3 hours)

★★★ Edison and Ford Winter Estates—Henry Ford and Thomas Edison were such good friends that in 1916 Henry Ford decided to come to Fort Myers and build his home next to Edison's on McGregor Boulevard. The interesting side-by-side estates are open to the public. Guided tours include Edison's botanical garden and laboratory, also on McGregor Boulevard. Details: 2350 McGregor Boulevard, Fort Myers; call (941) 334-3614 for schedule of guided tours. Admission is $10 for adults, $5 for children ages 6 to 12. (2–3 hours)

★★★ Edison Festival of Light—Fort Myers celebrates Thomas Edison's birthday from February 4 to 19 with the Festival of Light. There are upwards of 40 different events going on, all honoring one of the city's most famous winter visitors. Festivities include the largest nighttime parade in Florida.

★★★ **Fort Myers Historical Museum**—Area history is traced from prehistoric times through exhibits, artifacts, and miniature reproductions. This museum is a fully restored Atlantic Coast Line railway station. Details: Located at Peck and Jackson Streets, Fort Myers; museum hours vary, so call (941) 332-5955 before you visit. Admission is $2.50 for ages 12 and older, $1.50 for children ages 2 to 11. (1–2 hours)

★★★ **FunKruz**—A six-hour cruise departing from the Palm Grove marina, FunKruz features Las Vegas–style casinos with live entertainment and meals. Details: 2500 Main Street, Fort Myers Beach; (941) 463-5000; departures daily at 10 a.m. and 6:30 p.m. Price is $27 for day cruises, $32 for Friday and Saturday evening cruises. Reservations are required. (6–7 hours)

★★★ **Imaginarium**—Sensory attraction for children of all ages. Opened in 1995, the attraction includes a "walk-through" brain, surround-sound theater, and an aquaculture tank among its many exhibits. Details: 2000 Cranford Street, Fort Myers; (941) 337-3332; open From 10 a.m. to 5 p.m. Monday through Saturday, noon to 5 p.m. Sunday. Admission is $5.60 for adults, $3 for children ages 3 to 12. (2–3 hours)

★★★ **Manatee Tours**—Take a boat excursion to the Manatee Sanctuary in the Orange River, where the huge mammals congregate in winter near the warm water from the power plant. Details: 13828 Palm Beach Boulevard (Route 80), Fort Myers; call (941) 693-1434 for excursion times, scheduled November to May. (3–4 hours)

★★★ **Murphy–Burroughs Home**—Step back in time to 1918 with tour directors impersonating Jettie and Mona Burroughs. The meticulously restored 1901 Georgian Revival home was built to be the finest in Fort Myers at the time. Details: Located at the corner of 1st and Fowler Avenues, Fort Myers. For recorded tour information, call (941) 332-1229 or the Fort Myers Historical Museum office, (941) 332-5955, for tour schedules and special events information. Admission is $3 for ages 12 and older, $1 for children ages 6 to 11. (1–2 hours)

★★★ **Seminole Gulf Excursion Train**—Take a two-hour round-trip train ride from Fort Myers or Bonita Springs through the Florida countryside. The old-fashioned railroad cars follow the same route taken by Florida visitors in the past. A snack bar and narration are provided on the daytime excursions. Reservations only required for the dinner trains. Purchase tickets on the train or at the depots. Wedding parties, holiday trains, rail/boat trips, and special event trips are available. Daytime departures are at 9:30 a.m. and noon Wednesday and Saturday, and noon only on Sunday, from Metro Mall Station in Fort Myers. Fare for adults is $11 plus tax; children ages 3 to 12, $6 plus tax.

Dinner prices vary, ranging from $19.95 to $40 plus tax per person. Five-course gourmet meals are prepared on board and served elegantly. Departure times vary, from 6:30 p.m. for the Murder Mystery Train, to 5:30 to 8:30 p.m. for the Sunday Twilight Dinner Train. Details: Located off Colonial Boulevard (State Route 884) at Metro Mall, 3½ miles west of I-75 Exit 22 and 2 miles east of U.S. 41; (941) 275-8487 or (800) 736-4853. (2–4 hours)

FITNESS AND RECREATION

Baseball spring-training camps have long been big news in this area, and exhibition games between the Boston Red Sox and the Minnesota Twins take place from March through early April.

Fort Myers and Fort Myers Beach provide a variety of fitness and recreational activities. Eight miles of white sand Gulf beaches at Fort Myers Beach make swimming, running, and all kinds of sail- and power-boating available for everyone. **Sundance Sailing Tours**, at Palm Grove Marina, with licensed Captain Mike Richardson on the 42-foot yacht *Sundance*, offer half-day and sunset cruises ($25 per person) and full-day cruises ($75 per person). Boat rentals are also available at Sundance Sailing, 2500 Main Street, Fort Myers Beach, (941) 463-7333. Day and evening cruises on the *Europa SeaKruz* feature dining, dancing, and casino fun. Cruises depart from 645 San Carlos Boulevard on Fort Myers Beach. Call (941) 463-5000 for reservations and departure times. **Yachts of Fun** rents outboard powerboats, 15- to 24-feet-long at the Fish-Tale Marina, 7225 Estero Boulevard, (941) 463-4448. These are only a few of the many boating and water sports facilities available on Fort Myers Beach. Take time to browse through this old-fashioned beach's souvenir, T-shirt, beach toy, and scuba gear shops.

To reach **Fort Myers Beach** from Fort Myers, go south on U.S. 41 to Summerlin Road. Then travel 4 miles west on Summerlin Road, past College Parkway, and turn left onto San Carlos Road leading to Estero Island and Fort Myers Beach. Summerlin Road continues west to Sanibel and Captiva Islands.

Golfing fans find excellent courses on the Fort Myers mainland. Be sure to make reservations ahead, as golfing is a popular sport in Florida. **Gateway Golf Club**, 11360 Championship Drive, (941) 561-1010, is a 72-hole championship course designed by Tom Fazio, who combined bunkers and extensive mounding to create this unique course, unlike any other in Florida or the Southeast. The front nine holes are links-styled, with few trees and gently rolling fairways, dotted with a Fazio trademark of using both pot bunkers and grass bunkers. The back nine holes, instead, incorporate more trees and water areas, and the 10th, 12th, and 14th greens each have spectacular cypress trees as a backdrop.

Del Tura Country Club, 18621 N. Tamiami Trail, (941) 731-4125, is a fun yet challenging course in North Fort Myers with 27 holes. **Fort Myers Country Club**, 3591 McGregor Boulevard, (941) 936-2457, is a popular 72-hole course that gives the ladies a break with par 72, and the men a par 71. Tennis players, as well as golfers, are welcome at **Golfview Golf & Racquet Club**, 14849 Hole-in-One-Circle in Fort Myers, (941) 489-0909. Call to reserve courts or tee times.

To really see the area try **Classic Flight** biplane rides over the beaches and barrier islands including Sanibel, Captiva, and Fort Myers. The new Waco classic biplane holds the pilot and two passengers. Don't forget to bring a camera. For more information and reservations, call (800) 824-9464.

FOOD

One of Fort Myers' best restaurants is **Ballenger's Seafood Restaurant**, 4600 Summerlin Square Drive, (941) 446-2772, where the seafood is nicely cooked and served fresh daily seven days a week. Sunday brunch is served 10:30 a.m. to 2 p.m. Northern and Southern Italian cuisine are the specialties at **Capriccio's Cucina Abruzzese**, 4600 Summerlin Road, (941) 936-3555. Delicious crepes, soups, and sandwiches are featured at the **French Connection**, 2282 First Street, (941) 332-4443. Select your own health-conscious cuisine at **The Mill**

FORT MYERS BEACH

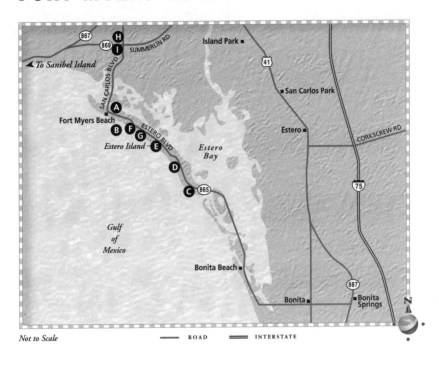

Not to Scale   ──── ROAD   ══ INTERSTATE

Sights

Ⓐ Europa FunKruz

Food

Ⓑ The Bridge

Ⓒ Channel Mark

Ⓓ Ernie's at the Beach

Ⓔ The Mucky Duck

Lodging

Ⓕ Best Western Pink Shell Beach Resort

Ⓖ Holiday Inn Ft. Myers Beach

Camping

Ⓗ Ft. Myers RV Resort

Ⓘ Siesta Bay RV Resort

Bakery Eatery and Brewery, 1149 S. Cleveland Avenue, (941) 939-2739, from grill-style pasta, pizza, sandwiches, freshly baked breads, seafood, prime rib, and the Mill's homemade beer. The Mill Bakery is also open late at night for snacks. Nothing is better than Southern cooking at **Veranda**, 2121 2nd Street, (941) 332-2065, served either in the courtyard or indoor dining room. Reservations are suggested.

In Fort Myers Beach, try **Ernie's at the Beach**, 7205 Estero Boulevard, (941) 463-4933, for a gourmet breakfast buffet on Sunday from 8 to 10:30 a.m. A family restaurant, Ernie's moderate prices and special buffets are the answer to finding the right-sized children's portions. Menu orders also taken. Ernie's serves lunch and dinner; brunch only on Sunday. For waterfront dining and a menu featuring steak and seafood (including fresh oysters), visit **The Bridge**, 708 Fisherman's Wharf, (941) 765-0050. The Bridge offers live entertainment until midnight on weekends; hosts Sunday "dock parties" with a reggae band, 4 to 10 p.m. Don't miss the delicious duck a l'orange at the **Mucky Duck**, 2500 Estero Boulevard, (941) 463-5519. Other specialties include bacon-wrapped barbecued shrimp and specially prepared grouper. Dinner is served 5 to 9:30 p.m., with a piano bar in the lounge. Reservations required for six or more. Arrive by boat to **Channel Mark** for casual waterfront dining on pasta and seafood. Lunch is served 11 a.m. to 4 p.m. daily; dinner, 4 to 10 p.m. Monday through Thursday, and 4 to 11 p.m. Saturday and Sunday.

LODGING

Just about any kind of lodging can be found on Florida's southwest coast. Five-star hotels with service second to none are waiting to pamper travelers in Fort Myers and Fort Myers Beach.

Tip: Some resorts have two or more facilities to choose from in this spread-out city with more than 10 miles separating the downtown/historic area from the beach. Be sure to check on the specific name of the hotel when making reservations with one of the larger chains.

Holiday Inn has four different hotels in the Fort Myers area. One of the most conveniently located for sightseeing is **Holiday Inn Central**, 2431 Cleveland Avenue, (941) 332-3232 or (800) 998-0466, close to area attractions and the connecting trolley car sightseeing bus. The inn has 126 rooms ($65 to $189) and three parlor suites, a heart-shaped heated swimming pool, plus a restaurant and lounge with live entertainment. Corporate rooms have in-room refrigerators and hair dryers. **Holiday Inn Fort Myers Airport**, located near the airport at 1305 Bell Tower Drive, (941) 482-2900, is handy for travelers arriving for group conferences. Some guest rooms ($59 to $119) are available in the special-access top floor. The newly renovated **Holiday Inn Sunspree** offers 152 rooms and suites on the Caloosahatchee River in historic downtown Fort Myers at 2220 W. 1st Street, (941) 334-3434. The inn's many exercise and fitness options include an outdoor pool, fitness center, and the welcome new addition of children's activities. Also available to guests are bike and water sport rentals and boat docks. Banquet and meeting space adjoins the restaurant and a tiki bar. The **Holiday Inn Fort Myers Beach** is located directly on the Gulf at 690 Estero Boulevard on Fort Myers Beach, (941) 463-5711. Guest rooms range from $65 to $331 per night.

Courtyard by Marriott, 4455 Metro Parkway, (941) 275-8600 or (800) 321-2211, offers 149 guest rooms and suites near both the beaches and downtown. Amenities include heated pool and hot tub, restaurant, lounge, exercise room, and laundry. The **Radisson Inn Fort Myers**, 12635 Cleveland Avenue, (941) 936-4300, provides a convenient airport shuttle. This sports-minded facility has newly redecorated rooms and suites ranging from $109 to $169. Outdoor activities include a heated pool, beach volleyball, horseshoes, and tennis. The whole family will be pampered at the **Best Western Pink Shell Beach Resort**, a 12-acre family-oriented waterfront resort, with 1,500 feet of beachfront, at 275 Estero Boulevard on Fort Myers Beach, (941) 463-6000. The facility has two- and three-bedroom cottages, hotel rooms, and efficiencies ($95 to $230). In addition, three heated swimming pools and a children's wading pool, two lighted Har-Tru tennis courts, bicycles, and water sports equipment are available to guests. Planned children's recreation programs help parents relax. The resort also has a marina, and golf courses are nearby.

CAMPING

The many RV parks in Florida provide a winter home for campers from the North. Most have a few sites, or even a separate section, for overnight travelers. On the road to Sanibel Island, **Fort Myers Beach RV Resort** has 305 shady sites, 216 pull-through sites, and all full-service sites. The park is 6 miles from Sanibel Island and 3½ miles from the beaches. From I-75 (Exit 21) turn right 4 miles on Daniels Road to

Cypress Lake Drive, continue straight ahead 1 mile to Summerlin Road, then left 5 miles to San Carlos Boulevard and right 7 miles to the park. For information call (800) 553-7484 and (941) 466-7171. Daily rate is $27.75.

Close to Fort Myers' attractions, **Siesta Bay RV Resort**, 19333 Summerlin Road, is an adult rental facility, no pets allowed. Tennis courts, horseshoes, pool tables, and fishing are only a few of the amenities in this planned-activities park. For information and reservations, call (800) 828-6992 weekdays 9 a.m. to 5 p.m.

To watch the baseball spring-training games and enjoy the many other Fort Myers sights, visit **Orange Harbor Mobile Home & RV Park** at 5749 Palm Beach Road, on the Caloosahatchee River in Fort Myers. For reservations and information, call (941) 694-3707.

14
NAPLES

Nestled between the Florida Everglades and the Gulf of Mexico, Naples attracts visitors for both its quiet sophistication and its diverse natural environment. With a population of 19,500, Naples is a cultural center, promoting the arts, exclusive shops, and laid-back, upscale living. Take a stroll down tree-lined 5th Avenue South in Naples, or down 3rd Street and The Avenues in Olde Naples for a little window shopping. Sample the assortment offered by intimate boutiques and galleries. Then get ready for some real exploration by visiting the area's outstanding public and private nature preserves. The Conservancy's Naples Nature Center, Big Cypress National Preserve, and the Everglades National Park offer the amateur naturalist the best glimpse of old Florida. The communities of Golden Gate and Immokalee, just outside of Naples, add to the list of natural and family-oriented attractions.

The Gulf of Mexico near Naples is dotted by a few large islands, including the inhabited Marco Island to the south and Sanibel and Captiva Islands to the north. The coastline is lined with mangrove-covered parks and features 7 miles of white sand beaches. Visiting families will find 20 off-beach parks and eight beachfront and beach-access facilities available for their enjoyment. ◪

NAPLES

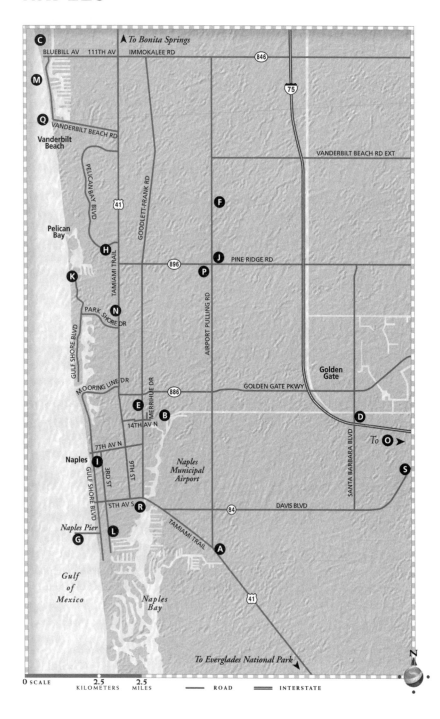

Sightseeing Highlights

Ⓐ Collier County Museum

Ⓑ The Conservancy's Naples Nature Center

Ⓒ Delnor-Wiggins State Recreation Area

Ⓓ Golden Gate Aquatic Center

Ⓔ Jungle Larry's Zoological Park at Caribbean Gardens

Ⓕ King Richard's Fun Park

Ⓖ Naples Fishing Pier

Ⓗ The Philharmonic Center for the Arts

Ⓘ Seminole Gaming Palace

Ⓙ Teddy Bear Museum of Naples

Food

Ⓚ Bayside

Ⓛ The Chef's Garden

Ⓜ Chickee Bar and Restaurant

Lodging

Ⓝ Best Western Naples Inn and Suites

Ⓞ Comfort Inn & Executive Suites

Ⓟ Naples Bath & Tennis Club

Ⓠ Ritz-Carlton Naples

Ⓡ Wellesley Inns

Camping

Ⓢ Naples RV Resort

A PERFECT DAY IN THE NAPLES AREA

The perfect day in Naples provides a sampler of the wonders the area has to offer. (Most of the tours and park areas are a full day's activity in and of themselves!) Begin at the Caribbean Gardens for a self-guided trail hike, winding through the 52-acre preserve and botanical garden. Wild birds and animals live here in a jungle-like setting. Spending three to four hours can easily take up the morning and the early afternoon.

Next, grab some lunch to go and head north of Naples to Barefoot Beach State Recreation Area, a beach area for purists. The sanctuary-like beach park offers an almost untouched stretch of sand and has no facilities or lifeguards, which keeps most of the tourists and families to a minimum. After a few hours of the quiet and sunshine, pack up any litter and head back towards Naples. Cool off while strolling the Olde Naples area around sundown. After a little shopping in a few of the quaint shops, finish this lovely day enjoying a leisurely dinner at one of the little restaurants or bistros in the area.

SIGHTSEEING HIGHLIGHTS

✯✯✯ **The Briggs Nature Center**—Part of The Conservancy, a non-profit organization dedicated to the preservation of Southwest Florida's fragile ecosystem, the Briggs Nature Center features an interpretive center, butterfly garden, canoe and kayak rentals, and a half-mile boardwalk for exploring the upland areas through the pinelands and mangroves of the Rookery Bay National Estuarine Research Reserve, located between Naples and Marco Island. The center is the launching point for regularly scheduled canoe and boat rides, guided bird-watching, and shelling on Key Island in Rookery Bay. Details: Located just a few minutes east of Naples at 401 Shell Island Road, off State Road 951 on the way to Marco Island; (941) 775-8569; open from 9 a.m. to 4:30 p.m. Monday through Friday year-round; open Saturday and Sunday at certain times of the year. Center admission is free, but boardwalk admission is $2 for adults and $1 for children. (3–4 hours)

✯✯✯ **The Conservancy's Naples Nature Center**—The Conservancy's nature center offers a microcosm of what can be explored throughout the Naples area. As a full educational center, the center's attractions include an aviary, a wildlife rehabilitation clinic (including a pelican/shorebird pool), a natural science museum, and a marine aquarium (which features a "touch tank" for visitors who'd like to pet sea life). Visit the "Snakes Alive" serpentarium or watch loggerhead turtles in the sea turtle tank; rent a canoe or kayak or take a boat ride to explore the tidal lagoon, including the Gordon River. Free guided trail tours and self-guided walks are offered. Details: 1415 Merrihue Drive, off 14th Avenue North and Goodette Road, Naples; (941) 262-0304; open Monday through Friday (and most Saturdays) from 9 a.m. to 4:30 p.m., Sunday during the winter from 1 to 4:30 p.m. The grounds are open to the public at no charge, but admission to the building is $3 for adults and $1 for children. (2–3 hours)

★★★ **Delnor-Wiggins State Recreation Area**—This popular beach was named one of America's top 20. The lifeguarded beach (wheelchair accessible) features a boat launch, barbecue grills, and showers. The accompanying park contains miles of crystal beach shoreline with sea oats and mangroves. Details: Located off Vanderbilt Drive, Naples; open from 7 a.m. to sundown. Admission is $3.25 per vehicle. (1–4 hours)

★★★ **Everglades National Park**—With an entrance 28 miles southeast of Naples, Everglades is the third-largest national park in the United States. A 1.5-million-acre expanse of grassy river, it's the perfect place for bird-watchers, nature photographers, and saltwater sportfishing fans.

The park is home to at least 14 endangered species, including the Florida panther, the southern bald eagle, the West Indian manatee, the wood stork, and the peregrine falcon. More than 400 bird species have been identified in the Everglades, along with dozens of orchids and 120 tree species.

See the park via a guided tram or boat tour, rent your own boat, or hire a local guide—several offer tours into the area. Don't forget your binoculars! Details: Head east on U.S. 41 until you reach Route 29, then drive south to park entrance. For more information, contact the Naples Area Tourism Bureau at (800) 605-7878, or call the park headquarters at (305) 242-7700. (4 hours)

★★★ **Jungle Larry's Zoological Park at Caribbean Gardens**—A self-guided trail winds through this 52-acre preserve and botanical garden where wild birds and animals live in a jungle-like setting. A 30-minute safari cruise takes visitors to islands where primates live in natural habitats. The park is one of the few places in Florida where visitors can view a rare collection free-roaming primates, from spider monkeys to gibbons to lemurs. Black bucks, cougars, servals, hedgehogs, wallabies, tigers, leopards, and kinkajous can also be seen during the safari cruise and tram rides. The park offers tram tours, lectures, elephant rides, and petting farms; kids and families will enjoy the playground and picnic facilities. Details: Caribbean Gardens, 1590 Goodlette-Frank Road, Naples; (941) 262-5409; open daily from 9:30 a.m. to 5:30 p.m. Admission is $12.95 for adults, $7.95 for children ages 4 to 15. (4 hours)

✪✪ **Collier County Museum**—The museum traces the history of Collier County, named for Barron G. Collier, and highlights Florida's last frontier, interesting people, and events from the Calusa Indian period to the present. The 5-acre museum grounds, part of the Collier County Government Center, also include a re-creation of a Seminole Indian village and a steam logging locomotive. Details: Located at the junction of U.S. 41E and Airport Road at 3301 Tamiami Trail E.; (941) 774-8476; open Monday through Friday from 9 a.m. to 5 p.m.; closed holidays. Admission is free. (1 hour)

✪✪ **Corkscrew Swamp Sanctuary**—This 11,000-acre protected area, maintained and operated by the National Audubon Society, features the largest-known stand of virgin bald cypress trees in the nation, some of which are said to be 500 to 700 years old. Home to alligators, bobcats, and otters, the sanctuary is also the winter nesting place of the North American wood stork. Photographers and outdoor lovers will enjoy taking a self-guided tour along a 2-mile boardwalk trail. And don't miss the 1,800-acre Lake Trafford County Park (located inside the sanctuary) for some of the best freshwater fishing in Florida, as well as boat rentals and charters. Details: Entrance to Corkscrew Swamp Sanctuary is off Immokalee Road, about 20 miles north of Naples and 14 miles west of Immokalee; call the National Audubon Society at (941) 657-3771 for more information. Open daily from 7 a.m. to 5 p.m. December through April, and from 8 a.m. to 5 p.m. May through November. Admission is $6.50 for adults, $5 for students with ID, $3 for minors. The preserve is wheelchair accessible. (1–2 hours)

✪✪**The Philharmonic Center for the Arts**—This multimillion-dollar center hosts an assortment of fine art galleries and studios, as well as professional theater troupes, and a variety of performers, syphony orchestras and programs that entertain as well as enrich.

The center has welcomed Itzhak Perlman and the Royal Philharmonic, as well as stage performances of *Crazy for You* and *Evita*, among others. Country greats Lee Greenwood and Chet Atkins have performed here. Also on the center grounds: a sculpture garden, four art galleries, and a museum shop with guided docent tours. Details: 5833 Pelican Bay Boulevard, Naples; (813) 597-1900.

✯✯ **Teddy Bear Museum of Naples**—This 8,000-square-foot museum is den to more than 3,000 teddy bears, from plain to fancy, miniature to giant, and antique to modern. There are even Baccarat crystal and Steiff mohair versions of this childhood toy. A reading library is stocked with books about nothing but bears, and a replica of the Three Bears' house is "just right" for young visitors. Changing exhibits and teddy bear memorabilia are also featured. Details: The museum is nestled in pinewoods at 2511 Pine Ridge Road, just ten minutes from downtown Naples and 1 mile from Exit 16 on I-75; (941) 598-271; open Monday through Saturday from 10 a.m. to 5 p.m. and on Sunday from 1 p.m. to 5 p.m. The museum is a nonprofit organization and welcomes a $5 donation for adults and $3 for children. (1 hour)

✯ **Barefoot Beach State Recreation Area**—This is a preserve for purists. The sanctuary-like state park north of Naples offers an almost untouched stretch of sand and has no facilities or lifeguards. Details: Located just north of Wiggins Pass, north of Naples; call the Naples Area Tourism Bureau at (800) 605-7878 for more information; open from 8 a.m. to sundown. No entrance fee. (1–4 hours)

✯ **Golden Gate Aquatic Center**—The Aquatic Center at Golden Gate Community Park makes a big splash with aquatic activities for the entire family. This state-of-the-art swim center sports a competitive pool, a water slide with separate landing pool, and a sloped activity pool for toddlers. The community park area also offers concessions, a picnic area, a playground, public restrooms, and courts and fields for volleyball, tennis, racquetball, basketball, baseball, football, and soccer. Details: 3300 Santa Barbara Boulevard, Golden Gate; (941) 353-7128. Admission is $2 for adults and $1.50 for children. (1–4 hours)

✩ **King Richard's Fun Park**—Highlights of this medieval-themed amusement park include bumper boats, go-carts, a video arcade, miniature golf, and a 9,600-square-foot castle. Details: 6780 N. Airport Road, Naples; (941) 598-1666. Admission to the park is free; rides cost $3 each. (2–3 hours)

✩ **Naples Fishing Pier**—A favorite fishing spot for catching snook, grouper, red snapper, and other regional species, the fishing pier extends 1,000 feet into the Gulf of Mexico. As a major city landmark, it's a perfect spot for visitors interested in a relaxing sunset stroll. There's a bait shack, snack bar, restrooms, and showers. Details: Located at 12th Avenue South in Olde Naples; the pier is open 24 hours, while concessions operate from 7 a.m. to 6:30 p.m. every day. Admission and parking are free.

✩ **Seminole Gaming Palace**—The recently built gaming palace, located on Seminole Indian reservation trust land in the heart of Immokalee, offers a variety of entertainment, from bingo, low-stakes poker, and video gaming machines, to fine dining at its continental dining room. Details: 506 S. 1st Street, Naples; (941) 658-1313. (3–4 hours)

FITNESS AND RECREATION

Naples almost seems to have been invented for recreation. In addition to its beaches and natural parks the area also offers ample opportunity and rental services for bicycling, racquetball, tennis, golf, canoeing, fishing, bird-watching, and short-distance hiking.

More than 40 golf courses, designed by some of the biggest names, are open for play. In fact, Naples was designated *Golf Digest's* "Golf Capital of the World" not long ago. The top public links include **Ironwood Golf Club**, (941) 775-2584; the **Lely Flamingo Island Club**, (941) 793-2223; and **Riviera Golf Club**, (941) 774-1081. Added to those, **Embassy Woods**, (941) 353-3699; **Highpoint Country Club**, (941) 261-4442; and **Palm River Country Club**, (941) 597-3554, which comprise some of the best of the semi-private courses.

Usually under heavy public use, area parks also offer many other recreational sports. **Cambier Park** offers lighted tennis courts, horseshoes, and shuffleboard, while **Golden Gate Community Park**, **Fleischmann Park**, and **Immokalee Community Park** feature tennis,

NAPLES REGION

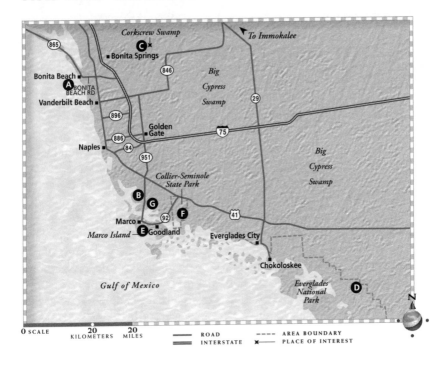

Sightseeing Highlights

A Barefoot Beach State Recreation Area

B Briggs Nature Center

C Corkscrew Swamp Sanctuary

D Everglades National Park

Food

E Apollo's Oceanview Restaurant

Camping

F Collier-Seminole State Park Campground

G Naples-Marco Island KOA

lighted racquetball, volleyball, and basketball courts.

For those who don't want to break established training schedules, Naples also has a number of weight-training gyms and fitness centers, many open to the public. Call the **Naples Area Tourism Bureau** at (800) 605-7878 for locations.

FOOD

Naples loves restaurants, and there are lots of them, offering food for virtually every preference. The **Chef's Garden**, 1300 3rd Street S., (941) 649-6554, is one of the best, serving classical cuisine (entrées $10 to $15). They've ranked in the top ten Florida restaurants for a decade. For seafood, don't miss **Apollo's Oceanview Restaurant**, 900 S. Collier Boulevard on Marco Island, (941) 389-0509, for lunch and dinner ($15 to $25). In Naples the best waterfront dining with some of the freshest seafood and oak-grilled meats is found at **Bayside, A Seafood Grill and Bar**, 4270 Gulf Shore Boulevard N., (941) 649-5552. Entrées range from $6 to $20. For a casual atmosphere on the Gulf of Mexico, serving lunch and light fare, stop at the **Chickee Bar and Restaurant**, 11000 Gulfshore Drive in Naples, (941) 597-3151. Meals cost from $10 to $18.

LODGING

Naples has a wide variety of overnight accommodations and weekly rentals, some with theme-park qualities. The traveler's choices are considerable, from the five-star **Ritz-Carlton Naples** on Vanderbilt Beach, 280 Vanderbilt Beach Road, (941) 598-3300, with rates of $300 to $500 per night in-season and $150 to $275 off-season, to the comfortable two-star **Best Western Naples Inn & Suites**, off U.S. 41 and Mooringline Road, 2329 9th Street N., (941) 261-1148, priced from $99 to $129 in-season and from $49 to $59 off-season. From Mediterranean architecture and *Fantasy Island* Gulf landscaping, to small, cozy Olde Naples motels, there are more than 100 hotels, motels, and resorts to choose from. Best buys include the **Comfort Inn & Executive Suites**, 3860 Toll Gate Boulevard, off I-75 and Exit 15, (941) 353-9500; **Wellesley Inns**, 1555 5th Avenue S. off U.S. 41 and State Road 84, (941) 793-4646; and the **Naples Bath & Tennis Club Resort**, with cottages at 4995 Airport Road N., off Pine Ridge Road, (941) 261-5777.

CAMPING

Naples RV Resort, (941) 455-7275, is one of the largest campgrounds in the area, with 424 grassy sites located on 40 acres. Facilities include a heated pool, whirlpool, bocci ball, horseshoes, volleyball, and other sports. An active winter rec program is planned each year. From I-75, take Exit 15 and head south on CR 951 to CR 84, then drive 1 mile east to the campground. Rates are $30 December 1 to February 28 and $18 May 2 to September 30.

Naples-Marco Island KOA, (941) 774-5455, one of the most interesting campground locations in the area, is near the Big Cypress Swamp and Gulf waters around Marco Island and Goodland. The campground has 172 grassy sites on 13 acres, with mangroves on the west side behind a fenced alligator pond. Features include 17 air-conditioned camping cabins, a heated swimming pool, whirlpool, boat ramp, playground, and grocery store. From I-75, take Exit 15, drive 7.5 miles south on CR 951 and turn left on Barefoot Williams Road. Watch for the KOA sign. CR 951, continues on to Marco Island and Goodland, on the edge of the Big Cypress Swamp south of Naples. Winter activities include canoeing and fishing. Rates are $37.95 to $39.95 March 1 to April 30; $24.95 to $26.95 May 1 to October 31. This KOA campground is a good base for a day trip to beautiful Collier-Seminole State Park (see below). To reach the park, take CR 951 to Marco Island, through the town of Goodland, then Highway 92 to the state park. Highway 92 takes you back to the Tamiami Trail (U.S. 41), about 8 miles south of CR 951, where you can complete the circle and return to the KOA.

The **Collier-Seminole State Park Campground**, (941) 394-3397, within 6,500-acre Collier-Seminole State Park, offers 150 public sites, 67 with electric and water, and flush toilets. A pontoon boat tour is also available. The park provides excellent opportunities to explore the mangroves and wildlife of this abundant region. It's resident manager, on duty 24 hours a day, can answer questions and recommend nature trails.

Scenic Route: The Tamiami Trail

The Tamiami Trail (U.S. 41) connects Naples and Miami, running along the northern border of **Everglades National Park**. The view in places can be spectacular, although the long drive may be monotonous. Take time to tour the park and, by all means, try the tram and airboat tours.

An excursion off the Tamiami Trail heads south on Route 29 towards Everglades City, Plantation, and Chokoloskee Island on the Chokoloskee Causeway. Area boat tours start from the **Ranger Station** in **Everglades City**. Don't miss the **Captain's Table Restaurant**. On the way back towards Naples, pull south off the Tamiami Trail onto Route 951 and follow it down the coastline and onto charming **Marco Island**.

THE TAMIAMI TRAIL

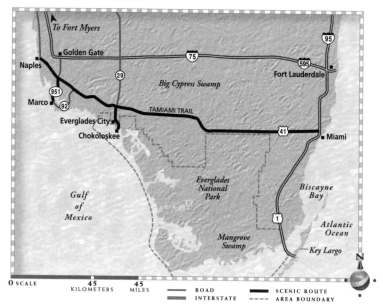

APPENDIX

METRIC CONVERSION CHART

1 U.S. gallon = approximately 4 liters
1 liter = about 1 quart
1 Canadian gallon = approximately 4.5 liters

1 pound = approximately $\frac{1}{2}$ kilogram
1 kilogram = about 2 pounds

1 foot = approximately $\frac{1}{3}$ meter
1 meter = about 1 yard
1 yard = a little less than a meter
1 mile = approximately 1.6 kilometers
1 kilometer = about $\frac{2}{3}$ mile

90°F = about 30°C
20°C = approximately 70°F

Planning Map: Florida's Gulf Coas

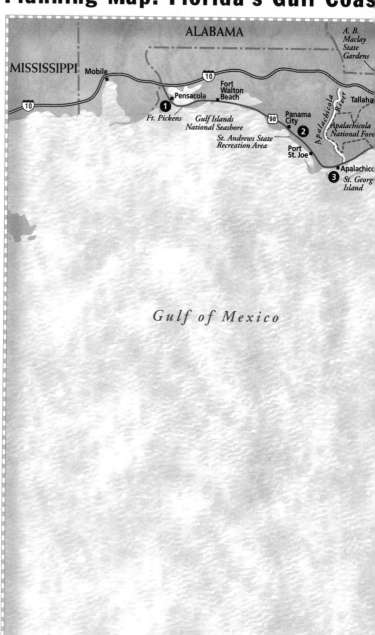

ALABAMA

MISSISSIPPI

A. B.
Maclay
State
Gardens

Mobile

10

Fort
Walton
Beach

Pensacola

10

1

Ft. Pickens   Gulf Islands
National Seashore

St. Andrews State
Recreation Area

98   Panama
City

2

Tallaha

Apalachicola
National Fore

Port
St. Joe

Apalachico

3   St. Georg
Island

Gulf of Mexico

SCALE

100
KILOMETERS

100
MILES

ROAD

INTERSTATE / TURNPIKE

AREA/PARK BOUNDAR
PLACE OF INTEREST

You have permission to photocopy this map.

GEORGIA

Jacksonville

Atlantic Ocean

Suwannee

Cedar Key 5
Yankee Town
Crystal River 6
Homosassa Springs
State Wildlife Preserve
Homosassa Springs

Weeki Wachee Spring

Tarpon Springs 7
Caladasi Island State Park
Clearwater 8
10
St. Petersburg 9

Tampa

FLORIDA

Orlando

FLORIDA TURNPIKE

Ringling Museums
Sarasota 11

Lake Okeechobee

Gasparilla Island

Boca Grande
Captiva
Captiva Island 12 13
Pine Island
Sanibel Island
Sanibel

Ft. Myers 29
Corkscrew Swamp
82
846

Ft. Lauderdale

Naples 14
Marco
29

Miami

Everglades City

Everglades National Park

Biscayne National Park

Everglades National Park

N

INDEX

Map Index

Other Books from John Muir Publications

Rick Steves' Books

Asia Through the Back Door, 400 pp., $17.95

Europe 101: History and Art for the Traveler, 352 pp., $17.95

Mona Winks: Self-Guided Tours of Europe's Top Museums, 432 pp., $18.95

Rick Steves' Baltics & Russia, 160 pp., $9.95

Rick Steves' Europe, 560 pp., $18.95

Rick Steves' France, Belgium & the Netherlands, 304 pp., $15.95

Rick Steves' Germany, Austria & Switzerland, 272 pp., $14.95

Rick Steves' Great Britain & Ireland, 320 pp., $15.95

Rick Steves' Italy, 224 pp., $13.95

Rick Steves' Scandinavia, 192 pp., $13.95

Rick Steves' Spain & Portugal, 240 pp., $13.95

Rick Steves' Europe Through the Back Door, 512 pp., $19.95

Rick Steves' French Phrase Book, 192 pp., $5.95

Rick Steves' German Phrase Book, 192 pp., $5.95

Rick Steves' Italian Phrase Book, 192 pp., $5.95

Rick Steves' Spanish & Portuguese Phrase Book, 336 pp., $7.95

Rick Steves' French/German/Italian Phrase Book, 320 pp., $7.95

A Natural Destination Series

Belize: A Natural Destination, 344 pp., $16.95

Costa Rica: A Natural Destination, 416 pp., $18.95

Guatemala: A Natural Destination, 360 pp., $16.95

City·Smart™ Guidebooks

City·Smart Guidebook: Cleveland, 208 pp., $14.95

City·Smart Guidebook: Denver, 256 pp., $14.95

City·Smart Guidebook: Kansas City, 232 pp., $14.95

City·Smart Guidebook: Minneapolis/St. Paul, 232 pp., $14.95

City·Smart Guidebook: Nashville, 256 pp., $14.95

City·Smart Guidebook: Portland, 232 pp., $14.95

City·Smart Guidebook: Tampa/St. Petersburg, 256 pp., $14.95

Unique Travel Series

All are 112 pages and $10.95 paperback, except Georgia and Oregon.

Unique Arizona

Unique California

Unique Colorado

Unique Florida

Unique Georgia ($11.95)

Unique New England

Unique New Mexico

Unique Oregon ($9.95)

Unique Texas

Unique Washington

Travel✦Smart™ Trip Planners

American Southwest Travel ✦ Smart Trip Planner, 256 pp., $14.95

Colorado Travel✦ Smart Trip Planner, 248 pp., $14.95

Eastern Canada Travel ✦ Smart Trip Planner, 272 pp., $15.95

Florida Gulf Coast Travel ✦ Smart Trip Planner, 224 pp., $14.95

Hawaii Travel ✦ Smart Trip Planner, 256 pp., $14.95

Kentucky/Tennessee Travel✦ Smart Trip Planner, 248 pp., $14.95

Minnesota/Wisconsin Travel ✦ Smart Trip Planner, 240 pp., $14.95

New England Travel✦ Smart Trip Planner, 256 pp., $14.95

Northern California Travel ✦ Smart Trip Planner, 272 pp., $15.95

Pacific Northwest Travel✦ Smart Trip Planner, 240 pp., $14.95

Other TerrificTravel Titles

The 100 Best Small Art Towns in America, 256 pp., $15.95

The Big Book of Adventure Travel, 400 pp., $17.95

The Birder's Guide to Bed and Breakfasts: U.S. and Canada, 416 pp., $17.95

Indian America, 480 pp., $18.95

The People's Guide to Mexico, 608 pp., $19.95

Ranch Vacations, 632 pp., $22.95

Understanding Europeans, 272 pp., $14.95

Watch It Made in the U.S.A., 328 pp., $16.95

The World Awaits, 280 pp., $16.95

Automotive Titles

The Greaseless Guide to Car Care, 272 pp., $19.95

How to Keep Your Subaru Alive, 480 pp., $21.95

How to Keep Your Toyota Pick-Up Alive, 392 pp., $21.95

How to Keep Your VW Alive, 464 pp., $25.00

Ordering Information

Please check your local bookstore for our books, or call **1-800-888-7504** to order direct and to receive a complete catalog. A shipping charge will be added to your order total.

Send all inquiries to:
**John Muir Publications
P.O. Box 613
Santa Fe, NM 87504**

Peg Armston

ABOUT THE AUTHOR

Jan Kirby was born in Minneapolis and grew up in Duluth, where her father designed and built boats. Boats continued to be a part of her life when she moved to Clearwater in 1957 and began exploring the Florida Gulf Coast and the Bahama Islands with her husband, Don, and friends.

A graduate of the University of Minnesota School of Journalism, Janet Spencer Kirby MacMichael is also the author of *Giant Steps*, the story of the Morton Plant Hospital in Clearwater. She is a freelance photojournalist contributing to local and national publications and a former newspaper editor and columnist for the *St. Petersburg Times*.

Jan is the mother of four grown children. Her hobbies include golf, fishing, sailing, camping, photography, gardening, and her schnauser-poodle dog, Patrick.